Intellectual Disability

Intellectual Disability

An Inability to Cope with an Intellectually Demanding World

Simon Whitaker
University of Huddersfield, UK and
South West Yorkshire Partnership NHS Foundation Trust

First published 2013 by
PALGRAVE MACMILLAN

Palgrave Macmillan in the UK is an imprint of Macmillan Publishers Limited, registered in England, company number 785998, of Houndmills, Basingstoke, Hampshire RG21 6XS.

Palgrave Macmillan in the US is a division of St Martin's Press LLC, 175 Fifth Avenue, New York, NY 10010.

Palgrave Macmillan is the global academic imprint of the above companies and has companies and representatives throughout the world.

Palgrave® and Macmillan® are registered trademarks in the United States, the United Kingdom, Europe and other countries.

ISBN 978–1–137–02557–9

This book is printed on paper suitable for recycling and made from fully managed and sustained forest sources. Logging, pulping and manufacturing processes are expected to conform to the environmental regulations of the country of origin.

A catalogue record for this book is available from the British Library.

A catalog record for this book is available from the Library of Congress.

Typeset by MPS Limited, Chennai, India.

To my father, who inspired me, my children, who admire me? my ex-wife and current partner, who tolerate me and my step-mother, who motivated me.

Contents

List of Tables

1
History and Definitions

Introduction

People are different in many ways. Some of these ways will be universally understood across cultures and time, for example whether one is a man or a woman or whether one is alive or dead. Although one could argue that the distinction between a man and a woman is not always clear-cut or that with modern medicine there are times when it is debatable whether somebody is alive or dead, as these constructs are generally used and understood they are discrete entities in that an individual is either one or the other. Other human conditions are what have been termed social constructs (Burr 2003), which are created by a particular society at a given time, and may well not be understood across time and cultures. Constructs such as 'witch' or 'possession by devils' were probably created to provide explanations for phenomena that were at that time not understood. These concepts would not have come into being without a widespread belief in the supernatural or the belief that it was possible to identify people who were witches or possessed by devils. What is commonly believed in western society today is different and these constructs no longer have relevance.

Examples of social constructs that are used today are fat and thin, young and old, and tall and short. Although it is likely that most cultures will have words for these conditions, it is also very likely that what constitutes thin, tall or old would vary between cultures and across time. Whether or not a particular society regards somebody as tall will probably depend on a number of factors, most notably the average height of people in that society and to what extent the individual stands out as being different. However, ultimately where the line is drawn between tall and average height is arbitrary. These constructs are what I have

1

called 'far end conditions' (Whitaker 2008a) in that they represent the end point of a continuum. In the examples of height, weight and age, once it has been decided where the line should be drawn, deciding if somebody is tall, fat or old is straightforward. There is a further group of constructs where either it is unclear what should be measured or the relevant variables do not lend themselves to measurement. For example, we all make use of the concept of beauty and ugliness, but most of us would not suggest that we could measure them objectively. Although there may be some commonly agreed factors that go towards something being beautiful, inevitably much of our judgment as to whether something is beautiful is determined by our individual history. It therefore would make no sense to count all the beautiful women or ugly men in a population. Conditions such as these I called 'judgment conditions' (Whitaker 2008a). In these cases it is a matter of judgment as to whether somebody has the condition or not, and of course different people may have different opinions.

The condition we now call intellectual disability has been acknowledged to be a social construct by influential writers on the subject (Greenspan 2006, Switzky 2006). What I want to do in this book is to consider if the construct of intellectual disability as it is currently defined is fit for purpose. In the rest of this chapter I look at how the current construct developed over the centuries, what purpose the construct has had in the past and what its purpose is today. In the rest of the book I analyse whether the assumptions on which the construct is based are valid and whether it fulfils its purpose.

Names

Over the centuries numerous terms have been used to describe people with low intellectual ability; many of these terms, although at one time technical, have now come into common language as terms of ridicule or abuse. In the English-speaking world the term 'idiot' was consistently used as the main scientific term well into the twentieth century. This was often subdivided into degrees of disability; for example, Howe (1848) in the US devised four levels of idiocy: 'Pure Idiots, Fools, Simpletons or Imbeciles as they are sometimes called'. He later refers to 'feebleminded' as a category more able than that of simpletons. Generally, in the nineteenth century the term 'idiot' was not only used as a specific term to describe those individuals with the greatest degree of disability but also as a generic term. Other terms were also used generically. In the early twentieth century 'feebleminded' was replaced by 'mental deficiency' as the generic term. Following a campaign from parents and others 'mental deficiency' was replaced by 'mental retardation' in the US in the 1980s, which in turn was replaced by 'intellectual disability' in the early twenty-first century. In the UK, mental defective was replaced in the mid-twentieth century by 'mental handicap', which was in turn replaced by 'learning disabilities/difficulties' in the 1980s. Although the term 'learning disability' is still in use in the UK, it is gradually being replaced by 'intellectual disability'. I have never liked the term 'learning disability', as in the US its meaning is different, referring to individuals who have specific learning disabilities such as dyslexia but whose intellectual ability is in the average range. As much of this book is written from a historical perspective and older terms may not have had exactly the same meaning as modern terms, I occasionally use the terms used by the authors I refer to or the term I refer to that was common at the time. However, when I refer to the current time, or require a general term to cover all times, I use the term 'intellectual disability', as this seems to be the main internationally accepted term and probably describes the people who acquire the label most accurately.

Early ideas about intellectual disability

The idea that there were people who could not cope because of apparent lack of intellectual ability is evident in all western societies that have left sufficient written records. There are references to it in Greek and Roman literature. It is referred to in the laws of medieval England; in the early 1300s Edward I and Edward II had a law decreeing that the property of idiots went to the Crown. This law also made a distinction between idiots (the intellectually disabled) and lunatics (the mentally ill).

In the main in the nineteenth century it was medical doctors based in institutions, such as Howe (1848) in the US and Ireland (1882) in the UK, who wrote about the condition, trying to classify and understand its aetiology. From the descriptions they give of their patients the impression is of people with what may today be considered to be a severe degree of intellectual disability resulting from medical conditions that are now rare in the west such as cretinism (hyperthyroidism) or that can now be treated, such as epilepsy. Given that the individuals written about were confined in institutions it is difficult to estimate what proportion of the population as a whole would be regarded as idiots, though Howe (1848) did cite a survey carried out in the state of Massachusetts. He reported the rate to be just under 0.2 per cent, which is less than the 1–3 per cent that the current rate of prevalence is considered to be. The intellectual demands of society at that time would also have been very different from those of today, particularly in the US, which in the nineteenth century was an agricultural society in which most people worked on the land. It is therefore likely that fewer people would have had difficulty coping as a result of low intellectual ability, but unlikely that the people who were then described as idiots would be exactly the same as those who today are labelled as intellectually disabled.

The attitude of society to people with an intellectual disability also changed over the nineteenth century in both the US and UK. Asylums were initially set up in the nineteenth century with the aim of protecting and educating the feebleminded and eventually retiring them to the community. By the late nineteenth century the primary aim of these institutions was to segregate the inmates from the rest of society and the two sexes from each other. By this time it was felt that there was no point in educating the feebleminded who, it was felt, could not learn and who were regarded as a burden on society (Noll and Trent 2004). Richards (2004) showed that there was not only a change in the official attitude to the feebleminded in the nineteenth and early twentieth centuries, but that this attitude was reflected in the popular literature of the time. The fiction of the 1840s depicted the families of such children as dedicated, loving, and spiritually improved by their challenge. By the 1870s things had changed to a negative view with an emphasis on protecting society from such people.

Although it was apparent from the writings of authors such as Howe (1848) and Ireland (1882) that the concept of intelligence was being used in describing the feebleminded, at that time it was not being used in a quantitative way. At the beginning of the twentieth century this changed with the development by Alfred Binet in France of the first effective intelligence test. This meant that intelligence could be measured and an individual's degree of disability could, in theory at least, be quantified. I discuss Binet and his assessment in more detail in Chapter 2 but what I want to show here is the impact this had on the concept of intellectual disability. The individual most responsible for this in the early twentieth century was Henry Goddard.

Henry Herbert Goddard (1866–1957)

Henry Goddard was born in the state of Maine into a family of Quaker farmers. His father died when he was young and the family lost the farm. He, however, obtained a scholarship to a Quaker boarding school and then went to university. After a spell teaching in 1906 he was made director of research at the Vineland Training School for Feeble-Minded Girls and Boys in Vineland, New Jersey, a post he held until 1918. In order to look for innovative ways of working with the feeble-minded in 1908 he went to Europe. While in France, almost by chance he came across Binet's scale. He brought it back to the US, translated it into English and gave it to 400 students at Vineland (Goddard 1910).

At that time the measure of intellectual ability produced by the Binet scale was a mental age, that is, the age of an average child who would obtain the score achieved by the individual being tested. Goddard looked at the relationship between mental age and the descriptions by staff of what the Vineland residents were able to do and concluded that a resident's mental age predicted how capable he/she was. He then categorised residents in terms of mental age, with idiots having mental ages between one and two years, imbeciles between two and seven years and the feebleminded who had mental ages between eight and 12 years. He, however, did not like feebleminded as a term for the most able group as it was commonly used as a generic term for all people with intellectual disabilities. He suggests the term 'moron' for this group, from the Greek word meaning foolish.

In 1919 Goddard proposed to the medically dominated American Association for the Study of the Feebleminded that they should adopt common criteria for defining different degrees of feeblemindedness based on the Binet intellectual assessment. Specifically, an idiot would have a mental age of two or less, an imbecile a mental age between three and seven and a moron a mental age between eight and 12 years. This was accepted and to this day a necessary criteria for having an intellectual disability for this organisation and its successors is having a measured intellectual level below a specified point.

Unlike Binet, Goddard believed the test measured a fixed intellectual ability that was inherited and due to a single genetic cause. He was particularly concerned about the morons who he felt were not easily distinguishable from the rest of society but were responsible for many of its ills, such as crime, illegitimacy and vagrancy. He introduced these ideas to the general public with the publication of a book *The Kallikak Family: A Study in the Heredity of Feeble-Mindedness*, published in 1912. The book traced the ancestors of a resident at Vineland, given the name Deborah Kallikak for the book. She had a mental age of about nine years, so in Goddard's terms would have been a moron. With the aid of a researcher Goddard traced 480 relatives both dead and alive going back six generations. Clearly it was not possible to do individual intellectual assessments on all these people, so it was determined whether they were feebleminded or not on the basis of what information was available. On the basis of this Goddard reported that 143 of Deborah's ancestors were clearly feebleminded, a further 291 possibly feebleminded and only 46 were normal. Of these there were 36 illegitimate children, 33 prostitutes and other sexually immoral types, three epileptics, three criminals, and eight who 'kept a house of ill fame'. It was therefore clear to Goddard that they were contributing to society's ills. But what was very worrying for him was that these feebleminded people had married into other families exposing a further 1,146 people to the destructive feebleminded gene. At that time Goddard felt that only 10 per cent of morons were in institutions, while the rest were in the community where clearly they could have a major detrimental effect on society. He therefore advocated identifying these people in the community and admitting them to institutions as the way of both caring for them and stopping them reproducing.

Goddard moved from his post at Vineland in 1918 to become director of the Ohio Bureau of Juvenile Research and then in 1922 he was made a professor in the Department of Abnormal and Clinical Psychology at the Ohio State University, which he held until his retirement in 1938.

Although Goddard's work and his book on the Kallikak family has since been severely criticised for poor method and false assumptions about feeblemindedness being the results of a single gene (for example, Zendaerland 2004) and for inaccurate reporting of information (see Smith and Wehmeyer 2012), it had a major impact in the first half of the twentieth century in creating a fear of people with low intellectual ability and consequential campaigns to prevent them from having children.

The fear of the moron

Goddard's ideas about the feebleminded were very much in line with the thinking at the time about racial superiority, genetic inheritance and the competence of the population as a whole. In 1859 Charles Darwin published *The Origin of Species*, a ground-breaking book that put forward the idea that living things, including humans, inherit their characteristics from their parents, that the members of the species who inherited attributes most appropriate to their environment survive resulting in evolution of the species. Gregor Mendel, working with pea plants, showed that a specific trait could be transferred from parents to offspring by means of single genes. These theories have since become the cornerstone of modern biology but in the late nineteenth and early twentieth centuries many people had simplistic ideas as to the mechanism of inheritance believing that a single gene was responsible for complex traits and in particular for feeblemindedness. This idea may have been given some further credence in the nineteenth century as at that time many people labelled feebleminded had conditions that were due to a single organic cause such as Down's syndrome, Cretinism, (hypothyroidism), or epilepsy, some of which were inherited.

In 1869 Sir Francis Galton (who is discussed in more detail in Chapter 2) published *Hereditary Genius* in which he suggested that intellectual ability was inherited and that people should be encouraged to reproduce in such a way as to improve the race, a policy that he later termed 'eugenics'. By the turn of the twentieth century eugenics was beginning to be accepted in the US and Europe and was supported by many prominent figures, notably H.G. Wells, Theodore Roosevelt, George Bernard Shaw and John Maynard Keynes. The First International Congress of Eugenics was held in London in 1912 with the support of Charles Darwin's son Leonard and had as its honorary vice-president Winston Churchill.

There were concerns in both the US and Europe that inferior genes may be introduced into the population. In Europe it was the time of empires in what would now be called the developing world, the native populations of these colonies being considered genetically inferior. In the US there was a fear that the current wave of immigrants from eastern and southern Europe were not as able as the original northern European settlers and the overall ability of the US population would be reduced.

These ideas may well have contributed towards the change in attitude towards people with mild intellectual disability from one where it was assumed that with the right help they could be improved, to them being regarded as unchangeable. However, a further probable factor was that people with low intellectual ability may well have been failing to cope in their communities and had resorted to crime and immoral behaviour in order to survive. A particular problem in the mid-nineteenth century was the need to adapt to the demands of work in factories set up as a result of the industrial revolution as opposed to the largely agricultural work that people with a mild degree of intellectual disability had successfully been doing for centuries. Within this context Goddard's suggestion that we should not allow the feebleminded to breed seemed obvious and reasonable.

In order to protect the general population, there were campaigns in the US to identify those with mild disabilities and institutionalise them.

Some states established travelling clinics to test suspected children and institutionalise them irrespective of their parents' wishes. There was an increase in the number of places in existing institutions and new institutions were built. Beginning with Connecticut in 1896, states began to enact marriage laws with eugenic criteria, prohibiting anyone who was 'epileptic, imbecile or feeble-minded' from marrying. Sterilisation was also advocated and became policy in many states starting with Indiana in 1907. Other countries throughout the world also introduced sterilisation notably Canada, Germany and Sweden where the policy was continued until the mid-1970s.

In the UK eugenic ideas were very much in vogue and had a big influence on the 1913 Mental Deficiency Act. This Act defined moral imbeciles as: 'persons who from an early age display some permanent mental defect coupled with strong vicious or criminal propensities on which punishment has had little or no deterrent effect' and allowed for the institutionalisation of such people. This category of moral imbecile included many people of whom society disapproved, such as women who gave birth to illegitimate children, and habitual drunkards. It is a similar concept to Goddard's concept of the moron and clearly shows the connection drawn by the legislators of the time between immoral behaviour and low intellectual ability.

In the UK although it was apparent that not all people who could be classified under the 1913 Act were sent to institutions, there was an increase in the number of institutional places (Dale 2003, Chester and Dale 2007). It is also probable that many people incarcerated under the Act did not have a significantly low intellectual ability even if the problems with the measurement of low IQ (discussed in Chapter 3) are taken into account. Mattinson (1970) followed up married couples who had been patients in Stipplefields Hospital, a hospital for the mentally deficient, in the 1940s, 1950s and 1960s, many of whom had been sent there under the 1913 Mental Deficiency Act. She reports that the measured IQs of these individuals when admitted to the hospital ranged from 38 to 93. Unlike the US and other countries, campaigns for both voluntary and compulsory sterilisation failed owing to strong moral arguments against. But what is apparent is the clear aim of the 1913 Mental Deficiency Act to identify people who it was felt should not be allowed to have children and were otherwise a menace to society, label them as Mentally Defective and keep them away from the rest of the community.

Eugenic ideas fell out of favour after the Second World War following the Nazis taking it to an extreme where undesirables were not only separated from the rest of society and sterilised but also killed.

The Second World War and beyond

The Second World War brought a change. There was a need for people in the armed services and the factories and many people with mental deficiency successfully served in the forces (Gelb 2004). Just after the end of the war, Weaver (1946) gave an account of how people with 'mental deficiency' fared in the US army, looking at a sample of 8000 men with measured IQs between 45 and 75. About half of them had a profitable military career. Of those who did not, the reasons seemed to be more to do with their personality than their intellectual ability.

After the war there was no longer a need to recruit to the services, industrial work was reduced and there were a large number of de-mobbed troops looking for work. Suddenly the opportunity for people with intellectual disability to play a useful part in society had gone. The old institutions were still there and the pre-war policies continued and, in the UK, institutions continued to be built up until the 1970s. However, gradually things were changing. There was a steady change in the national Zeitgeist with regard to individual rights in both Europe and the US. The 1960s saw the emergence of various campaigning bodies for individual rights. In Europe and the US the women's movement became increasingly vocal in demanding that women should be given equal rights under the law and in employment. In the US the Civil Rights Movements started campaigning for equal rights for African Americans and other ethnic minorities. In Northern Ireland, in the UK, Catholics campaigned for equal rights with Protestants. Later the Gay Liberation movement started to campaign for lesbians and gay men to be regarded as equal. As part of this general movement for individual rights, the disability rights movement campaigned to get equal rights and opportunities for people primarily with physical disabilities. They pointed to how the environment did not take account of their needs, for example, in allowing them access to public buildings or to transport, and that they were not able to gain employment owing to employers not making allowances for their disabilities. They campaigned for equal opportunities in employment, education and housing.

All this gradually changed how society saw minority groups from groups who needed to be legislated against, as in the case of gay men, suppressed in the case of black people, or kept in their place in the case of women, to being regarded more as equal members of society. Laws now exist in both the UK and the US so that it is now illegal to discriminate against people on the grounds of their race, gender or sexual orientation.

There had always been some people, groups and individuals, who campaigned for the rights of people with intellectual disabilities. But in the nineteenth century it was felt that the best way to help these people was to care for them in institutions and benevolent groups such as Quakers set up many of the original institutions in the UK. By the 1940s and 1950s groups began to campaign for the individual rights of people with intellectual disabilities. Castles (2004) points out that initially in the US these groups tended to be white middle-class parents concerned about the stigma of a diagnosis. For example, it was due to a campaign by parents that the American Association of Mental Deficiency changed its name to the American Association on Mental Retardation, which was felt to be a less demeaning name.

By the 1960s the tide was beginning to turn against institutionalised care. In addition to the new concern for individual rights generally, there began to be public concern about the standards of care in these overcrowded hospitals and there were a number of scandals with regard to abuse of patients. It was also becoming apparent that it would be cheaper to keep people in the community rather than have institutions staffed with highly paid doctors and nurses. In the UK in 1971 the White Paper, Better Services for the Mentally Handicapped, advocated moving from hospital care to care in the community.

Wolfensberger articulated the philosophy of care behind these changes with the ideas of 'Normalisation' (Wolfensberger 1972), which states that people with disabilities should not be regarded as objects of ridicule or pity but as valued members of society. The goal of services should therefore be to enable them to fulfil this role.

The hospitals began to close down and the residents were moved on to smaller homes in the community. In the UK the 1988 Griffiths Report continued to emphasise community care but with some suggested changes as to how it should be operated. It advocated that people should have their individual needs assessed and a care manager appointed to obtain the appropriate services to meet these needs. Griffiths also advocated more use of the private and independent sector to provide the care. Many of the suggestions were passed into law in the 1990 National Health Service and Community Care Act. This policy of helping people to live in their own community was continued in the last UK government White Paper, Valuing People (Department of Health 2001). By the 1990s many of the mental handicap hospitals had closed.

What these current ideas about intellectual disability have in common with those expressed in the nineteenth and early twentieth centuries is that they both accept that there are a number of people who are not able to cope with their environment without some degree of assistance. Where there is a major difference is that a hundred years ago feeble-minded people were regarded as a menace to society who needed to be kept separate and prevented from breeding. Today the philosophy and practice of care, as least as it is articulated, has changed dramatically to one of providing people with help and support to function as normally as possible. But what the legislation and to some extent the philosophy of care imply is that in order to gain this help and support one has to be recognised as having an intellectual disability. This means that one has to have a diagnosis. As I argued at the beginning of this chapter, intellectual disability is a social construct and so its diagnosis is determined by a socially constructed definition. This definition should therefore include people whom society deems to have the condition and exclude people whom society would not deem to have the condition. However, a diagnosis may not always be helpful or even benign as there is still stigma associated with it (Baroff 1999; 2006; Smith 2002 Snell and Voorhees 2006).

Definitions of intellectual disability

Early definitions of mental deficiency in the UK were usually based on a description derived by the medical profession. For example, the 1913 Mental Deficiency Act in the UK defined mental deficiency as follows:

(a) Idiots; that is to say, persons so deeply defective in mind from birth or from an early age as to be unable to guard themselves against common physical dangers;

(b) Imbeciles; that is to say, persons in whose case there exists from birth or from an early age mental defectiveness not amounting to idiocy, yet so pronounced that they are incapable of managing themselves or their affairs, or, in the case of children, of being taught to do so;

(c) Feeble-minded persons; that is to say, persons in whose case there exists from birth or from an early age mental defectiveness not amounting to imbecility, yet so pronounced that it required care supervision and control of their own protection or for the protection of others, or, in the case of children, that they by reason of such defectiveness appear to be permanently incapable of receiving proper benefit from the instruction in ordinary schools;

(d) Moral imbeciles; that is to say, persons who from an early age display some permanent mental defect coupled with strong vicious or criminal propensities on which punishment has had little or no deterrent effect.

As these definitions were criticised for lacking precision and not being scientific it was suggested that it would be better to make use of objective measures (for example, Binet and Simon 1905). In the US this was taken up by Goddard, who used intellectual assessment enthusiastically and it was largely due to his influence that the American Association for the Study of the Feebleminded adopted the criteria for defining different degrees of feeblemindedness based on measured intellectual ability, at that time mental age.

Although Goddard initially defined feeblemindedness in terms of mental age, by the 1920s the measure of intellectual ability being used was the intellectual quotient or IQ score, based on the ratio of mental age to chronological age. I give a more detailed explanation of IQ testing in Chapters 2 and 3. In 1916 Terman suggested the following definition based on IQ: Morons had IQs between 50 and 70, Imbeciles IQs between 50 and 20–25, and Idiots below 20–25. As shown in Chapters 2 and 3, theoretically there is a fixed proportion of the population at given IQ levels and a fixed proportion of the population below any given IQ level; for example, it would be expected that about 3 per cent of the population would have IQs below 70. So Terman's definition therefore limited the number of people with Feeblemindedness to about 3 per cent of the population as a whole. However, early American Association of Mental Deficiency (AAMD) definitions used the higher IQ cut-off point of 85 (Heber 1959, 1961), which would have included about 16 per cent of the population: this was clearly including many people coping without any difficulties and was clearly over-inclusive. In 1973 the AAMD changed the definition back to IQ 70 (Grossman 1973) and then in 1983 (Grossman 1983) it was extended up to 75 to take account of what they regarded as the five-point level of accuracy of IQ tests.

Goddard's and subsequent definitions in the first half of the twentieth century were based on the single criterion of intellectual ability. However, it became apparent that this definition was over-inclusive, with many people from lower social classes and ethnic minorities who were able to cope being given a diagnosis. People such as Doll (1941) argued that there needed to be a second criterion indicating that the individual was socially incompetent. The 1959 AAMD definition (Heber 1959) therefore had the additional criterion that the individual should have a deficit in adaptive behaviour (discussed more in Chapter 4). Although some writers have advocated a return to a definition based on IQ alone, for example, Clausen (1967), these two criteria of IQ<70/75 and a deficiency in adaptive behaviour together with a third criterion that the deficits should be apparent in childhood, has formed the basis of the internationally accepted definitions of intellectual disability ever since. For example, the International Classification of Diseases (ICD-10) (World Health Authority (WHO 1992)) and Diagnostic and Statistical Manual of Mental Disorders (DSM-IV-TR) (American Psychiatric Associations 2000), all use a definition similar to this.

In looking at how the definition has developed what is notable is that the definition changed when it was found not to be doing its job in including the people who needed to be included and excluding the people who needed to be excluded.

Current definition and assumptions

The major internationally accepted definitions of intellectual disability are based on the American Association of Intellectual and Developmental Disabilities (AAIDD) definition and so share many of the same assumptions with regard to why a construct is required, the nature of the condition and how it can be assessed. I therefore look at this definition in detail. The current UK definition as specified in the government White Paper, Valuing People (Department of Health 2001), is a bit different in not being so precise, and is considered later.

In the latest AAIDD diagnostic manual (American Association on Intellectual and Developmental Disabilities 2010) intellectual disability is defined as follows:

> Intellectual disabilities is characterised by significant limitations both in intellectual functioning and in adaptive behavior as expressed in conceptual, social and practical adaptive skills. The disability originates before age 18. (p. 1)

The definition therefore contains the three criteria of significant limitations in intellectual ability, significant limitations in adaptive/social functioning and an onset of these during childhood. The third criterion of an onset before the age of 18 years old is quite clear and unambiguous, the other two are less clear and are considered in more detail later in the manual. The details of these criteria and the assumptions on which they are based may well be crucial to whether the current definition is effective in including people who need to be included and excluding people who should be excluded.

Significant limitations in intellectual functioning

The first assumption that is made in the manual is that individuals have a true IQ that can be measured. This is apparent from the manual's clarification of what is meant by significant limitation in intellectual functioning.

> *Intellectual functioning*: an IQ score that is approximately two standard deviations below the mean, considering the standard error of measurement for the specific assessment instrument used and the instrument's strengths and limitation. (p. 27)

A standard deviation, which is explained in Chapter 2 in more detail, is a measure of how far a particular score differs from the average score. For modern IQ tests a score two standard deviations below the mean is equivalent to an IQ of 70. So for an individual to meet this definition they should have a measured IQ of 70 or less.

It is further specified that the assessment should be based on an individually administered IQ test:

> Although far from perfect, intellectual functioning is currently best represented by IQ scores when they are obtained from appropriate, standardised and individually administered assessment instruments. (p. 31)

Although it is acknowledged later in the AAIDD manual that there are some systematic differences in scores between different IQ tests whereby one test will on average score so many points more or less than another test, the assumption seems to be that the scores of different IQ tests are roughly equivalent. If this was not the case it would be necessary to specify which test should be used or at least which test should be regarded as the 'gold standard' against which the scores of other tests should be adjusted to be the equivalent of, which is not specified.

It is also acknowledged that measured IQ scores are subject to chance error, whereby a confidence interval is specified around the measured IQ score within which the 'true IQ' will probably fall.

> For well-standardised measurement of general intellectual functioning, the standard error of measurement is approximately 3 to 5 points. As reported in the respective test's standardisation manual, the test's standard of error of measurement can be used to establish a statistical confidence interval around the obtained score. (p. 36)

The Standard Error of Measurement is described in more detail in Chapter 3 on the measurement of intellectual ability but is a measure of the accuracy of an assessment. So what is being suggested here is that well-standardised modern IQ tests are accurate to within five points.

It goes on to further specify how the Standard Error of Measurement should be derived:

> Currently, the prevailing best practice standard in test construction, reporting, and interpretation is to use the internal consistency measurement of reliability (along with the test's standard deviation) to estimate the standard error of measurement. Reporting an IQ score with an associated confidence interval is a critical consideration underlying the appropriate use of intelligence tests and best practice; such reporting must be a part of any decision concerning the diagnosis of ID. (p. 36)

Again, Chapter 3 gives a detailed explanation as to what the internal consistency of an IQ test is; however, briefly it is a measure of the degree to which the different parts of the assessment agree with each other. It is one but not the only measure that test accuracy can be based on. The assumption therefore is that it is the best and most inclusive method of estimating test accuracy.

The manual therefore recognises that IQ tests are not accurate to within one IQ point, even if well standardised and individually administered. It is for this reason that it does not state that the measured IQ must be 70 or below but rather that this cut-off point should be approximate: 'The term approximate is there both as a recognition of error in measurement and to emphasise the need for clinical judgment' (p. 40).

However, it is also clear that there is an expectation that the tests will be accurate to within five points. There are therefore several assumptions made in the manual about our current ability to measure low IQ, that:

1. Individuals have a true IQ that can be measured.
2. Low IQ can be measured numerically.
3. Although IQ assessment is subject to error IQ can be measured to an accuracy of five points in the low range.
4. Standard Error of Measurement and confidence intervals should be based on internal consistency only.
5. Although different IQ tests may produce slightly different scores there is basic consistency between tests.

Adaptive behaviour

I consider Adaptive Behaviour in more detail in Chapter 4 but for now we need to be aware of the assumptions that are being made in the AAIDD manual with regard to our ability to measure it. The AAIDD manual gives details of the diagnostic criteria for adaptive behaviour from which a number of assumptions about adaptive behaviour are apparent. The manual gives guidance as to how significant limitation in adaptive behaviour should be established:

> For the diagnosis of intellectual disability, significant limitations in adaptive behavior should be established through the use of standardised measures normed on the general population, including people with disabilities and people without disabilities. On these standardised measures, significant limitations in adaptive behavior are operationally defined as performance that is approximately two standard deviations below the mean of either (a) one of the following three types of adaptive behavior: conceptual, social, or practical or (b) an overall score on a standardised measure of conceptual, social, and practical skills. The assessment instrument's standard error of measurement must be considered when interpreting the individual's obtained scores. (AAIDD 2010, p. 43)

Using the same logic as I did for IQ it therefore seems to be assumed:

1. That it is reasonable to measure adaptive behaviour.
2. That an individual's level of adaptive and social competence can be expressed in a single score in the case of an overall score or in terms of three scores in terms of conceptual, social or practical abilities.
3. That the measurement of adaptive behaviour can be made to a reasonable degree of accuracy.

The Valuing People definition

In the UK international definitions are used but not exclusively. Locally more ad hoc definitions are often used, often based on IQ alone. As for formal UK definitions, Valuing People (Department of Health 2001), which sets out the government's vision for services for people with intellectual disabilities, is probably the most relevant in a UK context. It refers to learning disability rather than intellectual disabilities but the terms can be regarded as synonymous. It defines learning disability as follows:

1.5 Learning disability includes the presence of:

- A significant reduced ability to understand new or complex information, to learn new skills (impaired intelligence), with;
- A reduced ability to cope independently (impaired social functioning);
- Which started before adulthood, with lasting effect on development. (Valuing People 2001, p. 14)

The definition has the three elements of low intellectual ability, low adaptive behaviour and both occurring in childhood common to the current AAIDD and other internationally recognised definitions. However, there is far less detail provided as to what constitutes low intellectual ability and adaptive skills.

1.6 This definition encompasses people with a broad range of disabilities. The presence of a low intelligence quotient, for example an IQ below 70, is not, of itself, a sufficient reason for deciding whether an individual should be provided with additional health and social care support. An assessment of social functioning and community skills should also be taken into account when determining need.
(Department of Health 2001, pp. 14–15)

Although an IQ criterion is not unambiguously stated, IQ 70 is given as an example and so is likely to be taken as the criteria, and the same assumption with regard to the accuracy to which it can be measured that applies to the AAIDD definition will also apply to the Valuing People definition. As for adaptive behaviour, there is no suggestion as to how this should be formally assessed so there seems to be considerable room for clinical judgment.

Cultural difference in Intellectual Disability

Although the current AAIDD definition is the basis of other internationally accepted definitions, it was developed in the US and based on ideas from the US and Europe to meet the needs of an increasingly educated industrial society. However, even within this context, what has been required from the concept has changed over time from identifying people in need of care in the early nineteenth century, to identifying morons that society needed protecting from in the early twentieth century, to labelling people who need help to play their full part in society as valued members, in the later twentieth early twenty-first centuries. The definition developed to meet the perceived needs of society at the time, which depended on the environmental demands, and the current philosophy of care. The western philosophy of care and environmental demands do not apply universally to all cultures.

There may be some commonalties between different cultures and societies with regard to how intellectual disability is perceived, with all societies recognising that there are some individuals who cannot cope and probably include those with the most obvious disabilities among them. However, there are also many differences in how different societies view intellectual disability. Some people live in very different environments, which make different demands on individuals. The Inuit of north-west Greenland, for example, live in a world in which survival is dependent on hunting so what is important is the ability to hunt. Academic ability is not seen as important and the indigenous population finds it difficult to understand why western-trained professionals give children labels of intellectual disability if they fail academically (Nuttall 1998).

In south India, although there is the recognition by most people that there are biological reasons for disability, such as poor diet, physical illness or marriage to a close relative, it is still believed by many that disability is punishment for sins committed by the person's ancestors. Parents of disabled children feel shunned by the rest of the community because of this and there is a tendency among poorer people to hope that the child dies if they are not going to get better (Edawardraj et al. 2010).

It is quite clear that the concept of intellectual disability is a function of the culture in which it is currently operating. It is different in different cultures, changes over time within the same culture and will continue to do so.

Is the current definition fit for purpose?

It seems to me that the main aim of the current definition in western developed countries is to identify and label people who are failing to cope owing to a low intellectual ability, so that they may be given the assistance they need to have a reasonable quality of life. However, there are also other reasons for having the construct that may be more relevant to specific groups who make use of the definition. Planners need to have a construct that helps them identify people who are likely to need a service in the future; the criminal justice system needs to have a construct that identifies people who are likely to be vulnerable to criminal behaviour, and researchers need to have a definition that clearly identifies the people they are researching.

There are therefore a number of questions that need to be considered:

- Is it reasonable to have a universal definition of intellectual disability that applies in all situations, in all cultures, or should we be considering other ways to define it?
- Are the assumptions with regard to our ability to measure low IQ and adaptive behaviour implicit in the current AAIDD definition of intellectual disability valid?
- Does the current AAIDD definition work in terms of identifying those individuals who need support to be able to become valued members of society and excluding those who do not?

I consider these questions in the rest of the book.

2
The Concept of Intelligence

The concept of intellectual ability has been evident in western literature at least since the time of Plato. In his history of mental retardation Scheerenberger (1983) cites a number of references to people who lack intellectual capacity in early writings. In Roman times it was recognised that people differed in terms of keenness of mind, which was thought to be dependent on fineness of brain substance. In the early Middle Ages Abu Ali al-Husayn ibn Sima (980–1037) defined various levels of intellectual functioning, and was aware that brain injury could affect memory and speech. In England during the time of Edward I and II, attempts were made to assess the intellectual capacity of idiots. In the *New Naturea Brevium* published in 1534, Sir Anthony Fitzherbert offered the following primitive intelligence test: 'And he who shall be said to be a sot and idiot at birth, is such a person who cannot account or number twenty pence, nor can tell who was his father or mother, nor how old he is, etc., so as it may appear that he hath no understanding of reason what shall be for his profit, nor what for his loss. But if he hath such understanding, that he knows and understands his letters, and do read by teaching or information of another man, then it seemeth he is not a sot nor a natural idiot.'

In the nineteenth century description of people with feeblemindedness clearly made use of the concept of intellectual capacity, for example, Howe (1848) and Ireland (1882) both referring to a lack of intellect when describing idiots. However, there was usually no suggestion that a numerical score could be put on an individual's degree of intellectual ability. On the whole, early reference to the concept treated it as a qualitative construct somewhat similar to beauty or ugliness, which everyone would have to some degree, but which we would not normally want to put the degree to which people have it on a numerical scale.

The first serious attempt to measure intellectual capacity was made by Sir Francis Galton.

Francis Galton (1822–1911)

Sir Francis Galton was a Victorian polymath. He was interested in various fields and made ground-breaking contributions in several; for example, he developed the first weather map and recognised that fingerprints were unique to individuals. He also developed a number of statistical concepts and methods that are key to the understanding and measurement of intellectual ability.

Galton was a second cousin to Charles Darwin and was greatly influenced by his book *The Origin of Species*. This led to an interest in why people differ from each other, most notably in intellectual capacity. In 1869 he published *Hereditary Genius*, in which he looked at the relatives of men who had clearly achieved eminence in a particular field such as law, science or the arts. He found that their relatives also tended to be high achievers but that the probability of being a high achiever decreased as the degree of their relationship decreased. So children and brothers were more likely to be achievers than cousins and grandchildren. He put forward the idea that eminence runs in families and suggested that this was due to inheritance. He advocated eugenics, a term he first coined in 1883.

He was probably the first person to seriously try to measure intellectual ability. However, before discussing this it may be useful to look at another of his innovations, the statistical technique of correlations. Correlation has been at the heart of the study of intelligence ever since the time of Galton and is a method that the reader will need to be familiar with in order to fully understand the arguments presented in this book.

Correlations

People vary in many different ways; for example, height, weight, the amount they earn and how long they live. Often these variables can be accurately measured; height can be measured to within a fraction of an inch, age at death to a few hours, weight at any one time to within a few pounds (though different scales may give different results and an individual's weight is likely to vary a little from day to day), and annual income to within a few pounds (though again this will fluctuate over time and the accuracy of its measurement may be affected by various factors such as whether one is filling in one's tax form or not). Things that vary are called, in statistical parlance, variables.

Some of these variables seem to have a relationship to each other: that is, people who measure high on one variable tend to measure high on a second variable and people who are low on a particular variable tend to be low on the second. A good example of variables that are related to each other are height and weight; people who are taller tend to weigh more, and people who weigh less tend to be shorter. There is not, however, an exact relationship between the two variables. We can all think of people who are short and weigh a lot and people who are tall but very thin and do not weigh a lot. Galton started to look for ways of quantifying the degree of the relationship between two variables and devised the correlation. This, in modified forms, is the basis of many areas of scientific research, particularly biology and social sciences. The statistic produced by a correlation is the correlation coefficient denoted by r, which indicates the degree to which two variables vary together. Correlation coefficients range between plus one, where there is a perfect relationship between two variables, for example, between an individual's age and the number of birthdays they have had, to minus one where the two variables change in opposite directions, for example, the relationship between the amount of one's salary one has left at the end of the month and the amount one spends over the month. If there is no relationship between two variables the correlation is zero, for example, there would be no relationship, hence a zero correlation, between individuals' heights and the amount of rainfall they experience on any one day in the UK. In most cases where we are interested in the relationships between variables, the correlation coefficient is less than one but greater than zero, or greater than minus one and less than zero. For example, a Google web search found a study that reported the correlation between height and weight to be .3 for 1501 12th grade (aged 17 to 18 years) males in the US. A correlation of .3 is generally regarded as a low correlation suggesting some relationship between the two variables but not a large one. Correlations between .5 and .7 may be considered moderate and those greater than .7 high, suggesting a strong relationship between the two variables. However, the degree to which one can apply these labels to correlations depends on the context in which they are being used.

Galton felt that intellectual ability was due to neurological efficiency and that neurological efficiency could be assessed by the effectiveness of an individual's senses. In order to get data to test this he set up a stand at the London International Health Exhibition of 1884. Members of the public were invited to pay three old pence to be measured on 17 different physical abilities. He assessed such things as 'Keenness of Sight and Hearing; Colour

Sense; Judgment of the Eye; Breathing Power, Reaction Time; Strength of Pull and of Squeeze; Force of Blow; Span of Arms; Height, both standing and sitting; and Weight' (Galton 1908 p. 245). In all he tested about 9000 people so had a lot of data. However, when he applied his correlations to this data he found there was virtually no correlation between the different measures, showing the tests were measuring different things and possibly that there was not a single trait of intelligence.

Alfred Binet (1857–1911)

Alfred Binet is credited with developing the world's first effective test of intelligence. Born in Nice, France, the son of a doctor and a painter, he was taken by his mother as a child to Paris and educated there. At university he initially studied law but, although enjoying his time as a student, he was unhappy with law and became interested in natural science and then in the newly emerging science of psychology. With a collaborator, Victor Henir, he published a series of papers between 1895 and 1898 in which they described a range of tests they had developed to distinguish between people and their attempts to measure higher mental processes in children and adults. During 1903 they reported an intensive study of the intellectual development of Binet's two daughters.

In 1904 the Minister of Public Instruction in Paris assembled a commission, which included Binet, to consider the problem of subnormal children in the public schools. The need was to develop a way of identifying the children who could not cope with the French school curriculum so that they could be given extra support. Together with Dr Simon, a young physician in an asylum for backward children, Binet did the initial work of developing a test to identify these children. Unlike Galton, whose tests were determined by his theory of intelligence, Binet and Simon took a pragmatic approach and looked for items. They wanted items that would distinguish children of different ages and different ability levels. To discover which items were useful they spent hours in schools checking how large groups of children of different ages performed on them. If the item did not distinguish between the bright and the dull children, or older from younger, it was abandoned. Items that worked were kept even though they may not have fitted with the theory. The first version of the 'Metrical Scale of Intelligence' had 30 items, mainly school-based tasks, arranged in order of difficulty. Early items were things such as following a moving light. More difficult items would be finding rhyme for words and constructing a sentence with three given words in it.

This first version of the test did not derive a score but instead categorised children according to their levels of intellectual disability: idiocy, imbecility, and moronaty. In a second version in 1908 the items were arranged according to the age at which 50–70 per cent of average children passed them. The grouping of test items according to the age at which a child would be expected to pass allowed Binet to produce what has become an important measure of intellectual ability: mental age (MA). A child's MA was the age of the average children who gained the same score on the test. Binet initially used the difference between MA and chronological age (CA) as a measure of disability and considered a two-year difference as significant. The problem with this is that a difference of two years for a five-year-old is proportionally much greater than it is for a 15-year-old. Because of this, in 1912 the German psychologist Stern suggested using the ratio between MA and CA instead, which when multiplied by 100 it gave an intellectual quotient or IQ.

$$IQ = (MA/CA) \times 100$$

Although IQ scores are calculated somewhat differently in modern intelligence tests the name has continued to the present day.

It is worth spending a bit of time looking at what this ratio means. If a child is average their MA will be the same as their CA so that their IQ will be 100 and will continue to be 100 until they reach the maximum average MA, the age at which MAs no longer increase, which is about 15 years old.

If at age five a child's MA was two years behind, that is three years, their IQ would be:

$$(3/5) \times 100 = 60$$

If, however, a child's MA is two years behind at age 12 years their IQ will be:

$$(10/12) \times 100 = 83$$

which is a greater IQ than the five-year-old would have with a two-year disparity between CA and MA.

The IQ score reflects the relative rate of development, so that if a child is developing at half the average rate they will have an IQ of 50, if he/she is developing at twice the average rate they will have an IQ of 200. The lowest possible IQ is zero if a child has a MA equivalent to a newborn baby. Theoretically there is no limit to the maximum IQ but in practice they are rarely greater than 150.

A further important feature of IQ scores is that they are normally distributed. Normal distributions together with the related concept of the standard deviation (SD) are statistical concepts that the reader will need to be familiar with so a brief description is given here.

Normal distribution and standard deviations

As Galton and many others have found, if a biological variable such as height or weight is measured in a large number of individuals, most people will score near the average, while far fewer people will score well above or well below the average. So for height, about 70 per cent of the population will be within three inches of the average height, which for western men is about 5 foot 9 inches, and only about 4 per cent of the population will be either six inches taller or shorter than the average. The same applies to most biological variables and many non-biological ones. The curve that fits over this distribution is called a normal curve. The equation giving its function is complex; however, what it comes down to is that all normal curves differ in terms of only two factors, the mean of the variable being measured and the standard deviation of the distribution. The standard deviation is a measure of the degree to which the distribution spreads: if there is a large standard deviation there is quite a flat curve, whereas if it is a small standard deviation it is a pointy curve. Mathematically, the important thing about the standard deviation is that it indicates the proportion of the individuals that will score in a particular range of scores. About 68 per cent of individuals will have a score between one standard deviation below the mean and one standard deviation above the mean. About 2.5 per cent of the population will score either above or below two standard deviations.

On the Binet test the scores were normally distributed around the mean of 100, and although the standard deviation varied between age groups, it was about 16 points, which meant that just less than 50 per cent of the population had IQs between 90 and 110 and about 2.5 per cent of the population had IQs above 132. The proportion of the population with IQs below two standard deviations or IQ 68 would also have been about 2.5 per cent; however, as is discussed later, the normal distribution does not apply at the very low IQ levels as there are more people with very low IQs than would be predicted by the normal distribution.

The major problem with mental age and IQ scores derived from the ratio of MA and CA is that it cannot be directly applied to adults. Mental age will stop increasing when a child is about 14–15 years old so that the average adult mental age will be about 14½. So an average adult of 20 years, who you might think should have a ratio IQ of 100, will have a MA of 14½ years and so will have an IQ of:

$$(14½/20) \times 100 = 72.5$$

And an average adult of 30 would have an IQ of:

$$(14½/30) \times 100 = 48.3$$

This has been dealt with in some tests by calculating the IQ for adults using the average adult MA rather that CA so that the IQ of the average 20-year-old would be:

$$(14½/14½) \times 100 = 100$$

But this is only a partial solution, as older adults tend to have on average lower mental ages. An IQ based on the ratio of MA/CA is therefore only really applicable to children.

As noted in Chapter 1, Goddard went to France in 1908 and came across the Binet Simon scale. He brought it back to the US, translated it into English, and then used it to assess the residents at Vineland Training School. He went on to have a major influence in making the American medical and psychological establishment aware of the scale and successfully argued that the definition of mental deficiency should be based on measured intellectual ability.

The Binet scale was further developed in the US by Lewis Terman, who in 1916 published the Stanford Binet scale. This was a substantial development on the original Binet scale with 90 more items and ratio-based IQ scores. The new items were mainly school-related knowledge such as vocabulary, reading comprehension, and word definitions. The items had been given to thousands of people in the states of California and Nevada and it was clear that the test could distinguish between children of different ages in schools. In spite of the educational nature of the test Terman believed it measured innate intelligence: a fixed, inherited trait, rather than just testing education or cultural background. The Stanford Binet scale has continued to be updated and is still in use today.

Charles Spearman (1863–1945)

Spearman served in the British army for 15 years before resigning and starting to study for a PhD in psychology in Germany. He later became professor of psychology at University College London. During the South African War at the turn of the twentieth century he was recalled to the army and was stationed on the Channel Island of Guernsey. It was there that he began to develop his ideas about intelligence. He used the children in the local school to look at the relationship abilities on different subjects. He found that there was a tendency for children who were good at one subject to also be good at others, so that a child who was good at maths also tended to be good at English. When quantifying these relationships using correlations he noticed that the more similar two academic subjects were the higher the correlation. Abilities to do language-based subjects such as Classics, French and English correlated quite highly but less so with maths, and only weakly with musical ability. It seemed that the more a task involved thinking the higher the correlation with other activities that involved thinking. These observations led to his two-factor theory of intelligence published in 1904. In this theory he suggested that an individual's performance on a mental task was determined by two factors: first, general intelligence, which is common to all mental tasks to some degree and, second, factors specific to that particular task. For example, an ability to do maths is determined by an individual's general intelligence and specific factors specific to do maths, such as a fascination with numbers. The reason why there is correlation between individuals' abilities on mental tasks is that they all involve intellect to some extent. The degree to which abilities on two tasks correlate is determined by the degree to which they both require intellectual ability. This idea has been the basis for much of the theory of intelligence and the development of IQ tests. However, Spearman's analysis of the data went further than simply using correlations: he developed the more sophisticated method of factor analysis to isolate the underlying factors in the correlations. This method has been extensively used not only in the understanding of what intelligence is and the development of intelligence tests but also in many areas of scientific enquiry ever since. The reader will need to develop a basic understanding of what factor analysis involves to fully appreciate some of the arguments developed later in this book.

Factor analysis

Factor analysis is a complex statistical procedure that is not that easily understood by people who do not have a grounding in statistical theory; therefore, what is presented here is a simplified description. Those readers who require a more thorough description of method could consult Mackintosh (1998), who gives a more detailed, though still relatively accessible, description of the method.

The start of a factor analysis is a matrix of correlations, which is produced by taking a large number of variables and correlating each with each of the others. The correlations are then placed in a matrix. If this is done it may well be found that there are clusters of relatively high correlations between some variables and relatively low correlations between others. It is assumed that if there is a cluster of high correlations this is due to all the variables sharing a common factor. Factor analysis is a method of isolating these factors and quantifying the degree to which the individual test items measure them.

When Spearman applied factor analysis to the scores of a large number of people on different mental tests he found a single factor common to all tests of academic and mental tests, that of general intelligence or what he termed g. Since Spearman's time, with the advent of fast computers, factor analysis has been become far more sophisticated, and nowadays there is a distinction made between exploratory factor analysis, similar to that used by Spearman, and confirmatory factor analysis which is used to quantify how well data fits a predetermined theoretical model of what it should look like.

The important things about Spearman's work are, first, that it provides good evidence that intellectual ability is a single factor g and so it is reasonable to quantify it in a single IQ score. Second, as it is possible through factor analysis to quantify the degree to which a test or a test item is measuring g, one can use this method to find tests and test items that clearly measure g and reject items that do not. This has been done in the development of IQ tests since and, although there are a number of valid criticisms of IQ tests, discussed in detail later, it cannot be claimed items in the test are arbitrary.

The US Army Alpha and Beta tests

Soon after the entry of the United States into the First World War a group of psychologists including Terman and Goddard persuaded the US army to have the IQs of all recruits and conscripts tested. Two separate tests that could be given to large groups of individuals at one time were developed. The Alpha was based on written questions and required the individual to be able to read and write English. However, as a substantial proportion of the US population was either illiterate or could not speak English effectively, the Beta test was developed based on non-verbal items. In order to get an indication as to how effective the tests would be with an average young adult population a trial was conducted in which the tests were given to 4000 soldiers. The officers were asked to rank the men in terms of intellectual ability, which was then correlated with the test scores and found to be between .5 and .7. The tests were then duly given to all conscripts and recruits. Although many officers did not feel the tests were much use at predicting who would make an effective soldier or sailor, by the end of the war they had tested over 1.5 million men. This gave a great deal of data on the intellectual ability of young men in the US. Looking at the whole 1.5 million assessments completed we see some interesting results: the average mental age of the conscripts was a lot lower than had been expected at 13.08 years. Indeed, nearly half the recruits would technically be classified as morons according to Goddard's criteria. There was a relationship between test scores and apparent intellectual competence with officers tending to score higher than enlisted men.

There was also a relationship between IQ and race, with Whites tending to score higher than African Americans. However, in spite of the assertions of Goddard and Terman that what was being measured was a genetically determined trait there was also a high correlation of .81 with level of education. Therefore to a large extent the tests were a measure of educational achievement. This raised the possibility that an individual's IQ is as a result of the education they received. If somebody had the opportunity for a good education he/she would score more highly on the test, if they were poorly educated they would score less well. There was clearly a lot of variation in level of education at that time; for example, just over a quarter of the conscripts could not read sufficiently to do the Alpha test and had to be given the Beta test and 20 per cent of the southern African Americans, who on average were the group to score the lowest on the test, had received no education at all, yet many of the officers were college graduates. It is therefore possible that an individual's measured level of intellectual ability is caused by the amount of education they received.

However, there are other possible explanations for the relationship between intellectual ability and level of education. First, that intelligence is inherited but that the more intellectually able parents would have better jobs and so be able to afford better education for their children. Second, it is also possible that the more intelligent children would do better in school and so want to have more education. This illustrates another important statistical point, which is that correlations do not show causality. In this case it is not clear if a better education results in higher scores on IQ tests or whether higher innate intelligence results in children achieving a higher level of education. This issue is discussed in more detail in Chapter 6 on the causes of intellectual disability but, briefly, the current evidence suggests that an individual's level of intellectual ability is partially due to genetic factors and in part due to what has happened to them over their life.

As a result of the mass testing during the First World War many people in the US had come into contact either directly or indirectly with IQ tests and they were being thought of as a useful tool not only for identifying those with mental deficiency but also for other things, such as job recruitment.

Sir Cyril Burt (1883–1971)

In the UK the main advocate of the use of intelligence testing in the first half of the twentieth century was Cyril Burt, the son of a country doctor who had as a patient a relative of Francis Galton. As a result of this, Burt met Galton on a number of occasions as a child. He studied psychology and philosophy at university. Then in 1913, influenced by Galton, worked on mental testing, he took a part-time job with London County Council with the responsibility of finding feebleminded children in accordance with the 1913 Mental Deficiency Act. This enabled him to work in Spearman's laboratory in University College London where he continued Spearman's work on factor analysis extending method. In 1921 he also translated the Binet scale into English and in 1931 he took over the chair of psychology at University College London from Spearman. In 1946 he became the first British psychologist to be knighted.

Like Galton and others he was convinced that intellectual ability was innate. In 1909 he published a paper in which he showed that children in a private primary school did better on mental tests than children in an ordinary state primary school. His explanation for this finding was that intelligence was innate ability. Beginning in the 1940s he started to publish papers that showed high correlations between the tested intellectual ability of identical (monozygotic or MZ) twins who had been separated at birth, supposedly showing that intelligence was mainly genetically determined. He was a member of the British Eugenics Society and he suggested in a 1946 radio interview that there should be a society for very bright people which led to his being made Honorary President of Mensa, a society for people with high IQs, in 1960.

Because of his prominence he had a considerable influence on UK educational policy and was influential in the introduction of the 11+ exam, given to children in the UK at age 10 and 11 years. This exam was used to select the most able children to go to the academically demanding grammar schools, from which it was expected that they would be able to enter university, a professional or managerial post. The other children would be educated in the less demanding secondary modern schools, which would lead to non-professional skilled trades at best. Part of this exam was a test of academic skills in subjects such as English and Mathematics; however, part was a direct measure of intellectual ability. A child's future could therefore be decided on the results of an assessment taken when he/she was only 10 or 11 years old. If Burt was correct that intellectual ability was innate and so could not be modified by education, and the 11+ exam was an accurate measure of intellectual ability, then the exam may well have been an efficient way of ensuring that a child got the right education. However, if these assumptions were not true then it was likely that many children who had had a relatively poor education up to taking the exam but had academic potential, or simply had a bad day when they took the test, would miss out.

There is a footnote to Cyril Burt's career. Soon after he died in 1971 as one of the UK's most honoured psychologists there were questions about the reliability of his data most notably on his work with twins, anomalies were noticed in his data together with a lack of procedural details that led some to question his integrity (Kamin 1974). For example, mysteriously the correlations in later papers were given to three decimal places and were the same as he had reported in earlier papers, suggesting that they were simply copied and not based on new studies. It now seems likely that much of his later work on the heritability of IQ using identical twins separated soon after birth was based on data that he fabricated (Mackintosh 1998).

David Wechsler (1896–1981)

The major innovator in the measurement of intelligence in the second half of the twentieth century was David Wechsler. He emigrated to the United States from Rumania as a child. He began to study psychology before the First World War and during the war was one of the psychologists involved in the administration of the Army Alpha and Beta tests. After the war he continued his studies in psychology. In 1932 he became Chief Psychologist at the Belleview psychiatric hospital where he began to develop a series of intelligence tests. During this time and as a student he came into contact with a number of prominent psychologists working on intelligence. At Columbia University, where he was completing his Master's he studied under James Cattell, who had

had previously worked with Galton. He came into contact with Edward Thorndike who believed intelligence was not a single entity but rather a set of independent and specific abilities. He also spent a few months in England studying with Charles Spearman.

As Binet had done, he took a somewhat pragmatic approach to the understanding and measurement of intelligence. He felt that intelligence was too broad a construct to be measured by an IQ test. He tried to develop an assessment that would measure as much of an individual's intellectual ability as possible. He therefore designed a test with a wide range of different subtests basing many on those used in the army Alpha and Beta tests. This resulted in a test that gave three IQ scores: Verbal IQ, corresponding roughly to the Alpha tests, Performance IQ, corresponding to the Beta test and the Full Scale IQ, which was derived from all the subtests. He was careful to demonstrate that the subtests correlated with each other and that the correlation between the verbal subtests and between the performance subtests was greater than between the verbal subtests and the performance subtests.

Wechsler's initial aim was to produce a test that could be used for adults. As was noted above, the MA/CA ratio method does not work for adults, as an adult will reach his or her maximum mental age in the teens, resulting in an individual's MA/CA ratio IQ continually going down after the age of about 14 years. Wechsler therefore based his IQ scores on how far the individual differed from the mean score of a representative sample of people of his/her own age rather than a mental age. It is worth going into how this was done in a little detail, as an understanding of this is necessary to appreciate the arguments outlined in the next chapter as to why these tests may be less accurate when used with people in the low intellectual range.

Until the most recent version of the test, the Wechsler's Adult Intelligence Scale (WAIS) had 11 different subtests, six of which measured Verbal IQ, five of which measured Performance IQ and all 11 measuring Full Scale IQ. On each subtest there was a different maximum number of points that could be obtained, so an individual's raw score on one subtest was not directly comparable with the raw score he/she obtained on another subtest. Subtest raw scores were therefore normalised, that is, they were converted to scaled scores that had an imposed normal distribution with a mean of 10 points and a standard deviation (SD) of three points. Tables are provided in the test manuals to convert raw scores to scaled scores but what is of interest is how these tables were derived. I think it would useful to give an explanation of this, though even a basic explanation is somewhat complex. Data is used from the standardisation sample, which is the large group of people who were representative of the US population as a whole. First the average raw score on a subtest is found: this will correspond to the middle scaled score of 10 on the normalised scale. The other raw scores are then allocated their equivalent scaled scores on the basis of the proportion of the sample who score higher or lower. So, if 16 per cent of the sample scored lower than a particular raw score, that raw score would be one standard deviation below the mean and that raw score would be equivalent to a scaled score of seven. A raw score that 16 per cent of the sample scored higher would be at the one SD above the mean point and would be given a scaled score of 13. In the more modern tests the sample that is used to convert raw scores to scaled scores is a representative sample in an age band of about 10 years in adults or one year in children, usually of 200 people. The test therefore compares an individual's performance with people of his/her own age.

Once the raw scores have been converted to scaled scores, the IQ scores are derived in a similar way from the scaled scores. The subtest scaled scores are added together to get a sum of scaled scores and is then converted into an IQ score which has an imposed mean of 100 and a standard deviation of 15 based on distribution of the sums of scaled scores of the standardisation sample. This method of deriving IQs has some advantages over the MA/CA x 100 ratio method: not only can it be used with people of any age but as standard deviation of the scores is imposed there will be no variation in standard deviation at different age ranges. This fixed standard deviation means that the proportion of the population who have IQs in a particular range is also theoretically fixed.

Although the current Wechsler tests only give Full Scale IQs between 40 and 160; however, 160 is not the maximum possible IQ that could be measured using this deviation from the mean method, though, unlike the ratio method there is a theoretical maximum. For IQs with a mean of 100 and a standard deviation of 15 the maximum possible IQ can be worked out as follows. First find the proportion of the population as a whole the single most intelligent person on earth would correspond to, then find how many standard deviations this is above the mean and then multiply this by 15 and add 100. As I write the population of the earth has just passed seven billion (7,000,000,000), so the most intelligent person on earth would make up 1/7,000,000,000 of the population, which is .00000000014286, which is equivalent to almost exactly six standard deviations above the mean. So the maximum possible IQ based on a mean of 100 and a standard deviation of 15, derived using the deviation method, would be six standard deviations or 90 points above the mean of 100, which is 190. This should be borne in mind when considering reports of people with much higher IQs.

Wechsler's first assessment for adults was the Wechsler Belleview Intelligence Scale produced in 1939. The Wechsler Adult Intelligence Scale (WAIS) was published in 1955; a revised version, the WAIS-R, was published in 1981; the third edition, the WAIS-III, in 1997 and the fourth edition in 2008. An assessment for children, the Wechsler Intelligence Scale for Children (WISC), was first produced in 1949, replaced by the WISC-R in 1974, the WISC-III in 1991 and the fourth edition, the WISC-IV in 2003. The Wechsler scales are now the most widely used and respected tests of intelligence and are seen as the gold standard tests.

The structure of intelligence

Spearman's theory that intellectual ability is a single factor of general intelligence (g) has been challenged by some who felt that intelligence was made up of a number of independent factors, notably Thompson (1916, 1939) in the UK and Thorndike (1925) and Hull (1928) in the US. Thurstone (Thurstone 1938, 1947 and Thurstone and Thurstone 1941) suggested that Spearman's factor solution was based on false assumptions and that IQ tests measured a variety of independent factors and set about using and adapting factor analysis to reveal these independent factors. He identified six 'Primary mental abilities' (PMAs): numerical, verbal comprehension, word fluency, space, reasoning, and memory. In his early studies he did not find a general factor equivalent to g in his factor analytic studies, that is, there were correlations between items that were related to specific PMAs but not between them. However, Mackintosh (1998) suggests that the reason Thurstone did not get a general factor in his early studies was that he used bright undergraduates, who, one would assume, would not vary on g that much. However, when he gave the test to schoolchildren he found the general factor. This debate has continued since and is somewhat complex though an accessible account is provided by Mackintosh (1998).

The generally accepted model of intelligence today and the one that underlies most commonly used IQ tests such as the Wechsler tests is hierarchical. In other words, there is a general factor of intelligence equivalent to g that can be summed up on a single figure such as the Full Scale IQ score but that there are also semi-independent factors that correlate with Full Scale IQ and to a lesser extent with each other. With the modern Wechsler tests (the WISC-IV and the WAIS-IV, see Appendix I) these semi-independent factors are represented by the four index scores: Verbal Comprehension Index, Perceptual Reasoning Index, Working Memory Index and Processing Speed Index. Each of these index abilities is measured by specific subtests. The subtests measuring a particular index correlate relatively highly with each other and much less so with subtests measuring other index abilities.

What intelligence predicts in the real world

If the g model of intelligence is correct we would expect that IQ scores would be predictive of other g-loaded activities and the degree to which they are an accurate predictor would be in proportion to the g loading of the task. This is largely what is found; for example, the US Army Alpha and Beta tests predicted educational achievement and occupational status. More recently a number of large studies have shown moderate to high correlation between IQ tests and tests of academic achievement. Zimmerman and Woo-Sam (1997) reviewed this evidence and reported that the average correlations of five studies that compared the WISC-III with the Woodcock Johnson Psychoeducational Battery – Revised Achievement Tests (WJ-R ACH), was .54 for reading and .68 for arithmetic/maths. There are also seven studies that compared the WISC-III with the Wechsler Individual Achievement Test (WIAT) where the correlations were .57 for reading and .79 for arithmetic.

Similar results have been reported for the latest standardisations of Wechsler tests. As part of the development of the WISC-IV (Wechsler 2003), 550 children were given both the WISC-IV and the second edition of the Wechsler Individual Achievement Test (WIAT-II). The correlations with FSIQ on the WISC-IV were as follows: Reading .78, Maths .78, Written Language .76, Oral Language .75 and Total Achievement .87. A similar study was done in development of the WAIS-IV, which was given together with the WIAT-II to 93 adolescents aged between 16 and 19. The correlations with FSIQ were: Reading .76, Maths .84, Written Language .65, Oral Language .79 and Total Achievement .88. There is also evidence that measured IQ is a relatively good predictor of intellectual achievements in the real world. Herrnstein and Murray (1994), in their controversial book *The Bell Curve*, look at the relationship between IQ and a number of real world variables, for example, the probability of getting into and graduating from college, getting into a profession and keeping a job.

However, IQ tests do not correlate with measures of abilities that do not seem to require intellectual ability, such some of the skills one would require on a daily basis. This evidence is reviewed in more detail in Chapter 4 on adaptive behaviour but recent evidence comes from the standardisation of the Vineland-II (Sparrow et al. 2005), a measure of adaptive behaviour, which includes daily living skills, socialisation and communication. As part of its standardisation it was compared with both the WISC-III and WAIS-III. The correlations between Vineland-II Composites score and Full Scale IQ were .12 and .20 for the WISC-III and WAIS-III respectively.

So the evidence suggests that IQ tests correlate with g-loaded tasks such as educational achievement and being able to get a professional job. However, they do not correlate highly with ability to do everyday tasks such as self-care or a manual job. It should also be noted that as these studies are based on correlations, they do not show causation. In the relationship between education and IQ, for example, we do not know if having a high IQ allows an individual to do well in education, or if having education causes a high IQ or whether both occur. A second point regarding this correlational data is that it tells us about the relationship for a group of individuals and not what will happen with a specific individual within that group. For example, a study may find that the correlation between IQ at entry to university and obtained degree class three years later is .60, showing that people who get higher IQ scores tend to get higher degree classes. However, there will still be individuals who score relatively low on the IQ assessment and still get a good degree, and individuals who gain a high IQ score who then go on to fail their degree.

James Flynn (1934–)

For me the next significant person in the understanding of intelligence is Jim Flynn. He was born in Washington DC and educated in Chicago, then emigrated to New Zealand in 1963 where he is now Professor of Political Studies at the University of Otago in Dunedin. In spite of not being a psychologist he has made a major contribution to our understanding of both the theory of intelligence and its assessment. His main finding was that the absolute intellectual ability of the population as a whole, at least in western industrialised countries, has been going up year after year for at least the last hundred years. In a now classic paper (Flynn 1984), he looked at US studies in which the same people had been given two different IQ tests. He found that there was a relationship between how old the test was and the IQ obtained. The longer it was since the test was standardised the higher the IQ it measured, the rate of increase being about three points per decade. The implications of this is that as tests go out of date they become easier for the population as a whole, demonstrating that the measured intellectual ability of the population is increasing at a rate of about three points a decade or .3 of a point per year.

In a second paper (Flynn 1987), he extended his analysis to 14 industrialised countries and found evidence of an increase in IQ in all of them. For some countries where there was a military draft (for example: Holland, Belgium and France) there was very strong evidence as data was available on very large samples of 18- to 19-year-old men going back decades. As part of their induction into the armed services the conscripts were given an IQ test. As these tests had not been changed for decades it was possible to compare the average scores obtained by the conscripts 10, 20 and 30 years ago with the conscripts of today. When this was done it confirmed the results of the earlier study that the intellectual ability of the conscripts as a whole was increasing at a rate of about three points per decade.

The Flynn effect in the low IQ range

In the low IQ range the indications are that the increase in intellectual ability has been even greater than in the average range. The early evidence for this again comes from a study by Flynn (1985) in which he used studies in which the WISC and its revised version, the WISC-R, standardised 25 years later, were given to the same individuals. He found that for those in the IQ range of 55 to 70 there was an average gain of .396 IQ point per year, which compared to .272 per year for those in the 125–140 IQs.

There are also now studies based on data from IQ given to military conscripts. In Norway, military service is compulsory for every able young man, who, as part of his induction process, is given an IQ test. This provides what amounts to a study on half the population, so sampling issues are not a problem. Sundet et al. (2004) used this data to compare the gains made for conscripts scoring above and below the median for pooled data for 1957 to 1959 with data from 1993 to 2002. For those scoring below the average ability there was an 11-point IQ point gain, which compared to a 4.4-point gain for those above the average. Teasdale and Owen (1989) used similar data from Denmark and found average gains in IQ over the 30 years up to the late 1980s of 7.5 IQ points. The gains were greatest in the lower 10 per cent with the maximum gains near the 11th per centile, where they were 41 per cent greater than those at the average point. There was very little gain for those in the top 10 per cent.

Is the Flynn effect real?

On the face of it, it does not seem that unreasonable that intellectual ability should be going up; after all, we have gradually been getting taller, living longer and leading healthier lives. But the gains in intellectual ability do seem dramatic. If the average gain over the past hundred years has been three points a decade, it would mean that the average intellectual ability of the population as a whole on today's standards a hundred years ago would be 70, the current cut-off point for having intellectual disability. Does it seem credible that a hundred years ago, in Britain, which at that time was one of the (if not the) major industrial, military and imperial powers on earth, half the population could have been regarded as having an intellectual disability on today's standards? Or is it possible that we are just getting better at doing IQ tests and our abilities in the real world have changed very little? If it is a real effect and people are behaving in a more intellectual way in the real world, then potentially whatever is causing the increase could be used to reduce the number of people who are failing to cope with the intellectual demands of their environment. Opinion is still somewhat divided as to whether the effect is genuine. Some have suggested that it is simply down to people becoming better at IQ tests, that is, greater test sophistication, for example Gottfredson (2008). Others have argued that the effect is genuine. Schooler (1998), for example, says the effect is genuine and suggests that it is due to increasing complexity in society. It certainly does seem that the environment is becoming more intellectually demanding and the number of intellectual demands that we meet increasing. A hundred years ago a working man or woman would learn a trade, the skills for which once learned, would change very little over the individual's working life. Similarly, leisure activities would usually make relatively low intellectual demands and be relatively unchanging. Today, jobs are constantly changing and the workers constantly have to adapt. For example, the laptop I am currently typing on is my third in the last eight years and works very differently from the one I had eight years ago. Each time I get a new laptop I am faced with the intellectual change of getting it to do what I need it to do. The same goes for TVs, DVD players, mobile phones and cars.

Flynn seems to have changed his mind on this issue; in earlier writings, for example, Flynn (1998), he emphasised that although measured intellectual ability had gone up the intellectual achievements of the population in the real world had not. However, since then he has begun to argue that the effect does have real world significance. Flynn (2007) has pointed out that the mean IQ of professionals, managers and technicians has gone down over the years as has the minimum required IQ to enter these careers and a higher proportion of the population are entering careers, suggesting that a greater proportion of the population are able to cope with intellectually demanding jobs. The intellectual demands of leisure activities have also increased over the years; for example, computer games now require prolonged concentration and on-the-spot problem solving. The evidence then seems to suggest that at least some of the effect is genuine. If it is genuine and we knew what caused it, it may be possible to change the environment so that the effect is enhanced and people become even more intelligent or we may be able to change the environments of people with intellectual disability to enhance their intelligence to a level where they are able to cope. So why does the Flynn effect occur?

What is causing the Flynn effect?

There are a number of hypotheses and much lively debate as to why the effect is occurring. Neisser (1998) is a good though somewhat old book of papers on this by all the major authors in the field. Greenfield (1998) suggests that the use of modern technology such as computer games, and the widespread use of computers has had an influence on the increased intellectual ability. Williams (1998) has suggested that improvements in education and at school may be a factor. She points out that there is more time spent in school than was the case earlier in the twentieth century; however, she also notes that there is a decrease in reading and the textbooks seem to be simpler than they were, which could have a negative effect.

Improved nutrition would seem an obvious probable cause and has been suggested as a cause by a number of authors notably Bergen (2008), Martorell (1998) and Sigman and Whaley (1998); however, the major advocate is Lynn (1990, 1998, 2009). There is evidence for improved diet being at least a contributory cause if not the sole cause of the effect, both the quantity and quality of diets having improved considerably in the last hundred years. Lynn (2009) has also demonstrated that the effect is evident in children less than one year of age, which would seem to exclude factors such as formal education, which would not have an impact until a child was older, at least as sole causes. Flynn (2006) himself has suggested that diet may be a factor for the intellectual gains before 1948, but not after. He suggests that diet did not improve very much after 1948 and that any further gains due to improved diet after that would be offset by the losses to average intellectual ability by those children who were saved at birth but had some brain damage. Flynn and a colleague (Dickens and Flynn 2001) have suggested a rather complex mechanism. They suggest that intellectual ability is enhanced by the increasing intellectual demands of the environment, particularly an increased need for on-the-spot problem solving. In addition, the environment has gradually become more intellectually demanding, as a result of being designed by a more intellectually able population. However, this model would predict that the intellectual gains would not start until a child began to interact with their environment in an intellectual way, which really does not start until the age of about two years. So, although having to cope with a more intellectually demanding world may be a contributory cause, it cannot be the only one as Lynn (2009) has found evidence for the effect in infants less than one year of age.

Another possible cause is the reduction in average family size over the years. Children in smaller families tend to have higher intellectual ability than children in larger families. The reason for this may well be due to the extra time and resources that parents may have to spend on children in smaller families. Sundet et al. (2008), in a study using intelligence test data from Norwegian conscripts, looked at the relationship between the Flynn effect and family size. They found that there was an inverse relationship between IQ and family size, with children with three or more brothers/sisters having progressively lower IQs. Over the years family size has reduced, hence there was an expected increase in average IQ. They say that this accounts for a proportion of the change but not all.

Although it would seem most likely that the Flynn effect is due to environmental causes, as the genetic pool of the population as a whole would not have changed that much in the last hundred years and the environment has changed significantly, Minogroni (2004) has proposed that some of the cause may be genetic. He argues that the Flynn effect is due to heterosis or hybrid vigour, which is the effect of breeding between two distantly related parents. He suggests that in the past people would marry someone in their locality so there was some degree of inbreeding. Now we mix much more widely within our own ethnic group and between ethnic groups resulting in more homogeneity in the gene pool. However, it seems to me that this is an unlikely mechanism as there is no strong evidence that communities breeding between genetically diverse groups has increased intellectual ability. One example that comes to mind is the United States, which was populated by immigrants from all over Europe who would interbreed and there is no evidence that intellectual ability of the children of these immigrants is any greater than those who remained in Europe. An even more potent example is the African American population who were descended from slaves brought from all over West Africa and so would breed with a wide group of other African slaves. In addition to this wide gene pool of Africans there was also a genetic input from the European population due to slave owners raping black women. But in spite of the mixing of genes, as was shown above, the measured IQ of the US African American population was significantly below that of the European American population. Flynn (2006) has suggested that what genetic effect that does occur from reducing the numbers of people who breed with close relatives would be offset by the effect of people with lower intellectual ability having more children, which should be responsible for a one point loss of IQ per generation.

The evidence therefore suggests that the main cause of the Flynn effect is likely to be environmental. There are a number of environmental factors that may be causing the effect, some of which will affect the child in the first year of life, such as improved diet or reduced family size. Others come into play in childhood and adolescence, such as the improved education system, the increased emphasis on a scientific approach to problem solving and the more cognitively demanding leisure pursuits people have today.

The end of the effect

Could the effect continue for another hundred years to bring the average IQ up to 130 on today's standards? The answer is almost certainly not. In simple terms, it is likely that everybody has a genetically determined intellectual potential, which then interacts with environmental factors to produce an individual's level of intellectual ability. If an individual is born into an optimal environment they will reach their maximum intellectual ability; if they are born into a less than optimal environment then their intellectual ability will be less. So when we come to a point when the factors in the environment responsible for intellectual development stop improving then the Flynn effect will stop. It also follows that if those aspects of the environment that are responsible for intellectual development change for the worse then the

Flynn effect will reverse. Currently Flynn (2007, 2009) has argued that in the US the Flynn effect is still continuing at all intellectual levels. However, there is now evidence that the effect may have stopped or even gone into reverse particularly in Scandinavia. Teasdale and Owen (2005), who had previously analysed the Danish data on the change in intellectual ability of conscripts up till the end of the 1980s and found greater gains in the low range, looked at the new data up to 2004 and found that there was a peak in average IQ in 1998 and then a decline until 2004. They also report that after 1995 there was an increased number of people scoring at the lower end of the tests showing a decline in IQ for people with lower IQ. Cocodia et al. (2003) looked at teachers' opinions as to whether children were getting brighter in Australia (a western country) and two Asian 'tiger' economies: South Korea and Singapore. In Singapore children were considered brighter and more motivated and in South Korea primary school children were felt to be brighter as were secondary school children, though to a lesser extent. In Australia teachers felt children were not getting brighter. I (Whitaker 2010a) used data from the last two UK editions of the WISC, the WISC-III, standardised in 1992 and the WISC-IV standardised in 2004, 12.5 years later. I found that for two of the three subtests, which were the same on both tests, there was evidence that the Flynn effect had continued in the average range but was much greater in the high ability range. However, in the low ability range it had gone into reverse. On the third subtest there was no difference between the performance of the two standardisation groups. Following a suggestion from Professor Flynn, who acted as reviewer for the journal, the analysis was repeated using the US standardisation of the WISC-III and WISC-IV (Whitaker 2011) and the same results were found.

The evidence for the end of the Flynn effect is currently small and, with the exception of the Teasdale and Owen (2005) study in Demark, may well have methodological problems; however, there are suggestions that the Flynn effect may well have come to an end in western countries and that in the low range may actually have gone into reverse. It may be possible to reverse this reversal if we can get a firmer understanding of what is causing the effect but further research will have to be done to do that.

Conclusions

The concept of intelligence has been about in western thought for thousands of years but was only seriously investigated and refined over the twentieth century. The evidence seems to suggest that it is a coherent concept in that it continually comes out of the factor analysis, is reportedly measurable and will predict how well people do in real world tasks. It feels almost the same as the physical human attributes of height and weight. However, IQ is very different from these tangible physical attributes; it may have some practical use in predicting what individuals or groups of individuals will be able to do but the concept may need to be used with caution as:

- It is not clear what the terms 'intelligence' and 'IQ' actually mean. There is a need to be careful with the language we use to describe intellectual ability. There are loose terms, for example: bright, stupid, dull, and quantitative terms, such as mental age, IQ, and true intellectual ability. These terms may be understood as equivalent but may not have the same meaning leading to misunderstandings. In later chapters I argue for a distinction to be made between genetic potential for intellectual ability, true intellectual ability and measured IQ.
- There is a relatively low relationship between intellectual ability and coping as measured on adaptive behaviour scales such as the Vineland-II. This may well limit the ability of IQ tests to predict if an individual will be able to cope or not.
- The studies that have been used to investigate the nature of intelligence and its measurement are largely correlational in nature and therefore do not show that IQ causes anything.
- An individual's IQ score only tells us something about the probability of them being able to do a g-loaded task and not whether he/she will definitely be able to do it or not.

This raises the question of what an IQ score can tell us about an individual in the low ability range. This will depend on two factors:

- How accurately one can measure IQ and from, the point of view of the theme of this book, how well it can be measured in the low range.
- The strength of relationship between measured IQ and what we are trying to predict.

This is considered in the next chapter on the measurement of IQ.

3
Measuring Intelligence

In Chapters 1 and 2, I made the point that the concept of intelligence, or specifically low intelligence, has been part of the construct of intellectual disability for centuries. Since the turn of the twentieth century the definition of intellectual disability has included having an IQ below a specified cut-off point. In the last chapter I looked at how the concept of intelligence and its measurement has developed over the years. In this chapter I want to examine in more detail how accurately intelligence, particularly low intelligence, can be measured with current tests.

We often talk about intelligence as though it is a human quality that can be measured in a similar way to height and weight. I hope I make the point in this chapter that I do not think they are the same; however, the analogy of height and weight will be a useful one to carry through the chapter. Both height and weight are physical attributes that can be measured accurately. If we specify the conditions under which an individual's height should be measured, for example, in bare feet and standing up straight, it can be measured to within a few fractions of an inch. Weight may be a bit different; although scientific instruments will measure weight to a fraction of a percentage, when it comes to measuring an individual's weight less accurate instruments are frequently used such as bathroom scales. On my bathroom scales my weight will vary from day to day depending on how much I have eaten or drunk in the last few hours and when I last used the toilet. So even though these scales could be giving me an accurate measure of my weight when I get on them they would only be able to predict what my weight would be in a few hours' time to within a couple of pounds. However, fluctuation in my weight on my bathroom scales is not the only reason to suggest that they may not be accurately measuring my true weight. I currently regularly use two other sets of scales in addition to the ones in my bathroom: the bathroom scales at my partner's house and the scales in the gym I use. My weight will vary systematically between these scales by about three pounds; I tend to have a lower weight on the scales in the gym, an intermittent weight on the scales in my bathroom and the highest weight on the scales in my partner's bathroom. I have no way of knowing which of these sets of scales is the most accurate so, although it is indisputable that at any one time I have a true weight, if I rely on these three scales I can only tell what it is to within a few pounds.

So I cannot measure my true weight on these three sets of scales; there are factors other than my true weight affecting my measured weight at any one time. It makes sense to divide these factors into two broad groups: chance and systematic. The chance factors are things that may be thought of as varying randomly from day to day, such as the time of day I weigh myself, how much I have eaten, when I last used the toilet and what clothes I'm wearing. These factors cause the variation in my measured weight from day to day. The second set of factors cause a systematic difference between scales so that on average one set of scales measured higher or lower than another set. These are factors such as how the scales are calibrated and whether the spring in the scales is wearing out. These two sets of factors both cause error in measurement, which we could call chance error and systematic error. The measurement of my true weight will therefore be subject to both chance and systematic error.

It may well be the case that I would not be so much interested in what my true weight is as whether my weight has gone down over time due to a diet. If this was the case then I could eliminate the effects of systematic error by always using the same scales. So I could set myself a target weight on my bathroom scales and not worry about what other scales were saying. But in order to get an estimate of my true weight I would need to take account of my varying weights on all three sets of scales. So one possibility for getting a more accurate idea of my true weight would be to take an average of my weight on all three scales over the last week. However, this would be assuming that my true weight falls within the range of the different weights on all three scales and although this is probably the case, it is definitely not certain. It is possible that all three scales are measuring low or high, or that one set of scales is very accurate and the others are not. The best we can truthfully say is that my true weight is probably within the limits of the different measures of my weight that I have obtained in the last few weeks and possibly close to the average.

The science of psychometrics

Psychometrics is the branch of psychology to do with the measurement of psychological variables such as intelligence and personality. When measuring any variable, first, you need to know if what you are measuring is what you think you are measuring and, second, you need to know how accurately you are measuring it. Technically this is establishing if the test is valid and reliable. These are concepts that the reader will need to be comfortable with in order to appreciate the arguments in the rest of this and the next chapters. I will therefore spend some time explaining them.

Validity

A scale is valid if it can be demonstrated that it actually measures what it is supposed to measure. This is not a straightforward thing to do with a hypothetical psychological construct, such as intelligence, as there is no independent true measure of intelligence that a scale can be compared against to check that it is accurate. But if intelligence is a coherent and real concept that can be measured, there are a number of things one would expect: that different measures of intelligence would be relatively highly correlated; that scores on the tests would correlate with real world measures of intellectual ability, such as academic performance, that test items are apparently measures of mental ability. Both the WISC-IV and WAIS-IV technical manuals (Wechsler 2003; Wechsler et al. 2008) give various lines of evidence that suggest that both tests do measure intelligence:

Evidence based on test content.
Evidence based on response processes.
Evidence based on internal structure.
Evidence based on relationships with other variables (other measures and special groups).

Evidence based on test content

As outlined in more detail in Appendix 1 both the WISC-IV and WAIS-IV give a score for the four Index Scales of Verbal Comprehension, Perceptual Reasoning, Working Memory or Processing Speed as well as Full Scale IQ. The issue with regard to test content is whether it appears to be measuring both general intelligence (g) and the more specific index abilities that it is designed to measure. The manuals point to both tests having a long history of development going back to the original Wechsler Bellevue (Wechsler 1939), and having been extensively researched over the years. So, according to experts' opinion and their interpretation of the research, the items in the test look as though they are measuring general intelligence and the index abilities.

Evidence based on response processes

What the test developers want to demonstrate here is that individuals will actually use the cognitive processes the assessment is intended to assess in responding to test items. Studying how individuals go about tackling test items, for example by asking them how they solved a problem, demonstrates this. Again evidence is presented that strongly suggests that items do tap the cognitive process they are designed to measure.

Evidence based on internal structure

What needs to be demonstrated here is that the structure of the tests is what the test developers would predict it to be, that is, that the sub-tests have the expected correlations with each other. All the subtests should measure general intelligence so should correlate with each other. In addition, specific subtests are designed to measure specific index abilities (see Appendix 1), so should correlate more highly with other subtests measuring that index ability and less highly with subtests measuring other index abilities. This is demonstrated in the first instance by presenting an intercorrelation matrix showing the correlations between subtests. Secondly, both the WISC-IV and WAIS-IV manuals give factor analysis showing that the tests both can be reduced to a single factor of general intelligence and that the predicted subtests measured the specific index abilities.

Evidence based on relationships with other variables

Irrespective of the evidence for the validity of test content, response process and internal structure, if any new scale of intelligence does not correlate highly with other established measures of intelligence, it cannot be said to be measuring intelligence. It is therefore vital to show that a scale does correlate with other IQ tests. It also needs to be demonstrated that it correlates significantly, though less highly, with measures of other related cognitive abilities such as memory. The test developers present evidence for this and then give evidence that individuals in specific clinical groups, most notably those with an intellectual disability, perform on the scales as they would be predicted to. The evidence presented in this section is fundamental to the validity of the WISC-IV and the WAIS-IV, the validity of the concept of intelligence generally and to some of the later arguments in this book. I will therefore go into it in some detail.

Comparison with other tests of intelligence

Both scales were compared with the tests they replaced, the WISC-IV with the WISC-III and the WAIS-IV with the WAIS-III. The results of this are presented in Tables 3.1 and Table 3.2.

Table 3.1 shows the comparison between the WAIS-IV and WAIS-III, in which both tests were given to 240 adults in counterbalanced order, that is, half the subjects were given the WAIS-IV first and half were given the WAIS-III first. The correlations between the two scales are high, with a correlation of .94 between the FSIQs, which is only slightly lower than the correlation of the WISC-IV with itself when it was given to the same subject twice. The lowest correlation of .85 for PRI is also still reasonable. This strongly suggests that both scales measure the same thing, which, given the other evidence from factor analysis studies and what the WAIS-IV predicts, is very likely to be general intelligence and related cognitive abilities.

The mean, and standard deviation, in brackets, of the IQ and index scores, are approximately 100 and 15 respectively for the WAIS-IV, as would be expected. What is also of note is that the mean score is higher on the WAIS-III than on the WAIS-IV. This is what would be predicted from the Flynn effect. As we saw in Chapter 2, Flynn in various studies has found that the intellectual ability of the population as a whole is going up by about three IQ points a decade. So for the six years between the standardisation of the WAIS-III and WAIS-IV one would expect there to be a two point increase in IQ. This is approximately what is found

Table 3.1 Comparison of the WAIS-IV and WAIS-III

	WAIS-IV	WAIS-III	dif	r
VCI	100.1 (14.9)	104.4 (15.5)	4.3	.91
PRI	100.3 (15.5)	103.7 (15.3)	3.4	.84
WMI	99.3 (13.7)	100.0 (14.5)	.7	.87
PSI	100.1 (14.9)	100.8 (17.2)	.7	.86
FSIQ	100.0 (15.2)	102.9 (14.9)	2.9	.94

Note: The mean scores and standard deviation of these scores, in brackets, for the Verbal Comprehension Index (VCI), the Perceptual Reasoning Index (PRI), the Working Memory Index (WMI), the Processing Speed Index (PSI) and Full Scale IQ (FSIQ) on the WAIS-IV and WAIS-III, together with the differences between the mean scores (dif) and the correlation between the scores (r). Data is derived from both scales being given to 240 adults in counterbalanced order.

Table 3.2 Comparison of the WISC-IV and the WISC-III

	WISC-IV	WISC-III	dif	r
VC/VI	103.0 (12.3)	105.4 (13.8)	2.4	.83
PR/PI	103.9 (14.0)	107.3 (14.9)	3.4	.73
WM/FD	101.5 (15.3)	103.0 (15.9)	1.5	.74
PS/PS	102.7 (15.1)	108.2 (16.3)	5.5	.81
FSIQ	104.5 (14.0)	107.0 (14.4)	2.5	.87

Note: The mean scores and standard deviation of these scores, in brackets, for the Verbal Comprehension Index (VCI), the Perceptual Reasoning Index (PRI), the Working Memory Index (WMI), the Processing Speed Index (PSI) and Full Scale IQ (FSIQ) on the WISC-IV and WISC-III, together with the differences between the mean scores (dif) and the correlation between the scores (r). Data is derived from both scales being given to 244 children, in counterbalanced order.

with a 2.9 point difference between FSIQs. However, the effect was not even across the index scales with 4.3 points for Verbal Comprehension and only a 0.7 increase for Processing Speed and Working Memory.

The WISC-IV and WISC-III were given to 244 children, counter-balanced order. The results are given in Table 3.2 above.

The correlations between the equivalent index scores and FSIQ are not as large as they were with the WAIS-III/IV comparisons though are still reasonable and provide evidence that both scales are measuring the same thing, which is very likely to be intelligence.

A Flynn effect is also apparent. With a 12-year interval between the standardisation of the two scales one would expect that individuals would score about 3.5 points more on the WISC-III than the WISC-IV. The differences vary between index scales and FSIQ, being greatest for Possessing Speed and lowest for Working Memory. What is interesting is that the highest effect of 5.5 points occurred for Processing Speed, which showed the lowest effect, of .7, on the WAIS-III and WAIS-IV comparison. It is not clear why this difference occurred. The gain in overall intellectual ability given by FSIQ is 2.5 points, which suggests that overall the Flynn effect may have slowed down for children.

Comparison between the two assessments

Both the WAIS-IV and the WISC-IV were given to 157 16-year-olds, the age at which both assessments can be used. The results are given in Table 3.3. Here again the correlations are reasonably good for FSIQ and Verbal Comprehension, suggesting that they are measuring the same thing. However, the correlations are only moderate for the other index scales, meaning that these index scales may not be tapping exactly the

Table 3.3 Comparison of the WAIS-IV and WISC-IV

	WAIS-IV	WISC-IV	dif	r
VCI	101.0 (13.3)	102.7 (12.3)	1.7	.88
PRI	102.6 (12.6)	103.4 (13.7)	.8	.77
WMI	100.9 (13.5)	101.1 (14.7)	.2	.78
PSI	101.3 (11.8)	100.7 (13.2)	−.6	.77
FSIQ	102.5 (12.2)	103.7 (12.7)	1.2	.91

Note: The mean scores and standard deviation of these scores, in brackets, for the Verbal Comprehension Index (VCI), the Perceptual Reasoning Index (PRI), the Working Memory Index (WMI), the Processing Speed Index (PSI) and Full Scale IQ (FSIQ) on the WAIS-IV and WISC-IV, together with the differences between the mean scores (dif) and the correlation between the scores (r). Data is derived from both scales being given to 157 16-year-olds, in counterbalanced order.

same abilities on the two scales. There is some evidence for a Flynn effect with an average score of 1.2 points higher on the WISC-IV for FSIQ, which is slightly less than would have been expected with the WAIS-IV being standardised six years after the WISC-IV.

Validity in the low range

Looking at the evidence for validity of the WISC-IV and WAIS-IV as a whole, it suggests that both tests are valid measures of intelligence for people with average intellectual ability. However, as these validation studies were not done using individuals with low intellectual ability they do not necessarily demonstrate that the scales are valid in the low range. However, there are studies that do suggest the assessments are valid in the low range.

There have been a number of factor analytical studies using earlier versions of the WISC and WAIS using people with low IQ, which produced very similar results to studies done with subjects of average intellectual ability. For example, Atkinson and Cyr (1988) did a factor analysis of 204 adults with IQs less than 80 on the WAIS-R and found good evidence for g and two or three additional factors. Huberty (1987) factor analysed the WISC-R scores of 171 children with a mean FSIQ of 71 and found that derived factors were very similar to those identified in standardised data and other studies using people with average intellectual ability, in addition to g they found evidence for three factors corresponding to Verbal Comprehension, Perceptual Organisation and Freedom from Distraction.

The WAIS-IV manual reports a study in which WAIS-IV and WAIS-III were given to 25 adults with a diagnosis of mild intellectual disability and 24 adults with a diagnosis of borderline intellectual disability. The results of these studies are shown in Table 3.4 for those with mild disabilities and Table 3.5 for those with borderline intellectual disabilities. Looking at the correlation between the two scales it is notable that they are lower than those found in the adults with average intellectual ability (see Table 3.1) but still acceptable.

In order to show the scales effectively assess people with low IQs, both the WISC-IV and WAIS-IV manuals report studies in which both scales were given to larger groups of people with intellectual disabilities and comparing their results with matched controls without intellectual disability. The WAIS-IV was given to 104 non-institutionalised adults with a diagnosis of intellectual disability: 73 to a mild degree and 31 to a moderate degree. The WISC-IV was given to 63 children with an

Table 3.4 Comparison of the WAIS-IV and WAIS-III in the mild range

	WAIS-IV	WAIS-III	dif	r
VCI	66.1 (4.9)	69.6 (6.8)	3.5	.78
PRI	65.0 (10.1)	69.4 (7.2)	4.4	.86
WMI	62.9 (7.6)	60.7 (7.0)	−2.2	.76
PSI	64.4 (11.9)	67.9 (8.0)	3.5	.89
FSIQ	58.5 (6.9)	62.6 (5.5)	4.1	.86

Note: The mean scores and standard deviation of these scores, in brackets, for the Verbal Comprehension Index (VCI), the Perceptual Reasoning Index (PRI), the Working Memory Index (WMI), the Processing Speed Index (PSI) and Full Scale IQ (FSIQ) on the WAIS-IV and WAIS-III, together with the differences between the mean scores (dif) and the correlation between the scores (r). Data derived from both scales being given to 25 adults diagnosed as having a mild intellectual disability, in counterbalanced order.

Table 3.5 Comparison of the WAIS-IV and the WAIS-III in the borderline range

	WAIS-IV	WAIS-III	dif	r
VCI	78.2 (7.4)	79.3 (8.3)	1.1	.79
PRI	75.3 (8.1)	80.4 (8.4)	5.1	.63
WMI	73.8 (9.3)	73.5 (13.2)	−.3	.89
PSI	80.1 (10.9)	78.7 (8.1)	−1.4	.50
FSIQ	72.5 (7.5)	74.7 (7.3)	2.2	.82

Note: The mean scores and standard deviation of these scores, in brackets, for the Verbal Comprehension Index (VCI), the Perceptual Reasoning Index (PRI), the Working Memory Index (WMI), the Processing Speed Index (PSI) and Full Scale IQ (FSIQ) on the WAIS-IV and WAIS-III, together with the differences between the mean scores (dif) and the correlation between the scores (r). Data derived from both scales being given to 25 adults diagnosed as having a borderline intellectual disability, in counterbalanced order.

existing diagnosis of mild intellectual disability and 57 with a diagnosis of a moderate degree of intellectual disability. The results are given in Tables 3.6 and 3.7. These results, though unremarkable, show that when the tests are given to people who have a diagnosis suggesting a low IQ, on average they do indeed score in the low IQ range.

So it seems that the WISC-IV and WAIS-IV specifically and probably IQ tests in general can be valid measures of intellectual ability in both the average and the low ranges. However, as the evidence for the validity of IQ tests is based on group studies, where groups of individuals

Table 3.6 Comparison of index scores and FSIQ between people with mild and moderate degrees of intellectual disability on the WAIS-IV

	WAIS-IV	
	Mild ID	**Moderate ID**
VCI	65.9 (6.3)	56.8 (4.8)
PRI	65.4 (8.7)	55.0 (5.1)
WMI	61.5 (7.7)	53.1 (4.6)
PSI	63.8 (12.6)	53.8 (7.3)
FSIQ	58.5 (7.5)	48.2 (4.7)

Note: The mean scores and standard deviation of these scores, in brackets, for the Verbal Comprehension Index (VCI), the Perceptual Reasoning Index (PRI), the Working Memory Index (WMI), the Processing Speed Index (PSI) and Full Scale IQ (FSIQ) on the WAIS-IV Data derived from both scales being given to 73 adults diagnosed as having a mild intellectual disability (Mild ID) and 31 as moderate intellectual disability (Moderate ID).

Table 3.7 Comparison of index scores and FSIQ between people with mild and moderate degrees of intellectual disability on the WISC-IV

	WISC-IV	
	Mild ID	**Moderate ID**
VCI	67.1 (9.1)	52.3 (7.5)
PRI	65.5 (10.3)	52.5 (9.2)
WMI	66.8 (11.1)	57.0 (9.2)
PSI	73.0 (11.6)	58.2 (11.0)
FSIQ	60.5 (9.2)	46.4 (8.5)

Note: The mean scores and standard deviation of these scores, in brackets, for the Verbal Comprehension Index (VCI), the Perceptual Reasoning Index (PRI), the Working Memory Index (WMI), the Processing Speed Index (PSI) and Full Scale IQ (FSIQ) on the WISC-IV Data derived from both scales being given to 63 children diagnosed as having a mild intellectual disability (Mild ID) and 57 as moderate intellectual disability (Moderate ID).

have been given tests and the results analysed, this leaves open the possibility that the tests are not valid for all the individuals in a group.

Reliability

In addition to establishing that a test is measuring what it is supposed to measure, it is also important to establish how accurately it measured it. This is the reliability of the test. What I do in this section is to look at how accurate IQ tests are particularly when used in the low range. As much of my own research has been concerned with test reliability in the low range and because of the implications of this for the whole concept of intellectual disability, this is a relatively extensive section.

If we are to make decisions on the basis of IQ score it is important to know how accurate the test is so that we are aware of the chances of making a wrong decision. The most striking example of IQ score being used to make decisions is when an assessment is being done in connection with an appeal against a death penalty in the US. I discuss this in more detail in Chapter 7 but, briefly, in the US it is unconstitutional to execute anybody with mental retardation, so if somebody is sentenced to death and it can be established that they have a mental retardation they cannot be executed. Although the definition of mental retardation differs between states, most have as part of their criteria having an IQ below a specified point. If the criteria is set to a single IQ point, yet the tests do not measure to an accuracy of one point, then people with true intellectual abilities above the criteria will get measured IQs below and be reprieved and some people with true intellectual abilities below the criteria will get measured IQs above and be executed.

It is generally acknowledged that IQ tests to do not measure IQ to an accuracy of one point. When reporting the results of IQ assessment it is recommended that a confidence interval be given that indicates what the range of scores within the 'true IQ' is likely to be. Although there are a number of ways that this can be calculated, which I explain below, the most usual way of reporting this is in terms of the 95 per cent confidence interval, which is supposedly the interval either side of the measured IQ in which the 'true IQ' has a 95 per cent chance of falling. The 95 per cent confidence interval reported in the WISC-IV and WAIS-IV manuals is about four points either side of the measured IQ. However, as I argue below, this may be a gross underestimate of what the true 95 per cent interval is.

The reason IQ tests are not accurate to one IQ point is because factors besides an individual's true intellectual ability affect the score. These non-intellectual factors are referred to as error as they cause error in measurement. Anastasi and Urbina (1997), in their influential text on psychometrics, divided these errors into two broad groups: chance errors and systematic errors.

Chance errors

Chance errors consist of a large number of relatively minor factors that affect an individual's score either way so that sometimes the score is increased and sometimes decreased. They are caused by variables such as how alert or fatigued the individual is when they take the test, how much distraction there is and whether the individual is lucky or unlucky in guessing answers to questions they are not sure about. Although an individual score will be in error, if the assessment is given to a group, or theoretically to the same person on several occasions, the positive and negative errors would cancel each other out and the mean score should be correct.

Correlations are used to quantify the degree to which a test is in error. If there were no error in a test then it would always produce the same result when given to the same individual, so the correlation between the score obtained when test was given on one occasion with the score obtained when the test was given on a second occasion would be one. However, as there is error the correlations are less than one. The degree to which a test score is accurate is given by the correlation and one minus the correlation gives the degree to which it is in error.

Anastasi and Urbina (1997) identify three different types of chance effort in the measurement of intellectual ability: that due to a lack of internal consistency of the test, temporal error and scorer error.

The internal consistency of a test. This is a measure of the degree to which the individual items in a test measure the same thing. Some test items will be relatively easier for some people irrespective of their intellectual ability. For example, if an individual likes watching nature programmes then they may well have an advantage with it comes to questions about animals in the Vocabulary and Similarities subtests; however, the same individuals may be at a disadvantage when it comes to questions about history. It is hoped that these errors will cancel each other out and that the final score reflects the individual's true ability. The degree to which this occurs represents the internal consistency of the test. It is measured in a number of ways though the conceptually simplest is the split-half reliability check. Here a test is effectively divided into two, with alternative items on each subtest being regarded as being in different tests. A key point here is that these two tests do not have to be given separately; the actual test is just given as normal and the items then regarded as coming from a different test when it is scored. Therefore, to get a measure of split-half reliability one simply gives the test once to a large number of people, which is usually done during the standardisation process, then divide the test into the two halves, score them up and correlate the scores from each half. In most modern IQ tests the results of this are quite high. Although the WISC-IV and WAIS-IV calculate internal consistency in a slightly different and mathematically more sophisticated way, it is pretty well equivalent to the split-half method. The internal consistencies for the WAIS-IV and WISC-IV standardisation samples are high at .98 for WAIS-IV and .97 for the WISC-IV.

Stability of a test. This is the degree to which a test will produce the same result on two different occasions. There are a number of factors that change between assessments that may well affect the score; for example, the amount of distraction in the setting the test was given in, the motivation of the individual being assessed and how well the psychologist giving the test administers it. Therefore it would be expected that if the same test was given to the same individuals twice the results would be different. The degree to which the results are the same is the stability of the test and the degree to which they differ is the error due to a lack of stability or, as it sometimes called, temporal error. The stability of a test is derived by giving the test to a group of people twice and then correlating the two scores. Both the WISC-IV and WAIS-IV manuals report relatively high stability scores of .96 for the WAIS-IV and .93 for the WISC-IV.

Scorer error. IQ tests have to be scored and so there is scope for error on the part of the scorer. The score consistency is calculated by getting two scorers to independently score a number of assessments and correlating the results. The scorer error is then one minus this correlation. Both the WAIS-IV and WISC-IV manuals report that that for most subtests there was little judgment required and the inter-scorer reliability was between .98 and .99. For those subtests where judgment was required it was .93 for Similarities, .95 for Vocabulary, .97 for Information and .91 for Comprehension on the WAIS-IV. On the WISC-IV it was .98 for Similarities, .98 for Vocabulary, .95 for Comprehension, .96 for Information and .97 for Word Reasoning. It therefore seems likely that the average scorer consistency, on the core subtests required to measure Full Scale IQ, is about .97 for the WAIS-IV and .98 for the WISC-IV.

So the error due to a lack of internal consistency, to lack of stability and a lack of scorer consistency can each be calculated in terms of a correlation. However, error is not usually given in terms of a correlation but is converted into a range of scores either side of the measured IQ where the 'true IQ' probably falls, usually the Standard Error of Measurement or the 95 per cent confidence interval.

The Standard Error of Measurement or SEM is one measure of the confidence interval. It is based on the assumption that because measured IQs are affected by chance error that, if the tests were repeated many times, the obtained scores would form a normal distribution around the 'true' score. The SEM is the standard deviation of that distribution. The SEM is derived from a reliability score of the test; although there are more complex formulas to calculate it, the one given by Anastasi and Urbina (1997) is the one that is the basis of other ones and is as follows:

$$SEM = SD \times \sqrt{(1-r)}$$

where SD is the standard deviation of the test, which for modern IQ tests is set at 15 and r is a reliability score of the test. The explanation for this formula is somewhat complex and we do not need to go into it here.

As SEM is the standard deviation of that normal curve, so 68 per cent of the scores fall between minus one and plus one SEMs. However, a 68 per cent confidence interval for most people sounds somewhat arbitrary and it is far more common to use the 95 per cent confidence interval, which is given by multiplying the SEM by 1.96:

$$95\% \text{ Confidence Interval} = SEM \times 1.96$$

The test manuals give figures for both SEM and 95 per cent confidence intervals and indicate that the 95 per cent confidence interval should be cited when reporting the results of the assessment. Although it varies a little with the age groups, the average 95 per cent confidence intervals are 4.23 for the WAIS-IV and 5.25 for the WISC-IV. Hence the two tests are considered to be accurate to within four to five points. However, what is curious about the SEM and 95 per cent confidence intervals cited in the manuals of both the WISC-IV and WAIS-IV, previous versions of these tests and most other commonly used IQ tests, is that the SEM and 95 per cent confidence intervals are based on only one reliability score, usually the internal consistency of the test. Therefore the confidence intervals cited in the manuals may not take into account all sources of error. If this is the case then the 95 per cent confidence interval of about four to five points cited in the manuals may well be a gross underestimate of the true confidence interval if all errors are taken into account. It is worth explaining this in a bit more detail.

The question is: does a measure of internal consistency such as split-half reliability not only include error due to a lack of internal consistency but also error due to a lack of stability? It seems to me that it does not and the reason for supposing this is very simple; when assessing internal consistency using a split-half reliability test or any other method, the assessment is only given once, so there is no opportunity for error due to a lack of stability to affect the score. So logically a measure of internal consistency cannot take into account error due to a lack of stability. It would be theoretically possible for an IQ test to have almost perfect internal consistency with a 95 per cent confidence interval of one point, yet have very low stability where the scores could differ by an average of 10 points between assessments. If this were the case then citing a confidence interval of one point in an assessment report would be very misleading.

So if a measure of internal consistency does not take into account error due to a lack of stability does an assessment of stability also take into account error due to a lack of internal consistency? Here the logic is not quite so clear-cut and there is a lack of empirical data on it. However, it does seem likely that to a large extent a test of stability, reflected in a test re-test study, would not be affected by error due to a lack of internal consistency. Error due a lack of internal consistency is due to people having specific knowledge or strategies for dealing with questions that are acquired over a lifetime and so are not likely to change significantly over the interval used in a test re-test reliability check, which is of the order of weeks. It therefore seems reasonable to assume that the error due to lack of internal consistency and error due to lack of stability are mutually exclusive.

This then leaves scorer error. It is possible that this is taken into account in the test re-test reliability, provided different people score the two assessments. The problem is that the studies that report on test re-test assessments do not usually report whether the two assessments have been scored by different scorers or not. However, having said this, when I look at total error below, I assume that they were scored by different people and that scorer error is part of the error due to lack of stability.

If IQ test scores are affected by error due to a lack of internal consistency, error due to lack of stability and scorer error, then one can find the total chance error affecting the test by adding the errors due to lack of internal consistency to the error due to lack of stability, which I assume includes scorer error. From this, the total chance error, the effective total reliability of the test, the effective total SEM of the test and the true 95 per cent confidence interval of the test can be calculated. Although test developers do not combine error in this way, it has been suggested by Anastasi and Urbina (1997). If it is done for the WISC-IV and WAIS-IV the results are as follows: for the WAIS-IV with a reliability score for internal consistency of .98 and for stability of .96, the error for internal consistency would be .02 and for stability .04, which would make the combined total error .06. This would then give a SEM of 3.67 and a 95 per cent confidence interval of 7.20. The equivalent for the WISC-IV with reliabilities for internal consistency and stability of .97 and .93 respectively would be a SEM of 4.74 and a 95 per cent confidence interval of 9.30. These figures are significantly greater confidence intervals than those given in the manuals.

Systematic errors

Unlike chance errors, which will cancel each other out if an assessment is given sufficient times, systematic errors will not and always affect a test result in the same direction. There are a number of systematic errors that will affect IQ assessments, most notably: the floor/ceiling effects, the Flynn effect and other error that is apparent from the difference between different tests.

The floor/ceiling effects are due to assessments having upper and lower limits on IQ scores that they give. I illustrate this for the ceiling effect. The WAIS-IV measures up to an FSIQ of 160. If somebody has a true IQ above this, say 170, and is given the WAIS-IV, then the measured IQ they have will be 160, so the test will have underestimated their true IQ by 10 points. The same effect occurs at the low end of the test causing the assessments to measure too high. As the effect is one that will really only affect scores at the high and low ends of the ability range, I will wait until I discuss systematic error in the low range before looking at the floor effect in more detail.

I looked at the Flynn effect in Chapter 2. It is the effect whereby, at least in western industrialised societies, the intellectual ability of the population as a whole has been increasing by about .3 of an IQ point per year. One effect of this is that the average score on an IQ test will go up by about the same .3 of a point per year for each year since the test was standardised. As IQ is a measure of an individual's intellectual ability relative to people of his or her own age at the time the test was taken, then tests will, on average, overestimate people's IQs by 0.3 of a point for each year since the test was standardised. If we had confidence that the rate of increase in IQ was .3 of a point per year we could correct IQ scores for the Flynn effect by subtracting the .3 of a point for each year since the test was standardised. However, it is not as simple as this as the Flynn effect varies over time, type of IQ test and, as we see later, ability level (Flynn 2007). So although we know there is a systematic error that is related to the age of the test we do not know exactly how much it is. From what we do know about the effect it will be between –.3 points and +.5 points per year depending on the type of test, the country it is being taken in and the ability level of the individuals being assessed.

There are other systematic errors in addition to the Flynn effect and the floor/ceiling effects that are apparent from the differences between some tests. However, these seem to be more serous in the low IQ level and so I discuss them below when considering the measurement of low IQ specifically.

Chance and systematic total error

If we know how much systematic error affects scores then we can correct for it. For example, as we saw above (Table 3.3) when the WAIS-IV was compared to the WISC-IV using a random sample of 157 16-year-olds the WISC-IV scores 1.2 points higher. So a WISC-IV score could be adjusted so that it is equivalent to a WAIS-IV score by subtracting one IQ point. Furthermore, in this case, if we assume that the difference was due to the Flynn effect, and the WAIS-IV was not subject to the Flynn effect as it was a brand new test, subtracting one point from the WISC-IV score would not only give a WAIS-IV equivalent IQ but also an estimate of IQ without this systematic error. However, there are often times when we do not know to what degree a systematic error affects scores. To take the Flynn effect, for example: we know it occurs and will affect scores in the order of .3 of a point per year; however, because of the variation in the Flynn effect over time, the type of assessment and degree of intellectual ability for those being tested, all we may know is that an IQ score will need adjusting by between –.3 and +.5 per year since the assessment was standardised. Therefore, although this is systematic error its effect could be anything between –.3 and +.5 points per year since the test was standardised. This is the same sort of information we have when we are talking about chance error, where we have a range of scores either side of the measured IQ where the 'true' IQ is likely to fall. Following this logic, I suggested (Whitaker 2010b) that it would be reasonable to add these ranges of different systematic errors together and then to combine them with the chance error to produce a confidence interval that takes account of all errors. To give a hypothetical example: suppose that we know that a particular measured IQ is likely to be too high by between zero and two points due to a floor effect, also that it may be too high by between zero and three points due to a Flynn effect, then adding both these systematic errors together means the assessment may be too high by between zero and five points. Once we have estimated this range of uncertainty due to systematic error it can then be added to the combined chance error to give a 'total' or 'true' confidence interval.

To illustrate how this could be done for the WISC-IV and WAIS-IV: if we take the combined chance error calculated above at 9.30 for the WISC-IV and 7.20 for the WAIS-IV, then the total error would be this plus the combined systematic error for each assessment. In actual fact, in the average ability range usually the only systematic error we would have to take account of would be the Flynn effect, which, as I write in early 2012, is probably increasing scores by between one and three points on the WISC-IV giving a margin for error of two points, and between zero and one point on the WAIS-IV giving a margin of error of one point. Adding these intervals would give approximate true confidence interval of about 11.3 points for the WISC-IV and 8.20 points for the WAIS-IV.

However, the concern of this book is not what the reliability of the test is in the average range but rather what it is in the low range. We cannot assume that the chance error will be the same, as very few people with low IQs were used in the studies deriving the reliability scores reported in the manuals. It is also apparent from what we have seen so far that there may be more systematic error affecting scores in the low range with the floor effect coming into play. What I look at in the next section is the evidence for the reliability of IQ tests when used in the low ability range.

The reliability of low IQ

Chance error in the low range

Internal consistency. When I first started to look at the reliability of IQ tests in the low range I could only find one rather old study that looked at the internal consistency of IQ tests in the low range by Davis (1966). He found split-half reliabilities of .90 for children with moderate ID, .91 for those with mild ID and .97 for those with borderline mental intellectual disability. Taking account of the different group sizes, the average was .92, which is acceptable though on the low side for internal consistency. However, there is now a far more up-to-date estimate of error due to a lack of internal consistency in the low range. As part of the validation of the WAIS-IV (Wechsler et al. 2008), it was given to a group of 75 adults with mild intellectual disability and 35 with moderate intellectual disability and the internal consistency reliability calculated. On average this reliability was approximately the same as the internal consistency reliability found for the standardisation sample, which means that the overall reliability for internal consistency in the low range is approximately .98. This means the error due to a lack of internal consistency in the low range is about .02. Quite why there was this very large difference between the internal constricts reported by Wechsler et al. (2008) and that reported by Davis (1966) is unclear, though it could be due to tests becoming more consistent as they developed or differences in the condition under which the tests were administered.

Stability in the low range. The current evidence suggests that temporal error may be greater in the low range than it is in the average range. I (Whitaker 2008b) did a meta-analysis of the test re-test reliability for Full Scale IQ (FSIQ) for assessments in the low IQ range (measured IQ<80) and found the weighted mean test re-test reliability figure to be .82. The temporal error is therefore one minus .82, which is .18, which is equivalent to a 95 per cent confidence interval of 12.5 points. As several of the studies in the meta-analysis reported the proportion of IQs that changed by specific amounts, I was able to check how accurate this 95 per cent confidence interval was in predicting IQ change when it was reassessed. It would be expected that, for a 95 per cent confidence interval of 12.5 points for stability, 61 per cent of IQs would change by less than six points and 13 per cent would change by 10 points or more. What actually happened in the studies that reported on this was that 57 per cent of the IQs changed by less than six points and 14 per cent changed by 10 points or more. This is quite a good estimate of what was predicted, suggesting that the 95 per cent confidence interval of 12.5 points is accurate for clients in the low ability range. However, the confidence interval is considerably greater than the corresponding 95 per cent confidence intervals for temporal error of 9.75 and 5.88 for the WISC-IV and WAIS-IV respectively (Wechsler 2003a, Wechsler et al. 2008) for people in the average ability range. Measured IQs therefore seem to fluctuate more in the low ability range than in the average range. One possible explanation for this greater change in IQs between assessments is that it may be due to a genuine change in an individual's intellectual ability between assessments. In some of the studies in my meta-analysis the intervals between assessments were much longer than is usual in test re-test studies: up to five years. However, if a change in genuine intellectual ability was a reason for the greater changes in measured IQ then one would expect the difference in scores to increase as the time between assessments increased, so that there would be a positive correlation between IQ change and test re-test interval. However, when I checked this I found that there was no significant relationship between the test re-test reliability and the interval between testing. This suggests the change was not due to a systematic change in intellectual ability over time. The most likely explanation for the change in scores is measurement error, though there is a possibility that intellectual ability fluctuates from day to day.

Total chance error. We therefore have values for the major sources of chance error: .02 for lack of internal consistency as reported in the WAIS-IV manual and .18 for lack of stability, found by myself in my meta-analysis (Whitaker 2008b), which I will assume includes error due to inconsistency in scoring. If these errors are added together we get a figure of .20, which is an estimate of total chance error, which means the effective score to total reliability would be one minus this which would be .80. This, when used to calculate a 95 per cent confidence interval, gives an interval of 13 points.

Systematic error in the low range

The Flynn effect. As we saw above, the Flynn effect may cause a test to measure too high by about .3 IQ for each year since it was standardised. It has therefore been argued by Flynn (2007, 2009) that it is possible to compensate for this error by subtracting .3 of an IQ point from the measured IQ for each year between the test being standardised and given. However, the rate of increase is not consistent over time or ability range. Flynn (1985) looked at comparisons of the Wechsler Intelligence Scale for Children (WISC) and its revised version (WISC-R) standardised 25 years later. He found that the gains appeared to be higher at the low levels, .396 per year for IQs 55 to 70 as compared to .272 per year for IQs in the range 125–140. In a more up-to-date review (Flynn 2006), he suggests that low IQs are still increasing by about .3 of a point per year in the US. In Norway, military service is compulsory for every able young man. As part of their induction process they are given an IQ test. This provides an opportunity to study what amounts to half the population of 18-year-olds. Sundet et al. (2004) used this data to compare the gains made for conscripts scoring above and below the median for pooled data from 1957 to 1959 with data from 1993 to 2002. For those scoring below the median there was an 11 point IQ point gain, which compared to a 4.4 point gain for those above the median. Teasdale and Owen (1989) used similar data from Denmark and found average gains in IQ over the 30 years up to the late 1980s of about 7.5 IQ points. The gains were greatest in the lower ability range. The maximum gains were near the eleventh per centile, at which point they were 41 per cent greater than those at the median. At the ninetieth percentile there had been very little gain over the years. However, when Teasdale and Owen (2005) looked at the new data up to 2004 they found that there had been a peak in intellectual ability for the population as a whole in 1998 followed by a decline. They found that after 1995 there was an increased number of people scoring at the lower end of the tests showing a decline in the intellectual ability for conscripts with lower IQ.

It therefore seems that the Flynn effect occurred at a higher rate for people with low IQs than for the rest of the population in the past. However, there is evidence suggesting that these gains may have now stopped or even gone into reverse in some parts of the world. It would therefore be an act of faith to assume that low IQ will continue to increase at .3 of a point per year or that subtracting .3 of a point for each year since the test was standardised would compensate for the effect.

The floor effect. A floor effect will put a lower limit on an individual's measured IQ irrespective of their actual intellectual ability. This is best understood in the light of how the Wechsler tests derive an IQ score. As we saw earlier, the Wechsler intellectual assessments measure IQ by giving the client a number of subtests measuring different aspects of intellectual ability (see Appendix I). As part of the calculation of FSIQ, the raw scores on these subtests are converted to scaled scores with a mean of 10, a standard deviation of three, and a range between one and 19. Allocating a scaled score of one to low raw scores or a raw score of zero could result in an overestimate of intellectual ability. This can be illustrated by looking at the relationship between raw scores and scaled scores for the Digit Span subtest for age groups 15:8 to 15:11 taken from WISC-IV UK Administrative Manual (Wechsler 2004):

Raw Score:	18	17	16	15	14	13	12	11	10	0–9
Scaled Score:	10	9	8	7	6	5	4	3	2	1

The relationship is linear between raw score 18 and raw score 10, a reduction in a raw score by one corresponding to a reduction in a scaled score by one. However, all raw scores of nine and less are then given a scaled score of one. There is no empirical reason to suppose that all raw scores below nine are equivalent to a scaled score of one, and logic suggests that the linear relationship between scaled scores and raw scores should continue for some way below raw score nine. Therefore a scaled score of one given for a raw score of less than nine is likely to be an overestimate of the client's ability. So generally, when a scaled score of one is given, there is a distinct possibility that the client's ability is being overestimated. This would clearly affect IQs in the 40s where scaled scores of one are inevitable but what was not clear was to what degree it would affect higher IQ scores. With a colleague I looked at this (Whitaker and Wood 2008). We plotted the distribution of scaled scores from WISC-III (UK) and WAIS-III (UK) assessments that had been given as part of clinical practice for people with intellectual disability in the previous few years. What we found was that distribution of scaled scores for the WAIS-III (UK) was approximately normal with very few scaled scores of one, suggesting that the floor effect would only be a potential problem for IQs in the 40s and 50s. However, with the WISC-III (UK) there was a skewed distribution with more scaled scores of one than any other scaled score. Scaled scores of one were found at all IQ levels up to and including those in the 70s, where they accounted for 10 per cent of scaled scores. One possible reason for this result was that the children who were given the WISC-III were less intelligent than the adults who had been given the WAIS-III, meaning that the children would have been more likely to get a scaled score of one. When we looked at the mean IQs for the children and the adults there was evidence for this, with the mean IQ for the children on the WISC-III being 57.72 and mean IQ of adults on the WAIS-III being 65.20. However, this did not explain why more children got scaled scores of one in IQs of 50 and above. So we looked to see if there was any difference between the tests that may explain this. As shown in Appendix 1, both tests have very similar subtests, and both tests can be given to 16-year-olds, so we were able to compare how well a 16-year-old had to do to get a scaled score of two on both assessments. There was no point in comparing the criteria for getting a scaled score of one as in both tests an individual is given a scaled score of one for a raw score of zero. When we looked at minimum criteria to gain a scaled score of two there seemed to be a major difference between the tests. It was immediately clear that the raw scores required for a 16-year-old to gain a scaled score of two on the WISC-III are considerably greater than those on the WAIS-III. This in itself is not surprising as the WISC-III is designed to test children as young as 6 years old and so will need to have items that six-year-olds with low intellectual ability will be able to pass. However, further examination of criteria for a scaled score of two suggests that the WISC-III is harder. On the Vocabulary, Similarities, Information and Comprehension subtests the WAIS-III requires an understanding of common concrete concepts that people would use in their day-to-day lives, for example knowing the days of the week, money and animals that are at least commonly seen on TV. On the WISC-III the concepts are more abstract, for example 'brave' and 'rule', or require an understanding of function, for example, that an elbow and knee are both joints and not just parts of the body. On the WAIS-III Arithmetic subtest the 16-year-old is required to take one from three, so needs an understanding of number to three, while on the WISC-III he/she has to add eight and six requiring an ability to deal with numbers above 10.

On the Block Design, Picture Completion and Picture Arrangement subtests the client has to complete more items, of which the final ones are more complex on the WISC-III than on the WAIS-III. However, the clearest indication that it is harder to get a scaled score of two on the WISC-III than the WAIS-III comes from the Coding (called Digit Symbol on the WAIS-III) subtest, which is virtually the same test on both assessments. On the WAIS-III the 16-year-old is required to fill in 14 symbols and on the WISC-III he/she is required to complete 39, a score that on the WAIS-III would get them a scaled score of five. All of this suggests that it is harder for a 16-year-old to obtain a scaled score of two on the WISC-III than it is on the WAIS-III. Therefore there seemed to be a clear possibility that one reason why WISC-III gives a greater number of scaled scores of one is because it is much harder to gain a scaled score of two than it is on the WAIS-III. This is somewhat paradoxical as it would also be expected that, given the high number of scaled scores of one on the WISC-III, it would be subject to a floor effect that would artificially increase IQ scores. Although the WISC-III and WAIS-III have now been superseded by the WISC-IV and WAIS-IV, a similar distribution of scaled scores to that found on the WISC-III (UK) has now been found on the WISC-IV (UK) (Whitaker and Gordon 2012), and the criteria for gaining a scale score of two still seems much more stringent on the WISC-IV than on the WAIS-IV (Whitaker 2012). There is therefore a distinct possibility that, particularly on the WISC-III and WISC-IV, IQ scores are increased at low ability level due to this floor effect.

Error apparent from the differences between IQ scales.   It is accepted that different IQ tests will give slightly different results (Floyd et al. 2008). In the absence of a test that is a clearly an accurate measure of true intellectual ability, the best that can be done is to decide which of the many IQ tests is likely to be the most accurate and take that as the 'gold standard' assessment against which other assessments should be compared. The WISC-IV and WAIS-IV and their predecessors should have a good claim to be regarded as the gold standard assessments. They have evolved over 70 years since the Wechsler Bellevue was first published in 1939 (Wechsler 1939), are apparently well standardised and are probably the most widely used tests of child and adult intelligence. However, it has been reported that early versions of the WISC scored systematically lower than the equivalent WAIS when used in the low intellectual range (Flynn 1985, Spitz 1986, 1989). There is also a recent study by myself and colleagues (Gordon et al. 2010), which compared the WISC-IV (UK) and the WAIS-III (UK) in the low range. Both assessments were given in counterbalanced order to a group of 16-year-olds receiving special education. In each case the FSIQ on the WISC-IV (UK) was less than that on the WAIS-III (UK). The mean FSIQ on the WISC-IV (UK) was 53.00, which compared to a mean of 64.82 on the WAIS-III (UK), a difference of just less than 12 points. The correlation between the two assessments was relatively high ($r = .93$), suggesting that the tests were both measuring the same thing and that the tests were given consistently. Of this 12-point difference between the two tests, it is likely that two points are due to the Flynn effect as the WAIS-III was standardised six years before the WISC-IV, while the remaining 10 points are due to yet unknown factors. As the degree to which either assessment is in error is not known, it is clearly possible that either the WISC-IV (UK) is systematically underestimating true IQ by up to 10 points, or the WAIS-III (UK) is systematically overestimating true IQ by 10 points or both assessments are making systematic errors of less than 10 points. Although this work was done with the UK versions of the WISC-IV and the WAIS-III, there is unpublished evidence (abstract is available, Bresnahan 2008) that the same effect occurs on the US versions of the tests.

Combined error in the low range

I published a paper (Whitaker 2010) in which I combined the error in the low range from lack of internal consistency, lack of stability, the floor effect, the Flynn effect and the error apparent from the difference between the WISC-IV and WAIS-III and estimated the 95 per cent confidence intervals for both the WISC-IV and WAIS-III. For the WISC-IV there was an effective confidence interval, which extends 16 points below the measured IQ to 25 points above it. For the WAIS-III the effective confidence interval extended 18 points above the measured IQ to 28 points below. This analysis is based on a number of assumptions with regard to combining measurement error and makes use of data from the UK versions of the WISC and WAIS. I also based the error due to a lack of internal consistency on a study by Davis (1966) in which a mean reliability figure of .92 was found for the low range on the original WISC, which is significantly lower than was found in the standardisation of the WAIS-IV referred to above. Because of this, the effective 95 per cent confidence for total chance error was 15 points rather than the 13 points suggested above, using the internal consistency of .98 taken from the WAIS-IV standardisation. Although I am sure that this very large margin of error will be questioned, I think it will be very difficult to escape the conclusion that the degree of error in the measurement of low IQ is much greater and the tests far less accurate than had previously been supposed.

Implications

What this chapter has shown is that modern IQ tests are valid in the low range, in that what they mainly measure is intelligence, however, their reliability is not nearly as good as the test manuals and most other writers on the subject would have led us to believe. This has a number of implications.

Distinction between true intellectual ability and measured IQ

These results mean that we should draw a clear distinction between measured IQ and true IQ. Usually when the term 'true IQ' is used in connection to psychometrics it means the IQ of an individual if the test was not subject to chance error. So they would talk about an individual's true IQ being the mean of several IQ test results. However, as an average score on the same test would not include systematic error a true IQ may well still be in error by a significant amount. It is for this reason I want to draw a distinction between measured IQ and 'true intellectual ability'. I would like to define true intellectual ability as follows: 'The intellectual ability an individual would be assessed as having if he/she were assessed on a perfectly reliable assessment of intellectual ability'.

I think it is reasonable to assume that most people have a true intellectual ability as intelligence has been consistently been identified as a major factor in factor analysis for the past hundred years. However, I should point out that this is an assumption that may not apply to everybody. Factor analysis, which is our main evidence for a true intellectual ability, is based on group data and so will not take account of individuals within that group who may be very different. There are some individuals who have very uneven intellectual profiles, notably savants, who have an apparently g-loaded ability, such as mathematical or memory, at a much higher level than the rest of their abilities.

Individual IQ scores are less accurate than mean IQ scores

As we have seen above, if a lot of IQ results are averaged then the chance error will tend to be cancelled out, meaning that the average score is far more accurate than most of the individual scores. So if we are dealing with average results such as in a research study then we could have more confidence in it. The major problems occur when we are dealing with individual results, which are subject to both chance and systematic error.

When a test is being used clinically it is usually used to get an individual IQ and one of the major reasons for doing an individual assessment is as part of a diagnosis of intellectual disability.

The assumptions made with regard to the measurement of low IQ in the AAIDD manual do not seem to be valid

At the end of Chapter 1 I listed a number of assumptions that seemed to have been made about our ability to measure low IQ in the AAIDD diagnostic manual, which are as follows:

1. Individuals have a true IQ that can be measured.
2. Low IQ can be measured numerically.
3. Although IQ assessment is subject to error, IQ can be measured to an accuracy of 5 points in the low range.
4. SEM and 95 per cent confidence interval should be based on internal consistency only.
5. Although different IQ tests may produce slightly different scores, there is basic consistency between tests.

I discuss these assumptions in more detail in Chapter 7, which deals with the problems with the current diagnostic system, but briefly it seems that Assumptions 1 and 2 may be valid in the average intellectual range but not in the low range as the reliability of the assessments is not good enough. Assumption 3 is not valid in either the low or average range. I have argued that basing the SEM and 95 per cent confidence interval only on the lack of internal consistency will underestimate the true accuracy of a test, so Assumption 4 is not valid. I have produced evidence that there can be large differences between the two main gold standard tests of the order of 10 points so Assumption 5 is not valid. I think that it may be valid to assume that most people have a true level of intellectual ability but that as we are not able to measure it with any accuracy it is not valid to define intellectual disability in terms of a specified IQ point.

4
The Concept and Measurement of Adaptive Behaviour

The second part of the current definitions of intellectual disability requires that the individual should have significant limitations in adaptive behaviour. Before the advent of IQ tests in the early twentieth century, definitions had largely been based on a lack of coping skills; for example, in 1910 the US government announced that:

> Feeble-mindedness has been broadly defined as comprising all degrees of mental defect due to arrested or imperfect mental development as a result of which the person so affected is incapable of competing on equal terms with his normal fellows, or of managing himself or his affairs with ordinary prudence. (c.f. Scheerenberger, 1983)

However, once IQ tests were introduced definitions tended to be in terms of measured intellectual ability. By the middle part of the twentieth century it was clear that basing the definition on measured intellectual ability alone resulted in a number of problems. In the US it was noted that a disproportionate number of people from lower social classes and ethnic groups were being classified as mentally deficient, which led to concerns from civil rights groups in the early 1960s (c.f. Greenspan 1997). It was also apparent that many people who have measured IQs in the low range were not only able to look after themselves but also were able to play a useful role in society, for example, Gelb (2004) points out that during the Second World War, when there was a demand for men, many people with low IQs successfully served in the US armed forces.

It was realised that the reason for this over-inclusiveness of the diagnosis was that it was entirely based on IQ. In order to remedy this, the 1959 American Association of Mental Deficiency added a second criterion of a deficit in adaptive behaviour. At this time the adaptive behaviour criterion was still qualitative in nature, referring to 'the effectiveness with which the individual copes with the natural and social demands of the environment': whether one met the criteria or not was therefore a matter of clinical judgment. However, by the tenth AAMR definition in 2002 there was a quantitative adaptive behaviour requirement: 'Significant limitation in adaptive behaviour can be established only through standardized measures normed on the normal population.' The current 2010 AAIDD manual devotes a whole chapter to adaptive behaviour, considering what it is, how it can be measured and what the criterion for a diagnosis should be. The following quote, however, sums up the essence of what is said in the chapter.

Adaptive behavior is the collection of conceptual, social, and practical skills that have been learned and are performed by people in their everyday lives. *For the diagnosis of intellectual disability*, significant limitations in adaptive behavior should be established through the use of standardized measures normed on the general population, including people with disabilities and people without disabilities. On these standardized measures, significant limitations in adaptive behavior are operationally defined as performance that is approximately two standard deviations below the mean of either (a) one of the following three types of adaptive behavior: conceptual, social, or practical or (b) an overall score on a standardized measure of conceptual, social, and practical skills. The assessment instrument's standard error of measurement must be considered when interpreting the individual's obtained scores. (AAIDD 2010, p. 43)

From this it is apparent that adaptive behaviour is regarded as a measurable construct and, although it is made up of a number of sub-constructs, it can be summed up in terms of a single composite score. As no specific test to measure adaptive behaviour is specified, it follows that the construct goes beyond the results of a specific test and is regarded as a coherent construct. That is, it is a construct that each individual has to a greater or lesser extent and is clearly understood by others. Also, given that this definition was produced after the Supreme Court of the United States ruled the execution of people with Mental Retardation unconstitutional in 2002, there must be an assumption that adaptive behaviour can be measured with sufficient accuracy for a life and death decision to be made on the basis of its assessment.

There have been a number of criticisms of how the adaptive behaviour criteria are used in the current and previous AAIDD manuals (Detterman and Gabriel 2006; MacMillan et al. 2006), most notably by Stephen Greenspan. While emphasising importance of other deficits besides IQ, Greenspan (1979; 1997; 1999) argued that adaptive behaviour is an invented construct, lacking in both theoretical and empirical support, and with the content of the scales designed to measure it being arbitrarily determined. He proposed a new, more theoretically sound, definition in terms of the three elements of adaptive intelligence: conceptual intelligence (a concept akin to intelligence as measured by IQ tests), practical intelligence (the ability to deal with physical and mechanical aspects of life, including both self-maintenance and vocational activity) and social intelligence (the ability to understand and interact in social situations). So in effect the construct of adaptive behaviour would be replaced with the constructs of practical and social intelligence. More recently (Greenspan et al. 2011) he has emphasised that the current adaptive behaviour scales do not take enough account of the vulnerability and gullibility of people with intellectual disability, which he regards as fundamental to the condition.

There are therefore a number of questions that need considering:

1. Is adaptive behaviour, as specified in the AAIDD and other definitions of intellectual disability, a coherent construct?
2. Are the scales that purport to measure adaptive behaviour valid and reliable?
3. Does a measure of adaptive behaviour actually tell us anything useful as to whether an individual is able to cope in the real world?

The evidence for the reliability and validity of the measurement of adaptive behaviour will be considered first.

Reliability of the measurement of adaptive behaviour

When reliability was discussed in relation to IQ in Chapter 3 it was noted that it is an estimate of how accurately a variable can be measured, or to put it the other way round, how much error there is in its measurement.

As with IQ, adaptive behaviour is presented as a measurable human attribute in the AAIDD definition of intellectual disability. Also, as with IQ it seems to be assumed that individuals have a 'true' level of adaptive behaviour. Although a number of tests have been developed to measure it over many years, there is considerably less literature on the measurement of adaptive behaviour than there is on the measurement of IQ. The following section will therefore try to piece together what evidence there is in order to draw a conclusion as to how accurately an individual's 'true' level of adaptive behaviour can be measured.

The current AAIDD definition of intellectual disability requires that the assessment of adaptive behaviour be done using a scale that has been standardised on the general population including people with intellectual disabilities. Probably the best standardised and most widely used scale of adaptive behaviour is the Vineland Adaptive Behavior Scale Second edition (Vineland-II, Sparrow et al. 2005). Like the Wechsler IQ tests it has a long history of development with several earlier versions dating back to the Vineland Social Maturity Scale (Vineland SMS) developed by Edward Doll in 1935 to assess the adaptive skills of people with mental deficiency. This scale was redeveloped in 1965, the Vineland Adaptive Behavior Scale was later produced and standardised by Sparrow et al. (1984) and the most recent version, the Vineland-II, by Sparrow et al., in 2005. It is applicable to an age range between 0 and 90 years and comes in a number of versions, the most commonly used one being the Parent/Caregiver survey form; there is also an expanded interview form and a teacher rating form. For children up to and including six-year-olds it has four domains: Communication, Daily Living Skills, Socialisation and Motor Skills as well as Composite or overall score. For the age groups older than six years the Motor Skills domain is not included but Communication, Daily Living Skills, Socialisation and the Composite score are. The scale is therefore regarded as measuring the areas of adaptive behaviour specified in the AAIDD 2010 definition of intellectual disability.

At the time of writing, the Vineland-II is the most recent standardisation of the scale. As its reliability has been checked under near optimal conditions, it is likely that the level of reliability found will be as good as one could get, better than has been found with earlier scales (c.f. Harrison 1987, 1990) and possibly better than would be found when the scale is used clinically. For this reason, in evaluating the reliability of adaptive behaviour scales generally, I focus on the Vineland-II (Sparrow et al. 2005).

The Vineland-II was standardised on a large and representative sample of the US population, comprising 3693 individuals. It therefore meets the specification made in the AAIDD 2010 manual that the measure of adaptive behaviour should be standardised on the mainstream population. The scores are produced and presented in a similar way to modern IQ scales with a mean of 100 and standard deviation of 15.

Measures of reliability such as the standard error of measurement (SEM) and 95 per cent confidence interval are also given. However, there are some differences in the ways adaptive behaviour and IQ are assessed, that mean adaptive behaviour scales are subject to more error than IQ tests. The major source of extra error comes from adaptive behaviour being accessed via a third party who reports what the client is able to do rather than by directly testing the individual.

As with major IQ tests, the Vineland-II reports reliability figures of SEM and 95 per cent confidence interval, based on the internal consistency of the scale with the full standardisation sample. A split-half reliability method is used whereby the items in the assessment are divided into two to create what amounts to two separate tests, and the scores of individuals on each of these tests are correlated. As I noted in Chapter 3 on the assessment of IQ, this method does not require these two assessments to be given separately: the data can be extracted from assessments that have been given once. The internal consistency for the Composite scale varied between age groups: from .93 for the adults aged 19 to 51 years to .97 for children aged between 0 and 11 years. So for adults aged 19 to 51 years the 95 per cent confidence interval would be 7.23, and for children aged 0 to 11 years it would be 5.09, which is a bit larger than the four points reported for IQ on the WAIS-IV and WISC-IV but nonetheless acceptable. But, as was emphasised in Chapter 3, a lack of internal consistency is not the only source of chance error in the measurement of an individual's level of adaptive behaviour. As with most other scales of adaptive behaviour an interviewer interviewing a respondent who knows the individual being assessed completes the Vineland-II. There is therefore scope for the following sources of error:

• There may be error due to the respondent not reporting what they know about the individual being assessed as accurately as they could, leading to variation in what is reported over time. This error will be referred to as 'respondent reporting error' (RRE). The degree to which this error affects the score can be assessed by a test re-test reliability check, where the same interviewer conducts the same interview with the same respondent twice. Correlating the scores and subtracting the correlation coefficient from one gives RRE:

$$RRE = 1 - r \text{ (test re-test correlation)}$$

where r (test re-test correlation) is the correlation coefficient of a test re-test study in which the same interviewer interviewed the same respondent.

- The way interviewers conduct the interview may have an influence on what the interviewee reports, for example asking supplementary questions to a greater or lesser extent or by making the interviewee feel more or less at ease. This will be referred to as 'interviewer error' (IE), which can be assessed by getting different interviewers to assess the same respondent about the same client. Correlating the scores and subtracting the correlation coefficient from one would give both IE and REE as respondents are interviewed and so what they report would still be subject to error. Therefore to get a figure for IE alone one must first subtract this correlation coefficient from one, which gives a figure for the combined error (IE plus RRE) and then subtract a previously calculated figure for RRE.

$$IE = (1 - r \text{ (inter-interview correlation)} - RRE)$$

where r (inter-interview correlation) is the correlation between scores in which the same respondent has been interviewed about the same client by two separate interviewers.

- There may be error due to the respondent not having full knowledge of what the client is able to do in all relevant settings. This may well be the major source of error as a single respondent may not know what a client is able to do in all the settings they visit. This will be referred to a 'respondent knowledge error' (RKE). Getting the same interviewers to interview different respondents about the same client and correlating the results could assess this error. Subtracting this correlation from one would give respondents RKE plus RRE. So to get a figure for respondent knowledge error alone one must subtract a previously calculated RRE.

$$RKE = (1 - r \text{ (inter-respondent correlation)} - RRE)$$

where r (inter-respondent correlation) is the correlation between scores in which the same interviewer has interviews different respondents about the same client.

Sparrow et al. (2005) give data that allows us to calculate the degree of error for each of these factors for the Vineland-II.

Test re-test reliability was assessed by getting the same interviewers to interview 414 respondents a second time. The assessed clients were aged between 0 and 71 years and the time between the two interviews was between 13 and 34 days. Unfortunately they do not report the results in terms of the same age groups as they did for internal consistency, however, across all age groups (adults and children) it was .92 and for adults only (aged 22 to 71 years) it was .95. The corresponding degree of respondent report errors (RRE) is therefore .08 across all age groups and .05 for adults only.

These figures are somewhat better than have been found by earlier studies on different scales, for example Harrison (1987) cites Mayfield et al. (1984), who looked at the test re-test reliability for 'educable mentally retarded children' and found .91 parent respondents, .75 for regular classroom teacher respondents and .85 for special education teacher respondents using the American Association on Mental Deficiency Adaptive Behaviour Scale, Public School Version (AAMD ABS PSV), which would have corresponded to RREs of .09, .25 and .15 for parents, classroom teachers and special education teachers respectively.

Sparrow et al. (2005) report an inter-interviewer reliability score of .78 based on different interviewers interviewing the same respondents about the same 148 clients. This makes the combination of IE plus RRE .22. So the IE alone would be this minus the respondent report error (RRE) of .08, which is .14.

Sparrow et al. (2005) also report the results of a study in which two different respondents were interviewed about the same client for 152 different clients. Unfortunately they do not say if the same interviewer interviewed the two respondents so we do not know if this error included variation in interviews, though it would have included error due to variation in interviewees over time. The mean reliability score over the full 152 pairs was .82. So the degree of respondent knowledge error (RKE) and respondent report error (RRE) and possibly interviewer error (IE) is .18. Given that this is less than the combination of respondent report error (RRE) and interviewer error (IE) of .22 reported above, it is likely that the same interviewers were used but in order to err on the side of caution when calculating the total error it is be assumed that different interviews are used. Therefore respondent knowledge error (RKE) would be .18–.08, which is .10.

Again this is lower than the error that was found in previous studies on other scales reviewed by Harrison (1987), who found only low to moderate correlations between the scores of parents and teachers. For example, she reported that Mayfield et al. (1984), in the study referred to above, found that the mean correlation between parents' scores and those of mainstream classroom teachers was .67, though for the scores of special education teachers it was lower at .50.

Total chance error

Total error in the assessment of adaptive behaviour should include error due to a lack of internal consistency, which is about .05; RRE, which is about .08; IE, which is about .14 and RKE, which is about .10. So, assuming that all these errors are mutually exclusive and are the only chance errors affecting the scores, then the total error is the sum of them all which is .05 + .08 + .14 + .10 = .37. This would give an effective reliability score of .63 (1-.37), an effective SEM of 9.12 points and a 95 per cent confidence interval of 17.88 points either side of the measured Composite Adaptive Behaviour score on the Vineland-II.

Other error

In addition to chance error there will also be some systematic error in the measurement of an individual's 'true' level of adaptive behaviour. As was seen in Chapter 3 on the measurement of intelligence, the assessment of human attributes is subject not only to chance error but also to systematic error, which cause different assessments of the same attribute to produce consistent higher or lower results than other assessments. Here the issue is that, if two measures purporting to measure the same attribute disagree, there may be no way of telling which scale is correct. So there may be no way of telling if the individual's true level on the attribute in question is the score provided by one test or the score provided by the other test or somewhere in between. There does seem to be some degree of systematic error in the uses of adaptive behaviour measures in general and with the Vineland-II specifically: a floor effect, a difference between measures, a difference between different groups of respondents and a problem with scores being faked.

A Floor effect

In the chapter on the validity of the Vineland-II, Sparrow et al. (2005) report a study in which the scale was given to groups of people who were described as having either mild, moderate or severe/profound degrees of intellectual disability. The scale was given to 45 children (aged 6 to 18 years) and 34 adults (aged 19 and older) with a diagnosis of 'mild mental retardation', 31 children and 33 adults with a diagnosis of 'moderate mental retardation', and 36 children and 20 adults with a diagnosis severe to 'profound mental retardation'. Although all groups scored well below average it was notable that the children's scores were considerably higher than those of the adults for all degrees of disability. For those with mild intellectual disability the Composite scores were of 66.3 (standard deviation of 10) as opposed to 49.9 (standard deviation of 12) for the adults, a difference of 16.4. For those with moderate intellectual disability the mean child score was 61.1 (standard deviation 11) compared to 33.6 (standard deviation 13) for the adults, a difference of 27.5 points and for those with severe profound disabilities the mean scores were 41.5 (standard deviation 10) as opposed to 20.4 (standard deviation 1.6) for the adults, a difference of 21.1 points.

Sparrow et al. (2005) do not offer any explanation as to why there was such a large difference between adults and children in all levels of disability; however, I think there are at least two possible reasons for the children scoring higher than the adults. First, it is likely that children would have been diagnosed on the basis of an IQ score obtained from the WISC-III and many of the adults on the basis of the WAIS-III or older version of the WAIS. As seen in Chapter 3, versions of the WAIS tend to measure higher than the equivalent version of the WISC, specifically I and my colleagues (Gordon et al. 2010) found the WAIS-III to systematically measure higher than the WISC-IV in the low range by about 12 points. The 'true intellectual abilities' (as opposed to the measured IQs) of the adults assessed on the WAIS-III would be about 12 points less than the children who gain the same measured IQ on the WISC-IV. Therefore a 16-point difference in the scores between adults and children, as found for those with mild degrees of intellectual disability on the Vineland-II is not so remarkable. However, this could not explain all of the much larger differences between adults and children at greater degrees of disability. A possible further explanation is that the difference is due to a floor effect, which has the effect of raising the child scores more than it does those of adults. As with IQ raw scores, the Vineland-II subdomains raw scores are converted to normalised scores, in this case called the v-scale score, which have a mean of 15 and a standard deviation of three points. Therefore there may be a floor effect in the conversion of raw scores to v-scaled scores at low levels where a minimum v-scaled score is given for all ability levels below a certain level. In order to test this I looked at the raw score v-score conversion tables of Vineland-II and found that raw scores of zero were given relatively high v-scaled scores, resulting in minimum standard scores for the domains and Composite scores being higher than the propertied minimum score of the test. What is more, the effect is much greater for children than it is for adults. Table 4.1 gives the mean standardised scores that would be obtained if all raw scores were zero for the age groups used in this study.

As noted above the children in the mild intellectual disability group had a mean score on the Vineland-II of 66.3, which is quite a bit higher

Table 4.1   Mean minimum standard score (for raw scores of zero) on the Vineland-II

	Age groups	
	6 to 18 years	19+ years
Composite	30.00	20.30
Communication	29.69	22.10
Daily living	33.08	22.00
Socialization	34.54	21.60

Note: The scores that would be obtained on the Composite, Communication, Daily Living, and Socialization scales of the Vineland-II if a client was to score raw scores of zero on all scales. For Age groups 6 to 18 years and 19 years and above.

than these effective floors of the test. It could be argued that with a standard deviation of 10 points none of the children would be scoring low enough for this floor to affect their scores. However, one should consider that the floor is the end point of the extrapolation of the relationship between raw scores and v-scaled scores down from where this relationship can be done on the basis of empirical data. It is therefore possible that, in order not to have a very large range of raw scores being given the minimum v-score, higher v-scores were also given to relatively low raw scores. So the floor effect could therefore affect higher scores.

The same arguments apply to the children in the moderate disability group, where the mean score was 61.1 with a standard deviation of 11.1 so again the floor would not be a direct effect. However, for the children with severe to profound intellectual disability, who had a mean standard score of 41.5 and standard deviation of 10.1, it is likely that some of these children would have had both standard scores and v-scaled scores at the floor levels, which would have given them a score above their genuine ability level. However, what is clear is that Vineland-II has a problem with the accuracy with which it can measure adaptive behaviour in the intellectual disability range because of a floor effect.

Differences between measures

As we saw in Chapter 3, one of the most obvious ways in which systematic error is apparent is when a significant difference is found in the scores produced on the same person by different tests. In the course of the standardisation of the Vineland-II, it was compared to other measures of adaptive behaviour but using subjects in the average ability range. With the Adaptive Behavior Assessment System: Second Edition (ABAS-II, Harrison and Oakland 2003), for a sample 82 people aged between 5 and 20 years there was virtually no difference between the Composite scores, with means of 99.7 and 99.8 for the Vineland and ABAS-II respectively. For another group comprising of 55 adults aged between 17 years and 74 years, the mean scores were 111.0 and 106.2 for the Vineland and ABAS-II respectively, a slightly larger difference of 4.8 points.

When the Vineland-II was compared with its predecessor the Vineland Adaptive Behavior Scale (Sparrow et al. 1984), the Vineland-II tended to measure higher, most notably in the 3 to 6 year age group, where the composite score on the Vineland-II was 91.4 compared to 82.7 on the Adaptive Behavior Scale. However, this may well have been due to changes in lifestyle over the years, for example, people no longer used phone boxes, which was an item on the Adaptive Behavior Scale. Neither of these studies suggests that there is any major systematic difference between the tests. However, the subjects were of average ability and it is clearly possible that, as with IQ, there are more differences in the low ability range, though on current evidence, apart from a floor effect, there is no major systematic error in the measurement of adaptive behaviour, at least in the average range.

Difference between parents and teachers

As I outlined above, Harrison (1987) reported that where the reports of parents have been compared with those of teachers, the parents tended to rate their children as more capable than did the children's teachers. There may be a number of possible reasons for this; for example, parents and teachers see different aspects of the children, parents may be motivated to project their child as more capable or teachers may be motivated to show the child as less capable in order to obtain more resources.

Faking scores

A further issue is the degree to which the results of assessments can be deliberately manipulated by the individual being assessed or the respondent. As noted above in the comparison between teachers and parents as respondents, different people may have particular motivations that the individual being assessed should get a high or low score. Doane and Salekin (2009) asked students to fake being intellectually disabled on two scales of adaptive behaviour scale, and found that the faking could not be detected.

Total error in measuring true adaptive behaviour

As was done in Chapter 3 for IQ it should be possible to add both chance and systematic errors together to get an estimate of total error from which can be calculated a true level of accuracy for adaptive behaviour scales.

The total chance error is about .37, which gives an effective reliability score of .63, an effective SEM of 9.12 points and a 95 per cent confidence interval of 17.88 either side of the measured Composite score. To this must be added various systematic errors evident from the floor effect, which could raise low adaptive behaviour scores by up to 20 points in children, differences between groups of respondents, notably parents and teachers, which could add another two to three points to the chance error, deliberately faking either low or high ability, which could change scores by 30 points without detection. Although these figures for systematic error are probably too vague to get a definitive figure for the accuracy of adaptive behaviour scales, it seems likely that the most generous assessment of the accuracy in the low range would be 20 points above the measured score for adults and children, 20 points below it for adults but 30 points below it for children who are subject to a greater floor effect.

Domain scores

In looking at the reliability of the Vineland-II, I have focused on the Composite score, however, according to the AAIDD definition of intellectual disability it is not necessary to have a Composite score below two standard deviations to reach the criteria, provided the client scores approximately two standard deviations below the mean on assessments of conceptual, social or practical adaptive behaviour. On the Vineland-II this would mean having a score below two standard deviations on Communication, Daily Living Skills, or Socialisation domains. It is certainly true that the much wider criterion for adaptive behaviour in the definition of intellectual disability would make the criterion easier to reach; however, there are a number of factors that should be considered. The reliability of the domains is less than it is for the Composite, for example on the Vineland-II for both the internal consistency and test re-test reliability. Therefore, although it only requires that one of the domains to be more than two standard deviations below increases the probability of meeting the criteria for having an intellectual disability, it also increases the probability of a wrong diagnosis.

Validity of the measurement of adaptive behaviour

The validity of a scale is the degree to which it measures what it is supposed to measure. So for a scale of adaptive behaviour the question is does it actually measure adaptive behaviour? In considering this I again focus on the Vineland-II (Sparrow et al. 2005).

Sparrow et al. (2005) define adaptive behaviour as: 'The performance of daily activities required for personal social sufficiency' (p. 6). The manual devotes a chapter to validity and presents a number of sources of evidence that show that the scale does measure adaptive behaviour:

Evidence based on test content
Evidence based on response process
Evidence based on test structure
Evidence based on clinical groups
Evidence based on relationship with other measures

Evidence based on test content

In developing the Vineland-II Sparrow et al. (2005) tried to ensure that the items in the test would actually assess adaptive skills in the four domains covered. Initially they looked at the items in the previous version of the Vineland and those in other scales of adaptive behaviour. The items were then tested and found to fall in to the predicted developmental sequence. Although Sparrow et al. (2005) looked at the requirements of the various definitions of intellectual disability such as the then AAMR and took this into account when choosing items, what they did not do was present evidence that the items related to real world coping.

Evidence based on response process

What the test developers wanted to demonstrate here was that the test did not perform differently for different subgroups or with different scorers. They present evidence to show there was no difference in scores between males and females. There was a small difference between people of different socioeconomic classes, with those in lower socioeconomic groups gaining lower scores. Once socioeconomic class was controlled for, there was no consistent trend across different ethnic groups.

Evidence based on test structure

As well as the Composite score the Vineland-II gives four domain scores for those aged up to six years and three for those aged seven and older. They present evidence in terms of an inter-correlational analysis and a confirmatory factor analysis that this structure is empirically valid. The domains themselves did not correlate overly with each other but all correlated with the Composite score and the best fit to the data from the factor analysis was a four-factor model (Communication, Daily Living Skills, Socialization and Motor) for the age group below seven years, and a three factor model for the domains (not including motor) was the best fit for the older age groups.

Evidence based on clinical groups

It would be expected that groups of people with a particular diagnosis would have a distinct profile on the Vineland-II. The most obvious example is that people with a diagnosis of intellectual disability would have lower scores as having low levels of adaptive behaviour is part of the definition of intellectual disability.

The scale was given to 45 children and 34 adults with a diagnosis of 'mild mental retardation', 31 children and 33 adults with a diagnosis of 'moderate mental retardation' and 36 children and 20 adults with a diagnosis severe to 'profound mental retardation'. For each level of disability, the score was well below the mean, and those with a diagnosis of moderate intellectual disability scored lower than those with mild and those with severe to profound scored below those with moderate. However, as noted above, for each ability level the adults scored significantly lower than the children. Sparrow et al. (2005) also give the percentage of scores at 70 or below for the three domains and the Composite scores. For those with mild disabilities 97.1 per cent of adults but only 71.1 per cent of children had Composite scores below 70. The manual does not say what percentage of the samples met the AAMR criteria for having mental retardation but there is clearly a possibility that a number of the children did not, which should raise questions as to the utility of the Vineland-II use as a diagnostic tool.

Evidence based on relationship with other measures

If a measure is valid then it should be highly correlated with other valid measures of the same ability; it should also correlate but to a lesser extent with measures of related ability and not correlate with measures of abilities that are unrelated. Sparrow et al. (2005) report a number of studies in which the Vineland-II was compared to other assessments.

Comparison with other measures of adaptive behaviour

The Vineland Adaptive Behavior Scale. The Vineland Adaptive Behavior Scale (Sparrow et al. 1984) is the predecessor of the Vineland-II. As both scales are designed to measure exactly the same construct, then if both scales are valid they should correlate highly with each other.

123 children aged from birth to 18 years, divided into three age groups: 0 to 2 years (N=24), 3 to 6 (N=29) and 7 to 18 (N=70), were given both the Vineland-II and Vineland Adaptive Behavior Scale.

The correlations between the Composite scores on the two scales were .87, .94 and .89 for the three age groups respectively. These correlations are only slightly less than Vineland-II correlated with itself in the test re-test study, which were .96 (0–2 years), .94 (3–6 years), .93 (7–13 years) and .83 (14–21 years). As a scale should correlate with another scale more highly than it does with itself these correlations clearly suggest that both scales are measuring the same factor.

Adaptive Behavior Assessment System: Second Edition. Adaptive Behavior Assessment System: Second Edition (ABAS-II, Harrison and Oakland 2003) is another measure of adaptive behaviour. As the domains and subdomains are somewhat different one would only expect moderate correlations between domains on both scales; however, as both scales claims to measure the construct of adaptive behaviour there should be a similar correlation between the Vineland-II and the ABAS-II as there is between the Vineland-II and the Vineland Adaptive Behavior Scale. Both the ABAS-II and the Vineland-II were given to 60 children aged between 1 and 5 years, 82 children and young adults aged between 5 and 20 years and 55 adolescents and adults aged between 17 and 74 years, the ages corresponding to the two parent forms and the adult form of the ABAS-II. The overall correlations between the Composites of the two scales for the different age groups were: .70 (age 0–5), .78 (5–20 years) and .69 (17–74 years), somewhat lower than that between the Vineland-II and the Vineland Adaptive Behavior Scale. This may well suggest that although the two scales measure a similar thing, it is not precisely the same thing. However, an alternative explanation is that the low correlations are due to measurement error, which will reduce correlations.

Harrison (1987) reviewed earlier studies in which different adaptive behaviour scales where compared. She found correlations ranged from .08 (AAMD ABS (school edition) and the Vineland Adaptive Behavior Scale (Survey form) with Developmentally Handicapped children) to .93 (AAMD ABS (School Edition) and the Vineland Adaptive Behavior Scale (Classroom edition) with Trainable MR). What is notable about these examples is that both were between the two major adaptive behaviour scales. She suggests that this is due to the lack of a general unitary adaptive behaviour factor, as well as the different theoretical frameworks on which adaptive behaviour scales are based, the different standardised samples employed to develop the scales, and the different methods of developing derived scores.

The evidence as a whole suggests that the correlations between different scales of adaptive behaviour are moderate, though better where the two scales are very similar, as is the case for the Vineland-II and the Vineland Adaptive Behavior Scale. Although these correlations may have been reduced by measurement error it is likely that different scales measure different things, which suggests that there is not a clearly agreed construct of what adaptive behaviour is.

Comparison with measures of intelligence

Adaptive behaviour and intelligence are different but to some extent related constructs, so one would expect significant but smaller correlations between measures of adaptive behaviour and measures of intelligence than one would get between IQ tests with IQ tests or Adaptive Behaviour Scales with Adaptive Behaviour Scales.

Sparrow et al. (2005) compared the Vineland-II with both the WISC-III and WAIS-III. There were 28 children (aged 6–16, mean IQ 105.7) and 83 adults (aged 16–68, mean IQ 110.6). The results of these correlations for the Vineland-II Composite and the domains with the Full Scale IQs is given in Table 4.2. Some of these correlations are effectively zero and others lower than would be expected for related variables, suggesting that IQ and adaptive behaviour are effectively unrelated constructs. However, somewhat higher correlations between IQ and adaptive behaviour have been reported in earlier literature. Harrison (1987) reported correlations ranging between .03 and .91, the majority falling in the moderate range between .3 and .7. There is no apparent relationship between the magnitude of the correlation and whether the assessed clients had an intellectual disability or with the scale that was used. Other more recent studies have also produced mixed results.

A further two studies that were not easily tabulated also showed similar results. Platt et al. (1991) gave the Vineland Adaptive Behavior Scale: Interview Form to 99 children aged between 5 and 19 years and got data

Table 4.2 Correlations between the Vineland-II and the WISC-III and WAIS-III

	WISC-III	WAIS-III
Composite	.12	.20
Communication	.36	.30
Daily Living	.25	−.02
Socialization	−.30	.12

Note: The correlations between Composite, Communication, Daily Living and Socialization scales of the Vineland-II and the Full Scale IQ on the WISC-III (with 28 children being given both scales) and the WAIS-III (with 83 adults being given both scales)

on IQ either from previous WISC-Rs or by giving then the WISC-R and/ or the Stanford Binet-IV (SB-IV). The mean measured IQ from all sources was about 59, with no difference between the WISC-R and SB-IV. The correlation with Vineland ABS Composite score and IQ was about .39. A study done in Germany (Bolte and Poustka 2002), gave the screening version of the Vineland ABS and the WISC-R or WAIS-R to 67 children and young adults with autistic spectrum disorder. Thirty-four of these clients had measured IQs less than 70 (mean IQ 53.4) and 33 IQs equal to or greater than 70 (mean IQ 93.2). Unfortunately they do not give a table of correlations, though it is apparent from the text that there was a higher correlation between IQ and the Vineland domains in the high functioning group than the lower functioning group. For the higher functioning group they cite a correlation of .65 for Communication. In the low-functioning group the correlations were less though there was still a non-significant correlation with Daily Living skills of .50. These correlations may well have been reduced not only by chance error in measurement but also by the assumption that the WISC-R and WAIS-R produced equivalent results in the low range which, as I argued in Chapter 3, is unlikely.

A further notable study can be found in the WISC-IV manual (Wechsler 2003) in which the WISC-IV was compared with the ABAS-II. The parents of 122 children (mean IQ 99.7) and teachers of a further 145 children who had been given the WISC-IV (mean IQ 100.5) completed either the parent or teacher form of the ABAS-II. The correlations are given in Table 4.3. Again the correlations are moderate at about .50. Therefore taking the data on correlations between adaptive behaviour and IQ as a whole, a correlation of about .50 is what seems to be generally found. Although these correlations will have been reduced by measurement error, it does suggest that IQ and adaptive behaviour are

Table 4.3 Correlations between the ABAS-II and the WAIS-IV Full Scale IQ

	Parent form	Teacher form
General Adaptation	.41	.58
Conception	.49	.63
Social	.35	.43
Practical	.28	.53

Note: The correlations between the WISC-IV Full Scale IQ and the General Adaptation, Conception, Social and Practical scales of the Behavior Assessment System: Second Edition (ABAS-II) in which 122 children were assessed on the Parent Form using information from their parents and 145 on the Teacher Form using information from their teachers.

separate but related constructs. It is not clear why Sparrow et al. (2005) found much lower correlations between IQ and Vineland-II.

This consistent finding that there is at best a moderate correlation between adaptive behaviour and IQ is at variance with what is frequently stated by other authors, that there is a strong relationship between IQ and adaptive behaviour, for example: Detterman and Gabriel (2006), Schalock (2006) and Simeonsson et al. (2006).

Validity as a whole

There is evidence but not proof that the items in the scales are appropriate. There is no unexpected bias as regards to subgroups, with no difference between sexes, ethnic group (once social class has been accounted for) and somewhat lower scores for lower social classes. A confirmatory factor analysis shows that the structure of the test, with three or four domains and a composite, is appropriate.

People with an existing diagnosis of intellectual disability score well below the mean, however, probably not all reach the AAIDD criteria for having a significant limitation in adaptive behaviour.

Evidence given in the Vineland-II manual shows that the correlation with the previous Vineland ABS is nearly as high as the correlation with itself, providing good evidence that the two scales measure the same construct. The correlation between Vineland-II and the ABAS-II, a different scale of adaptive behaviour, were not as high but still acceptable between .69 and .78, suggesting the two scales do measure the same thing. However, other evidence reviewed by Harrison (1987) shows that different adaptive behaviour scales often have only moderate correlations with each other, suggesting that there are different constructs of what adaptive behaviour is, which although overlapping are not synonymous. This lack of consistency between different scales of adaptive behaviour brings into doubt the degree to which any one scale measures an individual's true level of adaptive behaviour and whether it is reasonable to say that an individual has a true level of adaptive behaviour.

This same point is underlined by the variable correlations with IQ. Accepting that measurement error will reduce correlations, one would still expect that, if people have a true level of IQ and a true level of adaptive behaviour, and IQ and adaptive behaviour are separate but related constructs, there should be a moderate and consistent correlation between the two variables. The Vineland-II has low correlations with IQ suggesting that they are virtually separate constructs. However, this finding is different from previous studies reviewed by Harrison (1987) that have usually found a correlation of about .50, and does suggest the expected moderate association. It is unclear why the Vineland-II is less related to IQ.

What has not been demonstrated is that the Vineland-II or other scale of adaptive behaviour can predict how well an individual will cope in the real world, specifically that people with scores below two standard deviations are not able to cope. This would seem to be the main reason for using the assessments and the failure to produce that evidence would seem to be a major gap in demonstrating that the scale is valid. Finally, there does not seem to be sufficient evidence that any one scale is an accurate measure of adaptive behaviour or indeed that it is reasonable to have such a scale.

Conclusion

The current definition of intellectual disability requires that a significant limitation in adaptive behaviour should be established through the use of standardised measures normed on the general population, including people with disabilities and people without disabilities. I argued that this implies that adaptive behaviour is regarded as a coherent construct that is agreed upon and can be measured. What we find is that there is not agreement as to what constitutes adaptive behaviour. This is evident from the lack of agreement between scales, and unacceptable measurement error in individual scales. There are additional problems with the current criteria for adaptive behaviour in the definition. First, although it is likely there will be some relationship between coping and scores on adaptive behaviour scales, it is unclear what it is. There is no evidence presented that the scales actually predict coping in the real world, that is, that people who score below a given level, say below two standard deviations, are likely to be unable to cope. Secondly, as the scores on the test are produced by averaging what the client is and is not able to do, it seems possible for somebody to score above 70 on all domains and the Composite and yet still not be able to cope in a single critical way. For example, it is seems perfectly possible in the UK for a young woman with a low IQ to have gone through school without drawing attention to herself, to leave school when she is 16 and cope in a job that is not intellectually demanding, but then fail to cope with the demands of child-rearing. If she then came to the attention of social services she may well not get a service if they had a strict criteria for getting a specialised intellectual disability services requiring an adaptive behaviour score of less than 70 as well as an IQ scale of less than 70.

A further issue relates to the problem that may occur if scores on adaptive behaviour scales increase either as a result of measurement error or a genuine increase in ability, which Hamelin et al.'s (2011) meta-analysis suggested tended to happen following deinstitutionalisation. This could result in service users being excluded from a service that they previously had.

The current evidence suggests that Greenspan (1979, 1997, 1999) was right in his assertion that adaptive behaviour is an invented construct, with scales that are arbitrary in content and lacking both theoretical and empirical support. However, it is doubtful whether the solution he suggests of replacing the current construct of adaptive behaviour with the more theoretically grounded constructs of practical and social intelligence is viable, as these are also poorly defined and only theoretically measurable. The problem is that in the current definition of intellectual disability the adaptive behaviour criteria is too precise and crucially it specifies a numerical score. A strict adherence to this definition may well result in individuals who require a service not fulfilling the criteria and individuals who are basically coping fulfilling it and being given a label that they may well find demeaning.

5

Acquiring a Diagnosis and the Prevalence of Intellectual Disability

As I argued in the previous chapters the primary purpose of the current concept of intellectual disability is to identify people who are failing to cope. What I want to examine in this chapter is how well the current diagnostic system seems to be working in the real world; specifically, is the proportion of the population who have been given an intellectual disability diagnosis the same proportion that would be predicted from the definition? Are the individuals who have acquired the diagnosis actually in need of support in order to be able to cope? Are there other people who would not meet the current diagnostic criteria not coping with the intellectual demands of their environment? Does everybody who has acquired the diagnosis meet the current diagnostic criteria? And how do people come to acquire the diagnosis in the first place?

Mild and severe intellectual disability

In writing this chapter I have found it necessary to draw a distinction between mild and more severe degrees of intellectual disability. This presents me with a problem as degree of intellectual disability has been defined in terms of IQ, for example IDC-10 mild 50 to 69, moderate 35 to 49, severe 20 to 35 and profound below 20. However, as we saw in Chapter 3, we cannot measure IQ with a degree of accuracy to make these distinctions. I do not want to imply with my use of the terms mild, moderate and severe intellectual disability that I agree with this IQ-based definition. My use of the term is done less precisely. In part it reflects how the individuals have been labelled in any papers to which I refer. But it also refers to the degree of support the individual will need; so an individual with a mild degree of intellectual disability could be considered an individual who has the potential to live independently and somebody with a severe degree of disability as somebody who will always need some support or care.

Coping

Another concept that I need to explain is that of coping. The title of this book is *Intellectual Disability: An Inability to Cope with an Intellectually Demanding World* and the term coping is used throughout it. A failure to cope with many of the demands of the modern western world will clearly have a detrimental effect on an individual's quality of life. Not being able to use the Internet will mean that much of modern communication is not available; a failure to understand that a cold caller is trying to sell you something that you do not need at a high price could have financial consequences; a failure to look critically at food adverts and cope with the large choices available may result in not maintaining a healthy diet and possible poor health, and failure to understand and use modern computer technology will mean that many jobs even at a basic level will not be open to you. Although I do not think that coping is a term that can be closely defined, I mean more by the term than simply failing in some aspect of modern living, which we all do at times. I want to use it to reflect society's judgment as to what is an acceptable minimum of quality of life and a preparedness to put in resources to stop people falling below that level.

Whether somebody is coping or not will depend on two distinct factors: the environmental demands on them and society's judgment as to what is an acceptable quality of life. The environmental demands people have to cope with will vary depending on an individual's age and where they live. Children will have to cope with formal education, adults with the demands of caring for themselves. The environmental demands have also changed over time. As I pointed out in Chapter 2 when discussing the Flynn effect, it seems to me that over time the developed world is becoming a more intellectually demanding place. When I was a child in the 1960s one bought a television, brought it home, plugged in the power and aerial, pressed a button and it worked; to get the phone to work one picked up the receiver and dialled a number, and people only came across computers in films and did not have to worry about getting them to work. And, what is more, this situation did not change very much throughout the 1960s: once you had learned how to work the phone, TV or toaster you did not have to learn again. This is not the situation today. Now one has to read through a technical manual in order to get one's new TV, phone or computer to work, and, what is more, it will be out of date within a few years requiring one to buy a new one and re-learn how to work it. All this will require intellectual ability to read, understand and problem-solve. The intellectual demands of the environment will also vary between countries and may well be considerably fewer in many developing countries, where there is less need to use modern technology, and skills, once learned, can continue to be used over a lifetime. Therefore whether an individual is able to cope with the environment will in part depend on when and where he/she is trying to cope. Just because an individual is able to cope with one environment at one time does not mean that he/she will be able to cope with another environment at another time.

The other factor in determining if somebody is coping is what a society can tolerate, which in turn will depend on its political outlook, resources, priorities and desire to help people who it considers not to be coping. This again will change over time and place. In the nineteenth and early twentieth centuries in the UK and US poverty in the community and a minimum quality of life in workhouses and almshouses was acceptable (Ferguson 2004). In the later twentieth century a higher quality of life was felt to be necessary but, as we saw in Chapter 1, within institutions. Now, following the effect of the civil rights movements and the philosophy of normalisation, a reasonable quality of life is considered to be independent living within the community. Currently there is some guidance as to what is an acceptable quality of life for national legislation; for example, in the UK the Children's Act (Her Majesty's Stationery Office 1989, 2004) lays down guidance as to what are minimum standards of care for children, and Fair Access to Care (Department of Health 2003) gives guidance for social services as to the degree of need somebody should have before being provided with a service. However, a decision as to whether somebody is coping will also depend on the judgment of assessors, based on their assessment of the individual and interpretation of society's acceptance. As such, it may well vary over the life span, across cultural groups, between countries and between local regions within countries. The term coping should therefore be used as shorthand for what a particular society would be prepared to tolerate and fund at any given time. An assessment as to whether an individual is coping would have to be made on the basis of judgment as to how well an individual is dealing with his/her environmental demands, what is considered an acceptable quality of life and consideration as to what resources are available to help individuals who are deemed not to be coping.

Prevalence

One of the things about our current definition of intellectual disabilities is that it determines the minimum number of people in the population who will meet the definition. This is because the definition requires there to be IQ and adaptive behaviour scores below two standard deviations of the population mean. I will explain. IQ tests, such as the WISC-IV and WAIS-IV, are developed so that they are normally distributed with a mean of 100 and a standard deviation of 15. Therefore, if IQs continued to be normally distributed at the very low range, then the proportion of a population who fall below a specified number of standard deviations away from the mean is fixed, there would be 2.28 per cent of the population having an IQ below 70 (two standard deviations below the mean) and .04 per cent below 50 (3.33 standard deviations below the mean).

The same logic applies to adaptive behaviour. So if IQ and adaptive behaviour were perfectly normally distributed then 2.28 per cent of the population would have an IQ less than 70 and 2.28 per cent of the population would have a composited adaptive behaviour score below 70. In order to make the argument easier to convey I will assume that the only adaptive behaviour criterion is having a Composite score below 70. The proportion of the population who would meet both criteria would be determined by the correlation between adaptive behaviour and IQ, which as we said in Chapter 4 is about .30. This would mean that the percentage of the population who fit the criteria of having both a deficit in both IQ and adaptive behaviour would be about 1 per cent. And, as I show later, this would occur irrespective of how well this bottom 1 per cent of the populations is coping.

However, IQ at the low levels is not normally distributed, and there are far more people with severe degrees of disability than would be expected from a normal distribution. I will explain this. The developers of IQ tests such as the WISC-IV and WAIS-IV set the tests to have a mean of 100 and a standard deviation of 15. This is done by basing IQ scores on the per centile ranking of an individual's raw score on the test compared to the standardisation sample. In other words somebody who got an average score with half the sample scoring better than the individual and half scoring less well would be given an IQ of 100. Somebody whose score was better than the bottom 16 per cent and less than the top 84 per cent would be at an IQ of 85, equivalent to one standard deviation below the mean. Somebody who scored less well than the top 97.5 per cent and better than the bottom 2.5 per cent would be at two standard deviations below the mean point and be given an IQ of 70. However, this relationship between test score and IQ is calculated for each age group separately, uses a group of 200 people, in which theoretically there would be only about five people with IQs less than 70 and none with IQs less than 50. It is therefore not possible to allocate IQs on the basis of per centile scores for IQs much less than 70. Therefore, the only way they could get IQ figures for very low scores would be to extrapolate the relationship between scores and IQs down from IQ 70. In order to do this it seems to have been assumed that the relationship between ability and numbers of people in the population would remain the same as that predicted by the normal curve. However, it does not. As I show in the next chapter, the level of the average person's intellectual ability is determined by a multitude of small genetic and environmental factors, some resulting in a slightly higher IQ and some a slightly lower one. The result of this sort of mechanism would result in a normal distribution of IQs. However, at low levels there are additional more specific organic causes of intellectual disability where a single major physical/genetic/chromosomal cause, such as an extra chromosome leading to Down's syndrome or birth trauma. These organic factors result in there being far more people with a severe degree of intellectual disability than would have been predicted by the normal curve. The prevalence of severe to profound intellectual disability is found to be about 0.4 per cent (or 1 in 250) of the population as a whole (Abramowicz and Richardson 1975, Roeleveld et al. 1997), rather than the <0.04 per cent that would be predicted if IQ was normally distributed. Therefore, in order to correct for this breakdown in the normal curve at the low levels 0.36 per cent should be added to any estimate of the proportion of a population based on a normal distribution.

Taking this into account then we would expect there to be between 1 and 3 per cent of the population to meet the criteria for having a mild degree of intellectual disability. The actual figure depends on how strict the criteria for a deficit in adaptive behaviour was used and whether an IQ figure of 70 or 75 is used. In addition there would be a further 0.36 per cent of the population who would have a severe degree of intellectual disability. Therefore, one would expect that between 1 and 3.5 per cent of the population would meet the diagnostic criteria for having an intellectual disability.

It is not that easy to get a figure for the number of people in a whole population who meet the criteria for having an intellectual disability, as people are not routinely assessed for it. There are also potential methodological problems with studies that survey the IQs of a population, for example, getting an under estimation of those with low IQs because the IQ tests used are out of date or measuring too high as a result of the Flynn effect. However there are a few studies that have attempted to estimate the prevalence of intellectual disability in a population. In the UK Birch et al. (1970) looked at all 8–10-year-old children in Aberdeen and found that 2.74 per cent of then had an IQ below 75. Rutter et al. (1970) did a similar study in the Isle of Wight and found that 2.53 per cent of 10-year-olds had an intelligence level that fell two standard deviations below the mean of their peers. In the US, Mercer (1973) surveyed 2661 households to assess coping abilities and then gave IQ tests to those who were screened as having low coping ability. She found that 2.17 per cent had IQs below 70, but only 0.97 per cent met the then dual AAMR criteria for mental retardation. These figures are similar to more recent estimates of the prevalence. Emerson et al. (2001) suggested that the prevalent mild intellectual disparity is between 2.5 per cent and 3 per cent. The World Health Organization (1985) also put the figure of mild learning disability for children in industrialised countries at 2–3 per cent. In the UK the White Paper, Valuing People (Department of Health 2001), suggests that the prevalence of people with mild intellectual disability is about 2.5 per cent of the population. Although there seems to be some consensus that between 2 and 3 per cent of the western population should meet the diagnostic criteria, this does not mean that between 2 and 3 per cent of the population have a diagnosis, or whether those who have been given a diagnosis have been accurately diagnosed or whether they are unable to cope. There are a number of factors that could result in a wrong diagnosis and there will be a substantial number of individuals who may be eligible for a diagnosis at one time of their lives who are not eligible at other times.

The error in the measurement of IQ and adaptive behaviour will inevitably result in errors in diagnosis

People who have true intellectual abilities or adaptive behaviour abilities outside the intellectual disability range will be assessed as having an intellectual disability, and people who have true intellectual abilities and adaptive behaviour abilities inside the intellectual disability range will be assessed as not having an intellectual disability. However, this will not have an effect on the prevalence rate, as one would expect 2–3 per cent of the population to have both true intellectual abilities below 70 and 1–2 per cent of the population to have measured IQs below 70. The point is that those whose measured IQs that are below

70 will not be the exact same individuals with true intellectual abilities below 70; about one-third will be different.

The people who merit a diagnosis as adults will often be different from those who merited the diagnosis as children

It seems to me that there are three ways in which the criteria for a diagnosis of an adult differ from that of a child. First, it is likely that the assessment of intellectual ability for an adult will be made with the WAIS-IV which, as we saw in Chapter 3, is likely to measure higher than the WISC-IV in the low range, by the order of 10 points. This will make a considerable difference to the numbers that would meet the IQ criteria of the definition. In trying to quantify what the difference will be in terms of percentage of the adults and of children who would meet the diagnostic criteria for intellectual ability I am faced with the problem that we do not know if the WISC-IV is measuring intellectual ability accurately, or if the WAIS-IV is or if both tests are inaccurate. However, in order to illustrate the point I will assume that the true intellectual ability lies in the middle and that the WISC-IV is measuring five points too low, the WAIS-IV is measuring five points too high and that there are no other errors in measurement. If this were the case then, on the WAIS-IV, a measured IQ of 70 would be equivalent to a true intellectual ability of 65, which, if IQ was truly normally distributed in the low range, would mean that 0.99 per cent of the population would get this score or less. On the WISC-IV a measured IQ of 70 would be equivalent to a true intellectual ability of 75, which, assuming that IQ is perfectly normally distributed, would mean 4.75 per cent of the population would get this score or less. However, as showed above, IQ is not normally distributed in the low range, and about 0.36 per cent more of the population have a severe degree of intellectual disability than would be predicted by the normal distribution. When this is added to these figures for the WISC-IV and WAIS-IV it suggests that using the WAIS-IV 1.35 per cent of adults would meet the intellectual criteria; however, with the WISC-IV about 5.11 per cent of children would meet the same intellectual criteria, nearly four times more.

The second factor that will result in the adults who meet the current diagnostic criteria being different from the children relates to the adaptive behaviour criteria. The environmental demands on adults are different from those for children. Unlike children, adults are generally expected to care for themselves, to ensure that they get an adequate diet, are clothed, have somewhere to live, are not exploited by others and hold down a job, all of which children are not usually expected to have to do for themselves. On the other hand, adults do not have to meet the intellectual demands of school. The environmental demands made on adults are largely those that are assessed in adaptive behaviour scales, which, as we saw in Chapter 4, are only loosely related to intellectual ability with a correlation of only about .30 between IQ and adaptive behaviour. This is a lot lower than the correlation between IQ and academic ability, which I suggested in Chapter 2 is about .75. The fact that the correlation is lower between measured adaptive behaviour and measured IQ means there would be fewer adults reaching the dual criteria of being below two standard deviations in both IQ and adaptive behaviour than there would be children who had both low IQs and low academic achievement. However, the actual diagnostic criteria is not only met by having a Composite score for adaptive behaviour below two standard deviations, but can also be met by being two standard deviations on Conceptual, Social, or Practical adaptive behaviour on their own. Because of this it is not easy to calculate exactly how much greater the number of children one would expect to meet the diagnostic criteria than adults would be, but it is likely to be of the order of several times more.

Thirdly, as there is only a low to moderate correlation between academic ability and adaptive skills, it is likely that many of the children who fail academically will be able to cope with the demands of adult life and some of those who were able to cope with the academic demands of school would not be able to cope with the practicalities of looking after themselves as adults. In short how people coped as children may not be how they cope as adults and vice versa.

Prevalence in developing countries

These estimates of the prevalence of intellectual disability are only relevant to western industrialised countries where the intellectual demands of the environment are similar and where there is some consistency in the proportion of the population scoring below 70 on western standardised measures of intellectual ability and adaptive behaviour. In developing countries it is likely that the prevalence of intellectual disability will be much greater. Bergen (2008) suggests that between .5 and 2.5 per cent of the populations of developing countries have a severe degree of intellectual disability. As for an estimate of the numbers with mild degrees of disability, one would have to decide whether to use assessments that were standardised against the local population or against a western population. If one were to use locally standardised IQ and adaptive behaviour tests, then about 2.5 per cent of the population would fall in the mild intellectual disability range for IQ and about 2.5 per cent for adaptive behaviour. This means that, as in the west, there would be 2–3 per cent of the population with mild intellectual disability depending on the actual IQ and adaptive behaviour criteria. However, if one were to use western-normed IQ tests, there would be a much greater proportion of the population who would have measured IQs below 70 (Lynn and Harvey 2008). The other issue is that the intellectual demands of the environment in developing countries may not be as great as it is in the west, meaning that people with lower degrees of intellectual ability will still be able to cope and, possibly more significantly, what is seen as not coping by that society will be very different from what it is in the west. Therefore, although it is likely that the numbers of people with intellectual disabilities in developing countries is greater than in the west it is not clear how much greater, or indeed to what extent, a western definition of intellectual disability is applicable to developing countries.

The proportion of the population diagnosed as having an intellectual disability

If in the west 1–3 per cent of the population meet the criteria for having an intellectual disability, then one might expect that 1–3 per cent of the population would have a diagnosis of intellectual disability, and these same 1–3 per cent would have significant difficulty in coping without additional help. However, this does not seem to be the case. When I first began work as a clinical psychologist in an area of West Yorkshire in the UK, I was asked to take charge of the local register of people who had what we then called a mental handicap. There were about a thousand people on the register. However, I know that the population of the area was over 200,000 so that we had less than 0.5 per cent of the population registered. This worried me: I was concerned that we were not providing a service to everybody who should be given one. I therefore conducted a survey of the other areas of West Yorkshire to see what proportion of their populations was known to have mental handicap. What I found was that on average only 0.29 per cent of the populations registered as having mental handicap (Whitaker and Porter 2002). I therefore did a literature review of the proportion of the population with a diagnosis of intellectual disability in other parts of the UK and other western countries (Whitaker 2004). Briefly I found the following: Farmer et al. (1993) analysed data from the register of people with learning disabilities kept by the North West Thames Regional Health Authority, which had a total population of 2.69 million (about 5.3 per cent of the population of England and Wales). They reported having only 6625 people on their register, which was 0.23 per cent of the population as a whole. Studies done in the US also reveal similar rates of registered clients. Borthwick-Duffy and Eyman (1990) report an epidemiological study in which they examined the records of all 78,603 people on the California register. However, the population of California in the 2000 census was 33,871,648, which meant that only 0.23 per cent was registered as having a learning disability. Jacobson (1990) carried out a similar study in New York State. He examined the Developmental Disabilities Information System (DDIS), which effectively was a register of people with mental retardation, with 42,479 people on it. However, based on the 2000 census, New York has a population of 18,976,457, which means that only 0.24 per cent of the population was registered as having a learning disability. There is a degree of consistency between the different studies that have looked at the proportion of the population registered as having a learning disability: West Yorkshire, 0.29 per cent; NW Thames, 0.23 per cent; California, 0.23 per cent; and New York State, 0.24 per cent. The figures are considerably lower than the estimate of 1–3 per cent, suggested as the true prevalence.

There seemed to be a number of possible reasons for this disparity between the number of people eligible for a diagnosis of intellectual disability and the numbers who have got one. There may be up to 2.5 per cent of the population who are failing to cope, who, if assessed, would meet the diagnostic criteria for having an intellectual disability. For some reason they may not have come to the attention of services or having once had a service have now dropped below the radar. However, an alternative explanation is that a proportion of these people, in spite of technically reaching the diagnostic criteria for having an intellectual disability, are coping. Some support for this idea is provided by a some-what old Swedish study by Granat and Granat (1973) who looked at the proportion of young men with measured IQs below 70 who could not cope. The IQ tests were given as part of the army induction process so, as all 19-year-old men had to spend some time in the army, any sample taken from this population would be representative. Granat and Granat (1973) looked at a sample of 2000 conscripts and re-examined those who scored in the bottom 10 per cent on the IQ test. They found a lot of those who had a measured IQ below 70 had not been labelled as having an intellectual disability and apparently were coping. In a second study presented in the same paper, they did a wider survey of a sample of 5605 19-year-old men tested as conscripts in 1966. They found that the prevalence of conscripts who had not been given a label of intellectual disability with an IQ below 70 was 1.5 per cent of the population which, together with the 0.71 per cent who were known about, gave an overall prevalence rate of 2.21 per cent, a figure close to what one would expect from two standard deviations below the norm. So the evidence suggests that many people with measured IQs less than 70 are coping and that some people who meet the full criteria of scoring below two standard deviations on both IQ and adaptive behaviour may also be coping.

Acquiring a diagnosis

Although it is likely that most people with severe degrees of intellectual disability will get a diagnosis in their childhood, it is apparent that not everybody with a mild degree of intellectual disability is given a diagnosis. There may well be a number of reasons for this. In the UK there is no universal testing of children's IQs, so there is no way of formally identifying those children of low intellectual ability. The way that most children and adults with an intellectual disability are identified is that there is something about their behaviour that suggests a low intellectual ability. In other words they must be seen to be not coping with the intellectual demands of their environment.

The current AAIDD definition specifies a deficit in adaptive behaviour in terms of scores on a formal measure of adaptive behaviour and makes no distinction between what an individual would be required to do during different periods of life. However, the intellectual demands made on individuals will vary over a lifetime. Children are not expected to independently perform many of the activities necessary to provide a reasonable quality of life, such as ensuring adequate diet, clothing, somewhere to live, and protection from exploitation. It is the responsibility of parents and carers to ensure that this occurs. What children are required to do is to go to school and cope with the demands made on them there. As we saw in Chapter 2, there is a strong relationship between intellectual and academic ability on such tasks as literacy and numeracy with correlations of the order of .75. This would mean that about 2 per cent of children would meet the diagnostic criteria of being two standard deviations below the mean on both measured IQ and academic performance. Even in the early school years there is an emphasis on teaching children to read and do simple number work so one would have to expect that it would be apparent if a child was having difficulty acquiring these skills. In the UK some children are identified and given a statement of special educational needs and about 1 per cent of children go to special schools for children with learning disabilities. However, not all children with low intellectual ability are labelled as having intellectual disabilities. There may be a number of reasons for this. The school may feel that they are able to provide children with an adequate education in spite of apparent difficulties. It may be felt that there is some stigma associated with labelling a child as intellectually disabled; this seems to be particularly noticeable in the US where there has been an increase in the number of children labelled as learning disabled (which in the US refers to a specific learning problem such as dyslexia or dis-numeracy) and a decrease in the numbers given a mental retardation label (MacMillan et al. 2006).

Even though as a child an individual may be identified as having an intellectual disability, this does not mean that the providers of adult services will be aware of them once he/she leaves school. May and Hogg (1999) followed up the children identified in the Birch et al. (1970) study of all 8–10-year-old children in Aberdeen as having an intellectual disability and found that a significant number were no longer known to services in middle age. It is therefore likely that many children with diagnosed or undiagnosed intellectual disability will reach adulthood without being known to services and so will require to be identified and diagnosed before getting a service as adults.

Even if all children who met the diagnostic criteria were identified, and adult services informed about them when they got to adulthood, there would still be a number of people whose disability would not be apparent until they were adults. This is because the environmental demands on adults are very different from those on children. The relevant question with regard to getting a diagnosis, I think, is different for adults and children. Children are at school, are observed and have their academic ability regularly assessed, both informally via the performance in lessons, and formally via SATs tests. The relevant question for children is therefore: why do children with an intellectual disability fail to be identified? With adults who were not identified as having an intellectual disability as children, the situation is different, as people who could initiate a process that could result in a diagnosis do not closely observe them, so the more relevant question for adults is: why do adults with a mild intellectual disability get identified as possibly having an intellectual disability?

There seems to be a lack of research on how people come to be identified as potentially having an intellectual disability and then being diagnosed. What is in the literature suggests that it is often behaviour that is unacceptable to society in general that leads to questions being asked as to whether an individual has an intellectual disability. In the early twentieth century, when there was concern about the immoral behaviour of people with low IQs, it may have been immoral or criminal behaviour that brought people to the attention of the authorities. For example, a young woman may have been suspected of being a moron if she got pregnant outside marriage or a man if he was convicted of a minor crime.

Mattinson (1970) follows up people who had been patients in a UK mental handicap hospital in the 1940s, 1950s and 1960s and who had subsequently got married. Although with some individuals she interviewed it was apparent that their mental deficiency was recognised as children, with others it was clear that they had been initially admitted to hospital as their behaviour was considered immoral or in other ways unacceptable when they were adults or adolescents. For example, Mrs Hooper (an assumed name) was admitted at age 16 after it was discovered she had been having sex with American servicemen. Another man, Mr Bond, was hospitalised after having been found stealing. It was also apparent that having a measured IQ above 70 did not preclude a diagnosis and an admission to hospital. As part of the admission process all patients had their IQs assessed; in the group that were followed up these measured IQs ranged between 38 and 93. People were clearly getting labelled as having an intellectual disability because their behaviour was unacceptable. Mattinson quoted McCulloch (1947) 'What constitutes subnormality is to a very large extent socially determined by the threshold of community tolerance.' This statement not only sums up what was probably happening in the UK in the mid-twentieth century but also I think shows a recognition of something that will continue to happen, that society has a threshold of what it will tolerate, something that I also recognised in discussing what 'coping' is earlier in this chapter.

What brings somebody to the attention of services has probably changed since the early to mid-twentieth century. There is now less emphasis on immoral behaviour, for example, there is no longer any stigma in having a child outside marriage and there is more emphasis on ensuring that people are able to provide for themselves and have a reasonable quality of life. My own experience of working as a clinical psychologist in intellectual disabilities for 30 years suggests that there are a number of situations that bring adults to the attention of services for the first time. Occasionally, an individual, possibly even with a severe degree of intellectual disability, has been cared for at home without any other service involvement. The carer then becomes too old or ill to continue the care and relatives, friends of the family or relatives alert the services. Services may also be asked to become involved if an individual comes into contact with the criminal justice system and it is suspected that he/she has a low intellectual ability. But I think most requests for assessments of an adult new to services were of women who were due to have or had just had a baby and where there were concerns that they may not be able to cope with the demands of child-rearing. Child-care involves a set of skills that a woman with a mild degree of intellectual disability may well not have had to use until having a baby, such as ensuring an adequate diet for a young child, understanding complex spoken and written information given to her by professionals, organising the day to fit in with various and varying demands of child-care. Although some of these skills may be intellectually demanding and may well be far more difficult for somebody with a low intellectual ability, the evidence seems to show that people with mild intellectual disabilities can make successful parents and that measured IQ as such is not a particularly good predictor of how well they will do. It is possible that some of these women were coping adequately until they became pregnant, while others may not and have only been identified as failing to cope because of the current emphasis on ensuring that children are not left in abusive or neglectful situations. If this is the case it suggests there may be other adults in the community who are not coping and would meet the diagnostic criteria for having an intellectual disability but have not been identified, as they are not due to have a baby.

Types of intellectual disability

Given that there is clearly not a one-to-one relationship between being eligible for the current diagnosis of intellectual disability and having one, or between being eligible for a diagnosis and being able to cope, it seems to me that the term intellectual disability is actually quite ambiguous as it has different meanings in different situations. There are several groups of people who could be considered to have an intellectual disability:

• There are those people who, when assessed, would met the full diagnostic criteria for having an intellectual disability, who have been labelled as having intellectual disability and are known to services. This group will probably include almost all those with severe degrees of intellectual disability as well as some of those with mild degrees of intellectual disability. It is likely that most of this group will not be able to cope but some will. I would like to call this group the Labelled Intellectually Disabled.

- Based on my experience as a practising clinical psychologist in intellectual disabilities for 30 years, there is a small group of people who have acquired a label of intellectual disability who would not meet the diagnostic criteria of having a measured IQ below 70. These individuals have often acquired the label as it was abundantly clear that they were not able to cope and were given the label without a formal assessment being done. When an assessment is done it is often found that, although they may have a measured IQ above 70, they often have additional problems such as a mild mental illness or a mild autistic spectrum disorder. It may well be that it is the combination of a relatively low true intellectual ability and these other problems that result in them not being able to cope. I would like to call this group the Labelled But Non Intellectually Disabled. This group, together with the Labelled Intellectual Disabled, makes up the people who have a label and are known to services; the group as a whole are what have been called Administrative Intellectually Disabled. As I show in Chapter 7 it is this group of people who are usually used in research in order to find out the nature of intellectual disability, so that general statements can be made about the condition. However, the group does not include all those who, if assessed, would meet the diagnostic criteria and does include some individuals who, if assessed, would not.

- There are those people, who, if assessed, would meet the full diagnostic criteria for having an intellectual disability, but who have not been assessed and are not known to services. I would like to call this group the Unlabelled Intellectually Disabled. It may well be the case that a proportion of this group will be coping at any one time; however, it is also likely that a proportion will not be coping.

- There is also a group of people who would meet the criteria for having a low intellectual ability, that is a low measured IQ and true intellectual ability, but who currently do not meet the criteria of having a low level of adaptive behaviour and who have not been given a label of intellectual disability. It is clearly possible that any of these individuals may have a future deficit in adaptive behaviour and so reach the diagnostic criteria. This group I would like to call the Potential Intellectually Disabled. How large this group is will depend on the degree to which the error in the measurement of low IQ is allowed for. If a strict criteria of a measured IQ of 70 is used then it will be about 2 per cent of the population; however, if the error in measurement is allowed and it is accepted that people with measured IQs of up to 85 on the WAIS-IV may have a true intellectual abilities of less than 70 then this would be about 15 per cent of the population.

- There is a group of people who have been misdiagnosed as having an intellectual disability due to error in either the measures of IQ or adaptive behaviour. These I would like to call the Misdiagnosed Intellectually Disabled.

- Finally there is a group whose true intellectual ability and adaptive behaviour levels would meet the diagnostic criteria but when they were assessed were found not to fit the current diagnostic criteria as their measured IQ and/or adaptive behaviour was too high due to measurement error. I would like to refer to these as the Misdiagnosed as Non-Intellectually Disabled group.

Conclusions

What is apparent from the evidence reviewed in this chapter is that many of the people who would meet the current diagnostic criteria if they were assessed have not been identified as having an intellectual disability. It also seems likely that many, though not all, of these people will be coping. There is also a group of people who are not coping, in part due to a low level of intellectual ability, who have not been given a diagnosis either because they have not been identified as not coping, or because they have been assessed as not meeting the criteria. It is clear therefore that there is not an exact correspondence between those in society who are not able to cope owing to intellectual problems and those who meet the current diagnostic criteria. So, if meeting the current diagnosis criterion is necessary for getting a service, some people will be denied a service who need one. There are also people who cannot cope, who if assessed would not meet the diagnostic criteria but have been given an intellectual disability label. This to me does not seem unreasonable, as I have defined coping as failing to keep oneself up to the minimum standards that society deems to be acceptable. The reason we have a concept of intellectual disability at all is because it was clear that some people were falling below this level and so needed services. It somehow seems perverse to then deny them a service as they fail to meet a somewhat arbitrary definition that was created to include them in the first place.

The other thing that has become apparent from this chapter is that the people who are considered not to be able to cope and/or are included in the definition will change over age groups and over time. So a child labelled as having an intellectual disability in school as he/she failed to cope academically, which could be due to a low IQ, may well cope with the demands of adult life and vica versa. Although it is likely that people with severe degrees of intellectual disability will never be able to cope and always meet the diagnostic criteria, a substantial number of people who at one time in their lives get a label of mild intellectual disability will be able to cope most of the time. This underlines the notion that intellectual disability should not be thought of as a permanent condition. In terms of physical illnesses it may be more analogous to a cold than to diabetes.

What society considers as coping will also change over time. For example, in the past having an illegitimate child would be regarded as very good evidence of a young woman not coping; however, today social ideas on illegitimacy have changed and having a child with a partner one is not marred to is not considered wrong or particularly unusual. However, the standard of care one is expected to give to a child once it is born has increased.

What is considered to be coping will also be different in different cultures. It seems likely that the intellectual demands made on an individual living in an agricultural village in a developing country will not be the same as those made on somebody in a western city. It also seems likely that there will be more people in developing counties who would reach the current definition of intellectual disability, even if the assessments are based on the norms of the local population. However, to me the key question is whether people are managing to cope with the demands made on them in their environment. It is possible that the numbers of individuals in developing countries who would be considered to have an intellectual disability will be different than in the west because of the different environmental demands and the difference in what is regarded as coping.

The current definition is supposed to include people who are not able to cope and exclude people who are able to cope; therefore coping should be an explicit part of the definition. But this should be coping in the sense of not meeting society's current expectations, and not having a score below a given point on a scale of adaptive behaviour, which will be arbitrarily set and inaccurately assessed. It should also be remembered that what is regarded as coping will vary between cultures and countries and is changing over time.

6
Causes of Intellectual Disability

As we saw in Chapter 1, intellectual disability is arbitrarily defined in terms of having a low intellectual ability and low level of adaptive skills. Historically this definition developed for practical and administrative reasons with little consideration given to whether the people included within the construct were similar in any other respect than having low IQ and adaptive skills. From the point of view of evaluating the construct of intellectual disability however, understanding its causes and the different conditions associated with it is important for a number of reasons:

- If there is much similarity between people who are given the diagnosis then knowing that an individual has an intellectual disability will tell us a lot about them. However, if there is considerable variation, then simply being told that somebody has an intellectual disability will tell us no more than that individual has gained low scores on both measures of adaptive behaviour and IQ, which, as we saw in Chapters 3 and 4, may be quite inaccurate anyway.
- The extent to which everybody with a diagnosis of intellectual disability is similar should determine the degree to which they will require the same services or, to put it the other way round, the extent to which services will need to be flexible.
- The degree to which people with intellectual disabilities are similar will also determine the degree to which the results of a research study on one group of people with intellectual disability can be applied to another group of people with intellectual disability.

The degree of similarity of the individuals who are given the diagnosis is therefore a major factor in determining if the construct of intellectual disability is useful or not.

Organic and familial causes

In looking at the causes of intellectual disability Zigler (1967) and Zigler et al. (1984) made the distinction between organic and familial causes. An organic cause refers to a single biological cause resulting in significant neurological or biochemical changes. Familial caused intellectual disability occurs when there is no single factor causing the condition, but rather it is due to the same multitude of biological and social factors that determine the intelligence and adaptive ability of most people in the population. This seems a useful distinction and I will follow it here.

Organic causes

When there is a single organic cause it usually has a dramatic effect, the individual often has a significant degree of intellectual disability, with a true intellectual ability below three standard deviations and adaptive behaviour at a level that means the individual would require some form of support for life. It is because of these conditions that there are more individuals with severe to profound degrees of intellectual disability than would be predicted from the normal distribution of IQ. Organic conditions also seem to be evenly spread across social classes (Birch et al. 1970) with a similar proportion of children being affected in upper and middle-class families as in lower-class families.

Organic causes may be best thought of as falling into one of three sub-categories where damage is due either to: trauma, genetic/chromosomal disorders, or disease. Brain damage can obviously follow from trauma, whether this is due to a blow to the head or lack of oxygen at birth and this brain damage can result in a lower intellectual ability. Diseases that affect the brain, such as meningitis can also cause permanent damage. However, brain injury often results in a very uneven pattern of cognitive abilities and depends on which specific parts of the brain have been damaged. Genetic and chromosomal disorders, of which there are now hundreds identified which are associated with intellectual disability, also often present very differently from each other. What I want to do is to look at some of the more notable organic conditions that have resulted in intellectual disability over the years to see what they tell us about the nature of intellectual disability as a construct.

There are a number of conditions associated with intellectual disability, which, at least in western countries, have been considerably reduced by advances in medical science or social conditions. Cretinism, or as it is now known, hypothyroidism, was a major cause of mild to severe intellectual disability up until the mid-twentieth century. It is mainly due to a lack of iodine in the diet causing a failure in the thyroid gland. It used to be common in areas where there was a lack of natural iodine. However, since the cause has been identified and iodine supplements provided, people are no longer relying on locally produced food and the condition has reduced dramatically in western countries, though it is still common in developing countries (Bergen 2008).

Phenylketonuria (PKU) is a genetic disorder resulting in the inability to metabolise the amino acid phenylalanine. Its prevalence is somewhat different in different countries, although in the US it is about one in 15,000. If it is undetected and untreated it causes brain damage and severe intellectual disability. However, in most western countries it is now screened for at birth. Although the condition itself cannot be cured, provision of a diet low in phenylalanine and careful monitoring eliminate the symptoms and the affected individuals can expect to have intellectual abilities in the normal range.

Down's syndrome is one of the major chromosomal causes of intellectual disability due to an extra chromosome on the twenty-first pair, the chances of which happening increase with the age of the mother. It used to be associated with a moderate to severe degree of disability, which should mean that affected children would require special education and affected adults would never be fully independent. However, in the last 20 years or so it has become apparent that many people with Down's syndrome can live relatively independent lives as adults.

As Down's syndrome can now be detected before birth, one would have expected that both the number of babies born with the condition would have decreased and, consequently, so would the numbers of people with the condition in the population. As the incidence of Down's syndrome in the west is about one in a thousand and as the proportion of the population who have a moderate to severe degree of intellectual disability is about four in a thousand, the elimination of Down's syndrome could potentially reduce the numbers of people with moderate to severe degrees of intellectual disability by 25 per cent. However, what seems to have happened is that although the incidence of children with Down's syndrome fell in developed countries (Hansen 1978), the life expectancy of people with Down's syndrome has increased, meaning that the numbers in the population have not decreased. But, more puzzlingly, there is now an increase in the numbers of babies with Down's syndrome being born, at least in the US (Shin et al. 2009). It is unclear why this increase in births has occurred.

As with other conditions, in developing countries the incidence of Down's syndrome is much higher, and according to Bergen (2008)

94 per cent of those with Down's syndrome are born in low to middle income countries. This may well be due to not screening expectant mothers for the condition.

Despite the incidences of Down's syndrome not being reduced there is good evidence that other conditions such as hypothyroidism and PKU have dramatically decreased. One would therefore expect that the incidence of people with organically caused intellectual disability would have decreased overall; however, this may well not be the case. Although modern medicine has reduced or eliminated some conditions it has also increased the life span of people with other conditions such as Down's syndrome and is now able to save the lives of babies who decades ago would have died. It therefore is unclear if the incidence of organic conditions leading to intellectual disability is reducing overall, though the relative prevalence of individual conditions is changing.

Although all the people who suffer from an organic condition resulting in a significant reduction in intellectual ability will be classified as having an intellectual disability, the different organic conditions often present very differently. As I noted above, when an individual suffers brain damage it often does not affect all areas of the brain to the same extent, resulting in an uneven pattern of cognitive abilities. There are also genetic conditions that seem to have a particular personality type associated with them. In order to illustrate this I want to look at two conditions, Fragile X and William's syndrome.

Fragile X is the most common inherited cause of intellectual disability in boys, accounting for approximately one in 5000 male births (Coffee et al. 2009). As its name suggests it is a genetic condition involving changes to part of the X chromosome. As boys have only one X chromosome, the condition takes a much more severe form in boys, though it can occur to a mild extent in girls. Not only is Fragile X associated with intellectual disability but also with autism (Budimirovic and Kaufmann 2011, McLennan et al. 2011) with many sufferers showing autistic features, and between 15 and 60 per cent reaching the diagnostic criterion for autism.

William's syndrome is caused by missing genes; it affects both boys and girls and results in a moderate degree of intellectual disability. It used to be considered quite a rare condition with a prevalence of about one in 20,000; however, more recent work based on blood tests taken at birth suggests that it is about one in 7500 live births (Strømme et al. 2002). This discrepancy may be because the symptoms are not always obvious or, by implication, that severe, so individuals are not noticed as being abnormal. The interesting thing about the condition is that it is associated with a very affable personality being very friendly, empathetic with good social skills such as eye contact, which is very much in contrast to Fragile X where there is a tendency to an autistic personality. So although people with different organic conditions may all have a low intellectual ability they may well have very little else in common.

Familial intellectual disability

Whereas organic causes of intellectual disability are usually due to a single factor such as trauma or a faulty gene, familial intellectual disability is determined by the same multiple genetic and environmental factors that determine the intellectual and skills ability of the vast majority of the population. It can be divided into genetic and environmental causes, which may be best considered separately.

Genetics and the heritability of intelligence

Although I referred to genetic causes of intellectual disability in the last section on organic causes, these were due to a single fault in a gene leading to a very large negative effect on intellectual ability. Here I am talking about the effect of many intact genes acting together, some of which have a positive effect on intellectual ability, some of which have a negative effect on abilities. This is known as additive genetics and is responsible for the way people vary on a number of attributes such as height and weight. One of the key questions with regard to intelligence and this type of genetic influence is to what degree is intellectual ability determined by one's genes and to what degree is it determined by the environment one is brought up and lives in? There is a literature on this, although on the whole this work has been done on people with average intellectual abilities. I first explain the logic behind this work and what it shows and then look at what we know about the degree to which intellectual ability in the low range is genetically determined.

It is clear from what we have seen so far that both measured and true intellectual ability varies between individuals. Measured IQ is normally distributed with the standard deviation set at 15 points. The factors that are thought to cause one person's score to be different from another's are generally considered to be genetic and environmental. I would also suggest that specifically with measured IQ there is a third factor of test error, which as we saw in Chapter 3 is probably much greater than we had previously thought. However, in order to make the argument more straightforward for the time being I assume that IQ tests are accurate.

So how do we determine the degree to which intelligence is due to heritability and the degree to which it is due to environmental factors?

In broad terms this is done by comparing the correlation between the IQs of close relatives, such as siblings, with the correlations between the IQs of unrelated people living together, such as adopted children. If we were to correlate the IQs of people at random the correlation would be close to zero. On the other hand if we were to correlate the IQs of people with exactly the same genes and exactly the same environmental history then the correlation should be one, as their IQ would be determined by exactly the same factors, assuming no test error. If genes are the main factor determining intellectual ability we would expect close relatives living apart from each other, in random environments, to still have highly correlated IQs, as the relatives would still have similar genes. However, if the environment is a major factor, then the correlation between the IQs of close relatives living apart in random environments should be very low, as the genes they have in common would not be causing their IQs to be similar. The degree to which IQ is genetically determined, or as it is often referred to, is heritable, is therefore indicated by the correlation between the IQs of close relatives.

Genetically the closest relatives are identical or monozygotic (MZ) twins, who have identical genes. If we can find sufficient pairs of MZ twins who were separated at birth and brought up in different environments theoretically this would allow us to find out the degree to which their IQs are determined by their environment. Assuming no measurement error, any variation in their intellectual abilities would be due to environmental difference, as their genes remain the same. The correlation between the IQs of MZ twins brought up apart would therefore give a measure of the heritability of intelligence, that is, the degree to which it is genetically determined. An alternative way of referring to this is the proportion of the variance in IQ accounted for by heredity. One minus this correlation would give a measure of the degree to which IQ is determined by the environment. Although MZ twins separated at birth are rare, there are some studies that have used this method. There are, however, alternative ways of estimating the heritably of IQ. One would be to make use of both MZ twins and same-sex non-identical or dizygotic (DZ) twins. DZ twins have half their genes in common so one would expect that their IQs would correlate half as much as MZ twins, who have all their genes in common. So if we subtract the correlation of DZ twins brought up together from the correlation between the IQs of MZ twins brought up together, we get a figure for half the heritability, so doubling this gives a measure of heritability.

$$\text{Heritabilty of IQ} = 2 \times (\text{rMZT} - \text{rDZT})$$

where rMZT is the correlation between the IQs of MZ twins brought up together and rDZT is the correlation between DZ twins brought up together. Again, one minus this figure for heritability gives the proportion of the variance due to the environment.

Environmental influences on intellectual ability are usually considered in two parts: common environment, which is that part of the environment shared by siblings and is responsible for making their IQs similar and residual or idiosyncratic environmental factors that are not shared by siblings and make their IQs different. I think this requires some clarification. The common environment is that part of the environment that people living in the same family have in common, and may include factors such as the degree to which the parents encourage the children to read, to think about problems and provide a healthy diet. The idiosyncratic environment contains the environmental factors such as the effect of an individual's peers and teachers at school, what interests the individual, which are not shared by other siblings in the family. Theoretically it is possible to measure the proportion of the variance in IQ accounted for by the common environment by looking at the correlation in IQ between people living in the same family who are not genetically related such as adopted children living in the same family. Subtracting this from the figure of total environment influence would give a measure for the proportion of the variance accounted for by the idiosyncratic environment.

These methods of parcelling out the proportion of the variance determined by heritability, common environment and idiosyncratic environment are based on a number of assumptions, which may not be valid. Sometimes failure in these assumptions will result in the estimate of heritability being too high and on some occasions it will result in the estimation of heritability being too low. There are at least two invalid assumptions that would result in studies overestimating heritability. First, it is assumed that for twins separated at birth there are no common environmental effects on their IQs. However, the twins would have shared a common inter-uterine environment and often the separation of twins is not actually at birth but in the following weeks or months, so they do share the same environment for some time after birth. Secondly, it is assumed that the twins separated at birth and brought up apart are brought up in families randomly distributed across the intellectual spectrum. This may well not be the case and separated twins will be put in similar families. In both these cases some shared environmental influence on their IQs will be attributed to heritability, which will increase the figure for heritability.

There are also invalid assumptions that will reduce the estimation of heritability. First, it is assumed that DZ twins have only 50 per cent of their genes in common. However, at least as far as genes for intelligence are concerned, it is probably more than 50 per cent. This reason is associative mating, the tendency for people to marry individuals similar to themselves. So intelligent people will tend to marry other intelligent people and people of average intelligence will tend to marry other people of average intelligence. If we consider the equation of heritability above:

$$\text{Heritabilty of IQ} = 2 \times (\text{rMZT} - \text{rDZT})$$

if DZ twins have more than 50 per cent of their genes for intelligence in common then rDZT will be greater than it would have been if they had only 50 per cent of their genes for intelligence in common. So (rMZT − rDZT) would be less as would 2 × (rMZT − rDZT) and so there would be a reduced estimate of heritability.

Secondly, it seems to be assumed that IQ assessments test intelligence without any measurement error. So that if heritability of IQ was 100 per cent then correlation between the IQs of MZ twins reared apart would be one. However, as we saw in Chapter 3, there is significant measurement error particularly in the low IQ range. For illustrative purposes let us consider the test re-test reliability on the WISC-IV of .93, cited in the manual (Wechsler 2003). This is the correlation that is obtained when the same person takes the same test twice. On both occasions he/she will have the same true intellectual ability so if there was no test error the correlation should have been one. Given that the test would have been given in near optimal conditions, being part of the standardisation of the WISC-IV, this correlation of .93 must represent the maximum correlation between two WISC-IV scores. It is therefore underestimating the true relationship between the same true IQ by .07 or 7 per cent. So it is likely to be the case that when the WISC-IV IQs of two MZ twins are correlated that this correlation is also reduced by 7 per cent from what it would have been if there was no test error, so the estimation of heritability will be decreased by 7 per cent.

This same argument should also apply to reliability of internal consistency in the WISC-IV which, as we say in Chapter 3, for the WISC-IV is .97, meaning that test error due to a lack of internal consistency is .03. I argued in Chapter 3 that we should be able to add the error due to a lack of internal consistency to the error due to a lack of stability which is given by the test re-test reliability score, to get a figure for total error, which would give a figure for total error on the WISC-IV of .10.

This would mean that if the WISC-IV was being used to estimate heritability by looking at the correlations between MZ twins reared apart it would underestimate it by 10 per cent.

Even though there are some reasons to think that estimates of heritability are too high and some reasons to think that they may be too low, we cannot assume that these errors cancel each other out and that the estimates are about right without detailed information as to the degree to which each of the various factors affects the score. The best we can say is that the studies produce an estimate of the degrees to which genetics, shared environment and idiosyncratic environment affect intellectual ability.

People have been looking at the degree to which intelligence is inherited since the time of Galton in the nineteenth century and varying estimates of the heritability of intelligence have been produced. Herrnstein and Murray (1994) in their controversial book *The Bell Curve* suggested that in the average ability range it was between 60 and 80 per cent. Other works have supported this estimate, for example Bouchard (2009), Johnson et al. (2007) and Saudino et al. (1994). However, this relatively high figure for heritability has been disputed; notably by Nisbett (2009) and Devlin et al. (1997), who have pointed to the shortcomings of these studies. A more recent study by Haworth et al. (2010) with a large data set from twin studies done in several countries found that heritability of IQ increased from 41 per cent in childhood (mean age 9 range 4–10), to 55 per cent in adolescence (mean age 12 range 11–13) and 66 per cent in adulthood (mean age 17 range 14–34). Over the same period shared environment decreased from 33 per cent in children to 18 per cent in adolescents and 16 per cent in adulthood.

So, although there is considerable variation in estimates of heritability in the average ability range and certainly problems with the studies, the evidence suggests that intellectual ability is substantially determined by genetics by the order of 50–60 per cent.

These studies illustrate an important point about heritability of IQ: that it is not the same for different groups. It changes over the life span, being much greater for adults than for children. It may well therefore change for people in different ability ranges. So what happens at the extremes of the ability range? At the high end Haworth et al. (2009) looked at six large twin studies on the degree of genetic effect on high intellectual ability, done in four countries. They found that the effect was similar to how it is in the average IQ range at about 50 per cent.

At the low end there is a lack of good evidence as to whether heritability of intellectual ability is any different from the average range.

A study by Thompson et al. (1993) used 148 MZ and 135 same-sex DZ twins most of whom had average abilities but as there was a normal distribution of ability some would have relatively low ability and some relative high. They found no difference in the heritability of ability at the high or low end of the distributions.

In an early study, Nichols (1984) looks at the relationship between IQs of people with mild and severe intellectual disability and the IQs of their siblings for both European American and African American children. The IQs were measured on a variety of tests including the WISC. For the European American children there was little relationship for those with severe disabilities but a high relationship for those with a mild disability. For the African American children, when the dividing line between mild and severe was IQ 50 there was a relationship in both mild and severe, however, when the dividing line was changed to IQ 40 the relationship disappeared. He attributes this difference between the African and European American children to the lower distribution of IQs for African American children, that is, that they generally score lower on IQ tests. He also suggests that the reason he did not find a relationship between the IQs of those with severe disabilities and their siblings was that the children with severe disabilities had organically caused neurological damage which would have been the primary reason for their disability, whereas those with mild disabilities would have their IQs determined by a very similar environment to their siblings and similar genes.

So what evidence there is suggests that for people with intellectual disability not organically caused by neurological damage their intellectual ability is genetically determined to about the same extent as it is in the average range, about 50 to 60 per cent. Spitz (2006), who looked at some of this evidence would agree with this broad estimate of heritability but felt that considerably higher than is normally acknowledged and was concerned that many writers are ignoring it.

Environmental causes

The implication of this finding is that 40–50 per cent of the variance in IQ is determined by an individual's environment. This will include factors such as upbringing, education, diet, the cumulative effect of illnesses, poverty and wealth.

That only 40–50 per cent of the variance of intellectual ability is attributed to environmental causes is probably not as much as most people would expect. It may seem particularly surprising when one considers the Flynn effect, referred to in Chapters 2 and 3, whereby the intellectual ability of the population as a whole has been going up over the last hundred years or so at the rate of about .30 of an IQ point per year. There would seem to be a paradox: how can environmental causes only account for 40–50 per cent of the variance in IQ when they would seem to have resulted in a 30-point increase in average IQ in the last hundred years? One possible reason for this suggested by Minogroni (2004) is that the Flynn effect is actually due to genetic causes. He argues that, as we are all travelling more, people are now marrying and having children with people from diverse groups. There is therefore the possibility that the increase in intellectual ability is due to hybrid vigour, which is the positive effect of the introduction of new genes into a population. However, I have some difficulties with this idea, as it would suggest that populations that in the past had had new genes introduced would have shown higher IQs. For example, one would have expected that in the US, which had waves of immigration from various parts of Europe, there would have been much mixing of genes which, if hybrid vigour was to have a major effect, would have increased the IQ of the white US population in the early twentieth century. However, as we saw in Chapter 2, this did not seem to have happened. Furthermore, in the US one would have expected that hybrid vigour would have had a major effect on the intellectual ability of the African American population. This population was brought to the US from various parts of West Africa and sold as slaves when they arrived. There would therefore have been a mixing of people from different tribes from all over West Africa, which one may have expected to produce an increase in IQ. However, there is the additional effect of the introduction of genes from the European American population due to slave owners raping their female slaves. In spite of this mixing of genes the average measured IQ of the black population has always been less than that of the white population in the US. This suggests that the Flynn effect will be mainly due to environmental factors.

There would therefore seem to be a paradox with the environment only accounting for a relatively small proportion of the variance in intellectual ability and yet having been responsible for a gain of 30 IQ points, or two standard deviations, in the last hundred years. I am not sure that this has been fully resolved but it makes more sense and seems less paradoxical if we consider a bit more carefully what it means. The environmental influences on the variation of intellectual ability in the population at any one time are due to factors that vary in the population at any one time. The environmental influences that cause the mean intellectual ability of the population as a whole to change over time are environmental factors that have changed over time. The factors that change over time may not be the same ones that vary at any one time. An example of a factor that could cause change over time but not influence variation in the population at any one time may make this clearer. Air quality has improved over the last hundred years; as everybody breaths the same air one would expect that it would have an equal effect on the whole population at any one time. Therefore, as the air quality improved, everybody in the population would get roughly equal benefit from this improvement. So if air quality had a major effect on intellectual ability, and I am not suggesting that in reality it does, its improving would result in a Flynn effect but would not result in any variation in intellectual ability within the population. Factors that lead to the Flynn effect will have changed for the population as a whole, while factors that result in variation in IQ within the population at any one time will have to vary within that population at that time. It is possible that there are different environmental factors causing the Flynn effect from those causing the variation in intellectual ability at any one time, but this may not always be the case. For example, it is likely that the quality of obstetric care has an effect on the later intellectual abilities of babies. Obstetric care has also improved over the last hundred years so it is likely that it will have contributed to the Flynn effect. However, it will also vary from one hospital to another and from one expectant mother to another depending on how compliant they are with their own prenatal care. So general improvement in obstetric care over time may result in an improvement in average intellectual ability over time and variation in obstetric care at any one time contribute to variation in intellectual ability in the population at any one time. Therefore, in theory the paradox is explained, except that we do not know what factors are responsible for the Flynn effect and/or the variation in intellectual ability at any given time, but there are a number of factors that seem likely to do this, although there has been much speculation about this.

Lynn (2009) has found evidence of a Flynn effect within the first year of life, which means that there are environmental causes having an effect either in the first year of life or prior to birth. Apart from extreme poverty, clear evidence is lacking as to what pre-birth factors could affect intellectual ability; however, the following factors may well have an influences on both the Flynn effect and the variation in intellectual ability within the population: maternal health during pregnancy, maternal diet during pregnancy, smoking during pregnancy, and, as I mentioned above, prenatal and obstetric care. All of these have improved over time and vary within the population at any one time.

There is somewhat more evidence and speculation as to the environmental factors that affect intellectual ability after birth. A number of authors have suggested that a key factor is a child's diet. Lynn (1990) argues that once people started to farm and grow their own crops their diet was less varied and so did not allow intellectual ability and physical growth in terms of height to develop to its full potential. Over the twentieth and early twenty-first centuries diet in the west has become more varied and so has resulted in a more intellectually able and taller population. Lynn (2009) has continued to argue for nutrition being the major factor in the Flynn effect. Other authors have also presented evidence that nutrition is an important factor in intellectual ability. Sigman and Whaley (1998) suggest that nutrition is a factor but not the only one. Martorell (1998) reviewed the evidence for nutrition being a factor on both height and intellectual ability and suggested that there were two ways in which nutrition could affect IQ: first, poor nutrition *in utero* and childhood will affect development of the nervous system and, secondly, poor nutrition at the time the child is being assessed will affect performance on the assessment.

Family size is another factor that is related to intellectual ability in that people with fewer siblings tend to be more intelligent. Sundet et al. (2008) made use of the data on the intellectual ability and the numbers of siblings of Norwegian military conscripts and found that as family size dropped over time intellectual ability increased. They also found an inverse relationship between IQ and family size, with children with three siblings or more having progressively lower IQs. In part, this relationship could have a genetic cause, owing to less intelligent parents having more children; however, in this study there was no relationship found between the fathers' IQs and the number of children they had, which makes a genetic cause less likely. This therefore suggests that the number of siblings an individual has will have a direct effect on his/her intellectual ability. The mechanism by which family size results in higher IQs may well be due to parents who have fewer children being able to spend more time with children and possibly being able to devote more of the family's resources to them.

Less specifically, there is also a well-documented relationship between a family's income and the intellectual ability of its members. Although Herrnstein and Murray (1994) have attributed this to less intelligent people not being able get such highly paid jobs there is clearly a possibility that it is also the low income that prevents a child reaching his/her full intellectual potential. Bergen (2008) looks at the various ways in which poverty can result in low IQ. Factors such as malnutrition, deficiency in iron, iodine, zinc, Vitamins A and B12, are all associated with lower intellectual ability. These problems are chronic in the developing world but are also seen in lower socioeconomic groups in the western countries. Although Lynn's (2009) finding that the Flynn effect is seen in the first year suggests that there must be major environmental influences in intellectual ability prenatally or in the first year, this does not preclude factors that would only come into play later in childhood having an influence as well and there are a number that may be affecting intellectual ability. Education may well have become more intellectually demanding than it was in years gone by with more emphasis on problem solving and less emphasis on rote learning. Leisure activities also may well have become more intellectually stimulating; for example, Greenfield (1998) has suggested that the use of modern technology such as computer games, and the widespread use of computers has had a differential effect on non-verbal intellectual ability.

Dickens and Flynn (2001) and Flynn (2007) have suggested that since the middle of the twentieth century the major reason for the Flynn effect in developed countries is the increasing intellectual demands made by the environment. Life does seem to be getting more cognitively demanding: we have to use modern technology at work, and increasingly in our everyday lives and our leisure time. This can be a challenge, at least to me, finding out how technology such as smart phones, computers, the Internet, TVs, DVDs and microwaves, etc., work. These challenges seem to be continual as the technology goes out of date and has to be replaced with the latest more sophisticated version. This contrasts with how work, leisure and home environments would have been in the mid-twentieth century, when technology, jobs and leisure tended to remain the same and be less intellectually demanding and far more permanent. These frequent cognitive demands for on-the-spot problem solving is thought to work as a form of cognitive exercise increasing intellectual power.

Although there is more evidence for some of these environmental factors than others there are a number of implications that emerge from them. First, it seems likely that many of the environmental factors leading to a lower intellectual ability will not affect people randomly but will be associated with lower incomes. A child in a low-income family is more likely to have had a mother who had a poor diet and/or smoked during pregnancy. When a child is born he/she is less likely to have an adequate diet themselves, will have more siblings and so be less stimulated by their parents, and less likely to go to good schools. He/she will also be less likely to be given cognitively stimulating technology such as smart phones and computers.

Secondly, not only will these factors vary between social classes within countries but they will also vary between countries with developing countries having many more of the factors leading to low intellectual ability than in the west. It is therefore not surprising that the reported rate of intellectual disability in developing countries is higher than it is in the west (Bergen 2008).

Thirdly, as many of these factors in principle can be controlled, there is potential for increasing the intellectual ability of individuals and the average IQs of countries, for example, by improving nutrition, obstetric care, stimulation of children after birth and education.

So, in the absence of an organic cause of intellectual disability, whether or not an individual has an intellectual disability will be a function of both poor genetics and the environment in which they were conceived and raised. There are, I think, in reality two further factors: the demands of the environment and the tolerance of society as to how inadequately an individual is able to cope with them before they are regarded as being in need of a service. I return to these factors in Chapter 8.

Conclusion

What is clear from this chapter is that, for many people with mild degrees of intellectual disability, their low intellectual ability results from the same combination of environmental and genetic factors that determine most people's intellectual ability. They therefore have a similar diversity of skills and personalities to the rest of the population. For those whose low intellectually ability is organically determined, there is a wide variety of different causes, often resulting in a very idiosyncratic pattern of abilities and personality. It seems reasonable therefore to conclude that all people who have been given a diagnosis of intellectual disability will have in common a low measured IQ and possibly a low measured level of adaptive skills. The diagnosis as such therefore provides only limited useful information about an individual: that they will probably do poorly on intellectually loaded skills such as academic tasks and IQ tests and are more likely to show gullibility and naivety (Greenspan et al. 2011).

7
Problems with the Current Definition

As we saw in Chapter 1 there is now broad agreement as to what intellectual disability is, with AAIDD, ICD-I0 and DSM-IV all defining it as having a measured intellectual ability below a specified point, usually IQ 70 or 75, a deficit in adaptive functioning, also possibly below a specified point, all occurring before the age of 18 years. Intellectual disability is not, however, a naturally occurring condition such as, say smallpox or Down's syndrome; it is a social construct, devised to do a job. It is a condition created by definition. Therefore one should ask if the current construct and definition are doing the job for which they were created.

I argued in Chapter 1 that, currently, the primary reason for having the construct of intellectual disability is to identify people who are not able to cope as a result of low intellectual abilities, so that they can be helped to become valued members of society. The inability to cope follows from the adaptive behaviour part of the definition that implies a failure to cope. That this inability to cope is due to low intellectual ability follows from the first part of the definition that requires a low intellectual ability. That we want to assist these people become valued members of society follows from our current philosophy of care, based on normalisation, which emphasises supporting people to become valued members of society. What I want to do in this chapter is to look at all the issues of concern identified in previous chapters, and in the light of this consider if the current construct and definition of intellectual disabilities does the job it intends.

There seem to be a number of problems with the current construct and definition:

There is only a loose relationship between being eligible for a diagnosis and being able to cope

If the reason for having the construct and definition of intellectual disability were to identify people who are not able to cope, we would hope that there would be evidence that individuals who are given the diagnosis would not be able to cope and those who do not meet the diagnostic criteria would be able to cope. Surprisingly there is very little direct evidence of this. Whereas there is no doubt that people with moderate and severe degrees of intellectual disability cannot cope, it has not been demonstrated that most of those who would meet the criteria for having a mild degree of intellectual disability are not be able to cope. We saw in Chapter 5 that the majority of people who, if assessed, would meet the diagnostic criteria for having an intellectual disability are not known to services. It was also shown that the initial reason why people with mild learning disabilities are identified by services is that they were felt not to be coping. It is therefore likely that a significant proportion of those who would meet the diagnostic criteria, if assessed, are coping in the community at the current time.

There are also people who would not meet the criteria who are not able to cope. Some of these individuals may have been misdiagnosed as not having intellectual disability owing to measurement error; others may have true intellectual abilities and/or adaptive behaviour levels above the cut-off points, though still low. These people may not be able to cope for a number of reasons in addition to having a relatively low intellectual ability, for example, an autistic spectrum disorder, a mental illness, or sensory problems, but at such mild levels so that they do not meet the diagnostic condition for having the condition. It may well be the case that had they only one condition they would be able to cope; however, the combination of conditions prevents this. The problem is that if each service provider insists on people meeting strict criteria for their service, many of these individuals will not get a service. There will also be some people who have been able to cope for most of their lives and would be above the criteria for having a low level of adaptive behaviour, but who fail in a critical intellectual task such as providing adequate child-care or protecting themselves from exploitation, who may also denied a service.

The prevalence of mild intellectual disability is determined by the definition

A further problem with the definition is that it determines the minimum proportion of the population who will meet it. As we saw in Chapter 5, IQ tests and measures of adaptive behaviour are based on an imposed normal distribution with a mean of 100 and standard deviation of 15, meaning that there is a set relationship between an individual's score on the assessment and the proportion of the population that he/she scores higher or lower than. The problem with this is that, even if the intellectual ability of the bottom few per cent of the population increases, possibly due to the Flynn effect, and they have no problem in coping, they would still meet the current definition for having an intellectual disability and they would still be the bottom few per cent.

The definition was based on what was known when it was first formulated in the first half of the twentieth century

When earlier versions of the current definition of intellectual disability were first formulated in the early twentieth century, the concept of intelligence had been evident in western thought for centuries and the IQ tests had just been developed. It is likely that many of the people who were not coping had a low intellectual ability, so it would have seemed reasonable to define mental deficiency in terms of IQ. However, at that time, the concepts of autism and Asperger's syndrome had not been developed, with these conditions being described in the middle of the twentieth century by Leo Kanner in 1943 and Hans Asperger in 1944 respectively. People must have suffered from autism and Asperger's syndrome in the first half of the twentieth century and, as now, many of them would not have been able to cope. Autistic spectrum disorders, as these conditions are collectively known, have much in common with intellectual disability: they are both conditions that usually start early in life, often last for the rest of one's life and can seriously limit an individual's ability to cope. Evidence is lacking on this but I would guess that many of these individuals would have been labelled as having mental deficiency, in the early twentieth century, irrespective of their measured IQ. I therefore wonder if the concept of intellectual disability would have included people with autistic spectrum disorders, if the conditions had been known about at the time.

The concept of intelligence can be confusing

Much of this book has been devoted to the concept of intelligence and its measurement. In common language, the word intelligent is used to describe people in a similar loose way as words such as attractive or friendly. However, it also has a technical meaning or rather several technical meanings. I think confusion can occur, not only in the minds of lay people but also with some psychologists, if these technical meanings are not clearly differentiated. It therefore may be helpful to distinguish the several ways in which intelligence or IQ may be used and make a clear distinction between them.

- *Measured IQ.* This is the IQ score that is obtained when an individual is given a particular IQ test at a particular time. However, as was demonstrated in Chapter 3, the accuracy of IQ tests is not nearly as good as we had previously thought, particularly in the low range. Therefore a measured IQ cannot be assumed to be the same as an individual's true IQ or true intellectual ability, which may be of the order of 20 points different. The problem is that most people are not aware of this and assume that if an individual has had an IQ test that the resulting score is their IQ. To reiterate what I said in Chapter 3, I think it is important to draw a distinction between measured IQ and true intellectual ability.
- *True intellectual ability.* This is what I think most people mean by IQ or intellectual ability and what is referred to in the current definitions of intellectual disability. It is equivalent to a measure of g or general intelligence and is the score that would be obtained if an individual were assessed using a perfectly accurate IQ test, under perfect conditions, so there is no chance or systematic error. For the population as a whole, it has a mean of 100, a standard deviation of 15 and represents the intellectual ability of an individual relative to people of his/her own age. It may well change over life, as the environmental effects for an individual change. Knowing somebody's true intellectual ability should be important, clinically, for diagnosis and for research. However, as current IQ tests are subject to more error than we had previously suspected it cannot be measured with any accuracy and can only be estimated. I discuss how this can best be done in Appendix II.
- *Absolute intellectual ability.* IQ and true intellectual ability are measures of intellectual ability relative to people of the individual's own age; absolute intellectual ability is an individual's intellectual ability relative to the entire population. Some people with the same true intellectual ability at different ages will have very different absolute intellectual ability. For example, a child of 12 years with a true intellectual ability of 100 will be able to do far more intellectually than a child of 6 years with the same true intellectual ability. There may be times when it is important to predict what an individual is going to

be able to do; for example, if one needed to know which individuals were going to be able to benefit from an academic programme open to people of all ages, absolute intellectual ability would be a better predictor than true intellectual ability. Also in some scientific studies it is necessary to match adults with an intellectual disability with children of the same intellectual ability. The measure that is usually used for absolute intellectual ability is mental age. Mental age is a reasonable measure with which to compare individuals in a population at any one time and can be used to match adults with intellectual disability with children with the same mental age. However, it would not work over time, as absolute intellectual ability will be subject to the Flynn effect, so that somebody with a mental age of eight years today would be considerably more intellectually able than somebody with a mental age of eight years a hundred years ago, who on today's standards would have a mental age of about 5½ years.

- *Genetic potential.* As we saw in Chapter 6, genetics has a major influence on an individual's intellectual ability. These genes will be acquired at conception and cannot be changed throughout life. However, they are not the only influence on an individual's eventual level of intellectual ability; the environment also has a major influence. We could define genetic potential for intellectual ability as the true intellectual ability that would emerge if an individual were given an optimal environment for intellectual development. Assuming that there is an environment that cannot be improved on, then it will determine an individual's maximum level of intellectual ability. The distinction between genetic potential for intellectual ability and, say, true intellectual ability is that most people, particularly those with low true intellectual abilities, do not live in an optimal environment to develop their intelligence. Therefore, just because some groups, say African Americans, or people from lower social classes, have lower measured IQs than white middle-class Americans does not imply that they have lower genetic potential for intellectual ability or that they could not get similar measured IQs if their environments were brought up to the same standard as that experienced by white middle classes.

We cannot measure IQ and adaptive behaviour with sufficient accuracy

Not being able to measure intelligence as accurately as previously thought is a central problem with the current definition and I have devoted quite a bit of the book to this. In Chapter 1 I identified several assumptions that seem to have been made by the writer of the current AAIDD definition with regard to the measurement of both IQ and adaptive behaviour. Assumptions about the measurement of IQ were that:

1. Individuals have a true IQ that can be measured.
2. Low IQ can be measured numerically.
3. Although IQ assessment is subject to error IQ can be measured to an accuracy of five points in the low range.
4. SEM and 95 per cent confidence interval should be based on internal consistency only.
5. Although different IQ tests may produce slightly different scores there is basic consistency between tests.

In Chapter 3 I considered in detail how accurately we can currently measure low IQ. In the light of this, I now want to look at how valid these assumptions are. I will examine the assumptions in a slightly different order, which I think helps my arguments flow more logically.

Assumption 1. Individuals have a true IQ that can be measured

This assumption has two parts to it. First, that people have a true IQ and, secondly, that it can be measured. It seems to me that it is reasonable to assume that most people probably do have a true IQ or, as I call it, above a true intellectual ability. The main evidence for this being that a factor of general intelligence or g has consistently come out of the factor analysis over the last hundred years. However, it may not be reasonable to claim that everybody has a true intellectual ability. Factor analysis is based on data from large groups, and therefore, if there are individuals in the groups that are different from the trend, they will make little difference to the overall results and will not be apparent. There may well be some individuals for whom it makes less sense to say they have a single true intellectual ability; for example, people for whom there are very large differences between scores on the individual subtests, or index scales of an IQ test, or savants who have one area of ability far in advance of the rest of their development.

The second part of the assumption relates to whether intelligence is measurable. If this part of the assumption is not valid then Assumptions 2 and 3 will also not apply. I argued in Chapter 3 that we cannot measure low IQ to anything like the accuracy that is required to confidently say if an individual's true intellectual ability is above or below 70. So as things are at the moment this part of the assumption is not validated and therefore neither are Assumptions 2 and 3, though I shall expand on this below.

Assumption 4. Standard Error of Measurement and confidence intervals should be based on internal consistency only

Basing the 95 per cent confidence interval on internal consistency only seems to me to be disingenuous, as it suggests that the tests are accurate to four to five IQ points. It is my experience that most people, including many a practising psychologist, interpret this as saying that if the same test was given to the same person twice within a few days, the scores would be within four points of each other. This is not the case: the degree to which scores on the same test change from one assessment to another is indicated by the stability of the test and not internal consistency for the test. In Chapter 3 I calculated a 95 per cent confidence interval for the stability of IQ tests in the low range to be 12.5 points either side of the measured IQ. It seems to me that if an individual is given two assessments within a few days and the scores differ by ten points, as they very well might, then it is not possible to say that his/her true IQ is within four points of either of these assessments.

I argued in Chapter 3 that the 95 per cent confidence interval should be based on a combination of the errors due to a lack of internal consistency and a lack of stability. This to me seems a very reasonable approach: I have not come across any arguments against this; however, I'm aware that this is quite a novel approach and others may not accept it. However, if we are not going to base confidence intervals on a combination of error, I think it would make more sense to base them on stability rather than internal consistency. There are two reasons for this. First, a lack of stability is what most people who have not read the test manuals in detail feel that is meant by the confidence interval. Secondly, a 95 per cent confidence interval based on stability of 12.5 points is not very different from the 95 per cent confidence interval based on a combination of a lack of internal consistency and a lack of stability in the low range, which is 13 points.

Assumption 3. Although IQ assessment is subject to error, IQ can be measured to an accuracy of four to five points in the low range

This five-point accuracy implied in the definition refers to the 95 per cent confidence interval stated in the test manuals, which, as we saw in

Chapter 3, is based on the internal consistency of the test. Although, even in the low range, this confidence interval is about four to five points on the WISC-IV and WAIS-IV, it does not take into account the error due to a lack of stability, for which the effective 95 per cent confidence interval in the low range is 12.5 points either side to the measured IQ.

Assumption 5. Although different IQ tests may produce slightly different scores there is basic consistency between tests

This assumption may apply in the average range where there is a reasonable agreement between the two gold standard tests, the WISC-IV and the WAIS-IV. However, in the low range, what evidence there is suggests that this is not the case. Gordon et al. (2010) compared the WISC-IV with the WAIS-III, using 16-year-olds in special education, and found that on average the WISC-IV scored 12 points lower than the WAIS-III. Although I do not know of any studies in which both the WAIS-IV and WISC-IV have been given to adolescents in the low intellectual range, I (Whitaker 2012) compared what was required of 16-year-olds to get a scaled score of two on the common subtests in these two tests. It was apparent that, in the low range, the WAIS-IV was easier than the WISC-IV. It is likely that when the WISC-IV and WAIS-IV are compared in the low range the WISC-IV will still score significantly lower than the WAIS-IV. So if these two gold standard tests differ by the order of 10 points, and we have no clear idea which of these two assessments is likely to be correct, then we have no way of saying what an individual's true intellectual ability is. It seems like a reasonable assumption that the true intellectual ability would be somewhere between the two scores but this may not be the case. However, it is also possible that either the WISC-IV or WAIS-IV is spot on and the other is out by 10 points or that both assessments are measuring too high or too low and the true intellectual ability is either above the score on the WAIS-IV or below the score on the WISC-IV.

Assumption 2. Low IQ can be measured numerically

There are tests that will produce a numerical score for IQ, such as the WISC-IV and the WAIS-IV; however, it seems to me, that, at least in the low range, intellectual ability is not a quantity that should be measured numerically. Currently as the accuracy of IQ tests are so limited in the low range, I think we should regard an individual's level of intellectual ability a bit like an individual's level of attractiveness, as something that varies between individuals but that we cannot measure, in the sense of putting a numerical score on it. Where low IQ scores are used they should be interpreted with a great deal of caution.

So considering the AAIDD assumptions about intellectual ability as a whole, apart from individuals having a true intellectual ability as such, none of the assumptions seem to be valid. It therefore does not seem reasonable to specify an IQ figure in the definition of intellectual disability. It follows from this that if low intellectual ability is to remain part of the definition of intellectual disability, a cut-off point should not be specified and intellectual disability should be regarded as a judgment condition.

Assumptions about the measurement of adaptive behaviour

The assumptions made by the current AAIDD definition identified in Chapter 1 were as follows:

1. That it is reasonable to measure adaptive behaviour.
2. That an individual's level of adaptive and social competence can be expressed in a single score in the case of overall score or in terms of three scores in terms of conceptual, social or practical functioning.
3. That the measurement of adaptive behaviour can be made to a reasonable degree of accuracy.

Evidence with regard to whether adaptive behaviour is a meaningful and measureable construct is even less positive than it was for IQ. The concept of adaptive behaviour is far less coherent than that of intelligence, with the different scales of adaptive behaviour not correlating well with each other. Therefore, a significant number of people would reach the diagnostic criteria on one scale but not on another. Therefore, whether an individual met the criteria of having a deficit in adaptive behaviour would be a function of the scale they were assessed on, as well as their actual level of skills.

There are also problems with the reliability of even the most modern scales of adaptive behaviour. As I did with IQ in Chapter 3, in Chapter 4 I calculated a 95 per cent confidence interval based on combined chance error and found it to be just less than 18 points. In addition to this, there are a number of systematic errors, notably a floor effect, some differences between tests, the possibility of deliberately faking scores, and differences between groups of respondents, notably parents and teachers. All of these make the true confidence interval of these tests of the order of 30 points either side of the measured score.

It seems to me that none of the assumptions about the measurement of adaptive behaviour are valid. Therefore, neither intellectual ability nor adaptive behaviour can be measured with sufficient accuracy in the low range for them to be considered quantities that should be given a numerical score. This, together with the other issues outlined above, has a number of implications for clinicians and researchers working in intellectual disability, which I want to explore.

People who cannot cope may not get a service

The most obvious consequence of the error in the measurement of low IQ and adaptive behaviour and the wording of the current definition is that some individuals, who are not able to cope, will not be given a service. This may occur either because the individual's true level of intellectual ability and/or adaptive behaviour is above the cut-off points, so technically the individual does not meet the criteria, or it may be due to error in the assessment. However, for practical purposes there is no difference, as we are not in a position to say what an individual's true intellectual ability is. Webb and Whitaker (2012) give an example of just such a case. Sophie was a young woman who had been to special school. She had no self-care skills, never cooked, cleaned, budgeted or shopped for herself. However, after leaving school she got a job in a supermarket and ceased to have formal contact with services. While attending a youth club for people with intellectual disabilities she met her partner Gary. When she got pregnant she moved in with Gary. She was referred by her GP to the local social services learning disability team for support. As a result of this referral, a clinical psychologist assessed her cognitive abilities. He found her to have an IQ in the range 70 to 75, however, with deficits in memory and executive functioning. As her measured IQ was above 70 and as she had had a job, she was deemed by the local services to be 'too able' to be provided with specialist learning disability services. When she was seven months pregnant the social services child team assessed her. They concluded Sophie and Gary would not be able to keep the baby, as the level of support that they would need in the long term would be too great.

This case illustrates a number of points. Sophie was a young woman, who it was clear would probably not be able to cope and for whom there was evidence that she had an intellectual disability in that she had attended a special school and a special youth club. One may have thought that this would have been sufficient evidence to provide her with a service without the need for further assessment. However, an assessment was done and, in spite of it being clear that she did have specific problems in her cognitive ability, she was refused a service on the grounds of having a measured IQ over 70 and having had a job. This may well have resulted in her and her partner not being given adequate support to care for their baby and losing it. Even if we had confidence in the IQ tests and she clearly did have a true intellectual ability above 70, it illustrates how arbitrary an IQ 70 cut-off point is. What was clear was that she was not able to cope in a critical area of her life, and that a major reason for this was her cognitive deficits. Had her IQ been a couple of points less this would have probably made very little difference to her inability to cope but she may well have got a service. It could be argued that, as she had had a job, this provided some evidence that she did not have an intellectual disability. However, although it is less likely for people with intellectual disabilities to have a job than somebody with an average intellectual ability, it is certainly not unusual for people with intellectual disabilities to have jobs (Greenspan and Shoultz 1981). Many of the skills that would be required to do a basic job, say in a supermarket, are not intellectually demanding and doing them should not taken as evidence of a near average intellectual ability.

But there are errors in the measurement of low IQ and Sophie's measured IQ between 70 and 75 may well have been an overestimate of her true intellectual ability. First, there is a reasonable chance that, had the assessment been done on a different day, she would have scored six points lower putting her well within the learning disability range. Secondly, it is likely that as she was 21 when she was assessed she would have been assessed on the WAIS-III which, as we saw in Chapter 3, on average will measure 12 points higher than the equivalent child test, the WISC-IV. So had she been assessed at 16 on the WISC-IV, all other things being equal, she would have got an IQ between 58 and 63 and her learning disability would not have been questioned.

People may get wrongly diagnosed as having intellectual disability

It is also clearly possible for people to be wrongly diagnosed as having an intellectual disability on the basis of a measured IQ score below their true intellectual ability. Although this could lead to the individual receiving services, there are a number of negative effects of a wrong diagnosis. As I suggested in Chapter 1, there is stigma attached to having an intellectual disability label, which could reduce an individual's self-esteem. It may also mean that other significant reasons for the individual failing to cope may be missed, such as an autistic spectrum disorder or mental illness. Mental illness is an interesting example as not only could it reduce an individual's ability to cope, but it could also reduce his/her score on an IQ test, meaning that it makes it more likely that there would be a false diagnosis of intellectual disability and the mental illness would be missed and so not treated.

Possibly, as there is a general belief that the measures of IQ and adaptive behaviour are accurate, there is a lack of research on how individuals come to acquire a false diagnosis, but we can speculate about this. In the US there is often universal assessment of children's intellectual ability, therefore, a child may get a low score on IQ test and so get an intellectual disability label without any clear indication that he/she is not able to cope. In the UK there is no universal testing of the intellectual ability of either children or adults; therefore, in order to be identified as having an intellectual disability an individual must be behaving in a way that suggests that they are not coping in some respect. For example, in adults it may be noticed that they are not coping with a critical life task, such as failing to resist temptation to get involved in crime or to provide adequate child-care. It is more likely that the individual will be in a crisis and under stress when they are identified and so may well score low on an IQ test.

There are two additional factors that may make it easier for a child to acquire a false diagnosis. First, one of the major tasks of childhood is to cope academically. This is an intellectually loaded skill, so failure academically may be attributed to low intellectual ability. However, although academic ability is related to intellectual ability, there are other reasons why children may fail: there may be a lack of motivation to succeed, they may have other conditions that may interfere with learning such as Attention Deficit Hyperactive Disorder (ADHD), undiagnosed sensory problems, a behavioural disorder, or a specific learning disability such as dyslexia or dysnumeracy. Some of these factors may not only cause them to fail academically but may also affect the child's performance on an IQ test; for example, if a child has ADHD then he/she may not be able to concentrate for the hour to hour and a half necessary to do the WISC-IV. The second issue specific to childhood is that the WISC-IV probably measures systematically lower than the WAIS-IV by the order of 10 when used in the low range, so may well underestimate true IQ by a significant amount. Once the label is acquired it may well remain into adulthood, by which time he/she will no longer have to cope academically and may be as capable as anybody of coping with the general demands of daily living.

The US death penalty

In 2002 the US Supreme Court, in the case of Atkins vs. Virginia, prohibited the execution of individuals with mental retardation. However, they did not say what mental retardation was, leaving it up to individual states to produce their own definition. There are therefore numerous definitions loosely based on the AAIDD definition (Duvall and Morris 2006; DeMatteo et al. 2007). All the 38 states that allow capital punishment require a sub-average level of intellectual functioning as part of their definition of mental retardation. Twenty of these states specify an IQ figure above which a convicted individual would not be considered to have mental retardation and so could not be reprieved from execution on the grounds of mental retardation. Therefore, establishing that an individual has an IQ below this point is critical in showing that a defendant has an intellectual disability. Clearly the errors in the measurement of IQ outlined above and in Chapter 3 will mean that there is likely to be error in the diagnosis in some cases; however, there are other factors that make the diagnosis even more of a lottery. In addition to the above sources of error, which I added together to get an estimate of the true confidence interval of the WISC-IV and WAIS-III (Whitaker 2010b), the literature on the measurement of IQ in forensic cases highlights two additional sources of error, malingering and the practice effect.

Malingering.   This is deliberately underperforming on an assessment in order to get a low score. An individual appealing the death penalty on the grounds of having an intellectual disability may be motivated to do this. It is clear from the literature (Salekin and Doane 2009) that courts are well aware of the possibility of this error in assessment; however, currently there does not seem to be a reliable way of detecting when it occurs when assessing an individual with low intellectual ability.

The practice effect.   This occurs when an individual performs better on a test the second time he/she is given it, owing to having had the opportunity to practise when they were first given it. This is more of an issue in forensic cases as both prosecution and defence psychologists may well assess the defendant. The amount the practice effect increases test scores can be estimated from test re-test reliability studies that have given the same test to the same clients on two occasions. Both the WISC-IV and WAIS-IV manuals (Wechsler 2003, Wechsler et al. 2008) describe such studies, with mean Full Scale IQ increasing by 5.6 points on the WISC-IV over an average test re-test interval of 32 days and by 4.3 points on the WAIS-IV over a mean interval of 22 days. However, the practice effect is likely to decrease as the interval between testing increases and may well also be a function of ability level. In this respect it is notable that my meta-analysis (Whitaker 2008b) of test re-test reliability in the low range found a mean increase in FSIQ of only .41 of an IQ point for a mean test re-test interval of 2.3 years.

It is up to the defence to establish, usually on the balance of probability, that the defendant has an intellectual disability. However, the prosecution will challenge the evidence presented by the defence. This may mean both defence and prosecution employing their own psychologists. This can result in the defence and prosecution psychologists getting very different scores. Although clearly the responsibility of an expert witness is to give impartial advice to the court, it is possible that they may be unconsciously swayed to produce a particular result, or that the attorneys employing them may have chosen them for their apparent views or track record in obtaining certain results. Therefore, if the assessor is commissioned by the defence it is possible that they may want the client to have a measured IQ less than the specified figure. This could be made more likely if they did the following:

- Put emphasis on WISC-IV rather than WAIS-IV scores. Although in a death penalty case the defendant would be over 16-years-old, and so there would be no scope for assessing them on the WISC-IV, the defence psychologist could still make use of earlier WISC-IV or WISC-III assessments done during childhood and argue that greater weight should be given to these assessments as they would have been done before the offence was committed and so would be less likely to be subject to the problem with malingering. It could also be suggested that the WISC-IV may be a more accurate assessment in the low range than the WAIS-IV, as it is easier to get a representative sample of children with low intellectual ability than it is of adults to standardise the test (Flynn and Weiss 2007).
- Allow the assessment to be done under sub-optimal clinical or forensic conditions. It likely that if an IQ assessment is done under sub-optimal conditions, such as may occur in some prison or clinic settings, the score will be reduced. In order to obtain a lower score the

assessor may therefore not insist on a distraction free environment or that the defendant is in a state to give of his/her best.

- Ensure the defendant is aware of the consequences of a high score. For example, in death penalty cases, the assessor could make it clear to the defendant that a high score will increase the likelihood of being executed.
- Avoid using an assessment that the client has been assessed on recently so the score is not increased by the practice effect.
- Correct for the Flynn and floor effects. As we have seen test scores can be artificially increased by both the Flynn effect and the floor effect; however, these effects could be corrected for to some extent.

However, if the assessor was working for the prosecution he/she may wish to ensure a high score, in which case he/she could:

- Put emphasis on the WAIS-IV rather than the WISC-IV. It could be argued that emphasis should be put on a more recent WAIS-IV score than older WISC-IV or WISC-III scores as the WAIS-IV results reflect how the individual is now and that higher scores are less likely to be subject to error.
- Ensure that assessments are done under optimal conditions. Rather than accepting poor conditions such as may be offered in a prison setting the assessor could insist on as near to optimal conditions as possible. They could also put off an assessment if the defendant was not in an optimal condition to be assessed, for example, angry, depressed or non-cooperative.
- Ensure that the individual is motivated to do well on the assessment. Rather than emphasise the negative effects of doing well on the assessment, emphasis could be put on the positive consequence, such as showing that you are smart.
- Re-assess on a test that has been used recently in the past. By using an assessment that the individual has only recently been assessed on, possibly by the defence assessor, the score should be increased owing to the practice effect.
- Do not correct for the Flynn or floor effects. The obtained scores could simply be presented without any correction. Also, if possible, the assessor could use an older version of the test in order to maximise the Flynn effect.

Although it is not be possible to put an exact figure on the degree to which it would affect scores, if an individual were assessed under these two extreme sets of conditions, it is likely that the two obtained IQ scores would differ in the order of 25 points. Twelve points would be attributable to differences between the tests used due to the Flynn effect and other factors, 10 points to temporal error due to difference in assessment conditions, one point for the floor effect, two points for the practice effect, as well as some effect due to malingering. However, both assessments would produce a measured IQ score. If a court was unaware that these manipulations could have such a large effect on measured IQ and regarded measured IQ as a good indicator of true intellectual ability, then it would be likely to accept an IQ score as a good indicator of the defendant's true intellectual ability.

The judge and sometimes jury have to decide, on the merits of the case presented to the court, whether a defendant has an intellectual disability. Juries and to some extent judges, will have a lay understanding of what intellectual disability and IQ are. They may feel that if somebody has got some adaptive skills that are in the normal range in one area, such as being able to drive, this rules out a diagnosis of intellectual disability. They may well feel that IQ tests are accurate and suggestions that they may need adjusting to take account of the Flynn effect, and the floor effect, or that an assessment such as the WAIS-IV may systematically measuring too high, are simply attempts by the defence to exempt their client from death penalty. Whether these corrections are allowed may well be as much a function of the relative eloquence of the defence and prosecution lawyers as the scientific merits of the case.

Each part of the definition may have to be established so that the defence would have to show that the defendant had a low level of intelligence and adaptive behaviour both now and before he/she was 18 years old. There may well be an issue in establishing that an individual had intellectual disability in childhood. School records may therefore be examined for evidence that the defendant either had or did not have an intellectual disability in childhood. However, for a number of years there has been a reluctance to diagnose mental retardation in children in US schools (Baroff 1999; 2006; Gresham 2009; Reschly 2009). In part this is because of the stigma associated with the term mental retardation. The term learning disability has often been used instead; however, in the US use of the term learning disability means a specific learning disability such as dyslexia, which is not necessarily associated with a low level of intellectual ability. Therefore, whether or not a defence lawyer can convince the court that his/her client reaches the full diagnostic criteria could depend on how the school chose to label the individual years earlier.

So, in death penalty cases, whether or not somebody is accepted as having an intellectual disability will be dependent on a lot of factors in addition to their actual ability and test error: the abilities of the defence and prosecution lawyers to put over their cases to the court, the prior opinions of judge and jury, what has been recorded at school and, probably, what assessments have previously been given. And this determines if somebody lives or dies. Clearly there are going to be miscarriages of justice, with some individuals whose true intellectual ability and level of adaptive skills are in the intellectual disability range not being able to establish this and being executed, and some individuals who have abilities outside the intellectual disability range convincing a court that they do have an intellectual disability and being reprieved. In part this will be due to the current definition that gives the impression that both IQ and adaptive behaviour can be measured precisely.

The effect on scientific research

This lack of precision in the measurement of IQ and adaptive behaviour can have implications for the scientific literature. First, if people are simply described as having an intellectual disability or having a particular measured IQ score, it does not convey very much information about the individual. Secondly, the error in measurement of IQ will affect the results of scientific studies.

Description of people in the scientific literature

Laird and Whitaker (2011) looked at how people with intellectual disabilities were described in two leading intellectual disability journals: the *American Journal on Mental Retardation* and the *Journal of Applied Research in Intellectual Disability*, examining all the papers in the 2008 editions of both journals.

The concept of intelligence was used in 81 of the 91 papers, with measured IQ scores frequently being reported. A few studies indicated that there may be some errors in the measurement of low IQ and that different intellectual assessments may not be equivalent to others; the majority, however, gave little or no indication as to the accuracy of IQ assessments. There seemed to be an implicit assumption that one IQ assessment, done with a particular test, under a particular set of conditions, is equivalent to another assessment, done with a different test, under a different set of conditions. This failure to take this lack of accuracy in the measurement of low IQ into account could have varying impacts on studies, and may on some occasions lead to false conclusions being drawn.

The chance and systematic errors will have different effects. If a study gives the average IQ of a group of participants then the chance error will be greatly reduced, as the errors on the individual assessments will be cancelled out. However, a mean score will be still subject to systematic error. On the other hand, chance error will reduce correlations and the chances of getting a statistically significant result but systematic error will not. It may be useful to consider some examples in more detail to illustrate how this may work.

The greatest impact of the error will occur when the measured IQ of a single individual is reported, for example in a clinical case study. This IQ score will be subject to both chance and systematic errors and so true intellectual ability may vary by up to 25 points either side of the measured IQ. If there is a large disparity between measured IQ and true intellectual ability the study could give the false impression that the factor under investigation had a particular effect with individuals at that IQ level. For example, if a case study was reporting on the successful use of a cognitive method of treating depression and the individual was described as having an IQ of 50, it may be assumed that this treatment method was applicable to individuals with moderate degrees of disability. However, it is clearly possible that the client's true intellectual ability would be in the 70s, meaning that the case study only demonstrated that the treatment method could be successfully used with individuals with borderline degrees of disability.

As I argued in Chapter 6, chance error will also have the effect of decreasing the correlation between measured IQ and other variables. I made the point in Chapter 6 that the maximum correlation one can expect between two measured IQs is the correlation one would get when the test is given to the same person twice, that is, the correlation found in a test re-test study. This is because the individual's true intellectual ability will be the same on both occasions he/she is assessed, so the true correlation should be one. Therefore, any reduction from one must be due entirely to test error. This error will occur every time the test is given, so will reduce any correlation by the same amount. For example, if a study was looking at the relationship between IQ and ability on a spelling test, the correlation obtained would be reduced due to the error in measurement in IQ and possibly also in the measurement of spelling ability. So the obtained correlation between measured spelling ability and measured IQ will underestimate the true relationship between true intellectual ability and true spelling ability and reduce the chances of getting a statistically significant result.

A failure to recognise that different IQ tests produce different scores because of systematic error may lead to wrong conclusions being drawn. Russell et al. (1997) is an example of a study where this may have happened. Working in the UK, Russell et al. (1997) investigated whether schizophrenia reduced IQ. They compared the IQs of adults who had developed schizophrenia with their IQs before developing schizophrenia when they were children. As children the patients had been mainly assessed on the WISC-R, though some were assessed on the WISC; however, as adults they were assessed on the WAIS-R. Russell et al. reported the mean WISC-R/WISC IQ to be 84.1 and the mean WAIS-R IQ to be 82.2 and concluded that schizophrenia did not result in a significant reduction in IQ. They make the point that previous studies claiming schizophrenia reduced IQ had been flawed and that it was just that schizophrenics had a lower pre-morbid IQ. However, they fail to consider that the WISC-R may systematically measure lower than the WAIS-R at these IQ levels, which is likely for two reasons. First, it is probable that the scores on the WAIS-R would have been elevated far more by the Flynn effect than those on the WISC-R they took as children. This is because the majority of the assessments on the WISC-R occurred in the mid-1970s, soon after the UK version of the test came out, so would have been subject to about a one point Flynn effect. As the paper was published in 1997 and the WAIS-R assessment was used on adults, one assumes these assessments took place in the mid-1990s, about 18 years after the test was normed, meaning it would be subject to about a six-point Flynn effect. The paper does not report how many participants were assessed on the WISC as children, which would have been subject to a Flynn effect of about 10 points. However, assuming that only a small proportion of the children were given the WISC, it is likely that the WAIS-R scores were systematically elevated by the Flynn effect on average by about four points above the WISC and WISC-R assessments. Secondly, there is an additional four point systematic difference between the WISC-R and WAIS-R found by Spitz (1988) at this IQ level. Therefore, in order to get an estimate of true change in IQs between the participants when they were children and later as adults, one needs to subtract from the WAIS-R score four points for the Flynn effect, and four additional points for the systematic error found by Spitz (1988), in order to make it comparable with the WISC-R scores. Therefore, with the 1.9 points difference that was found in the measured scores in the study, it would appear that as adults the participants were effectively scoring 10 IQ points lower than they did as children. This may well be seen as good evidence that schizophrenia does reduce intellectual ability.

Conclusions

The current construct and definition of intellectual disabilities is clearly not doing the job for which it was designed. Even if it were possible to measure IQ and adaptive behaviour to the level of accuracy suggested in the definition, the definition would still not include all those who were not able to cope for reason of a low intellectual ability and would include many who were able to cope. However, the assumptions about our ability to measure IQ and adaptive behaviour are not valid and many people who have true intellectual abilities and adaptive behaviour levels within the intellectual disability range will be assessed as not having an intellectual disability, and many people who have true intellectual abilities and or adaptive behaviour levels outside the range will be assessed as having an intellectual disability.

This will clearly lead to misdiagnoses and people not getting the services they need or being given a stigmatising label that they should not have. It may also lead, in extreme cases, to individuals being executed when they should not be. The scientific literature may also be misleading if IQ assessments are treated as being accurate and equivalent to each other. The definition therefore needs reconsidering.

8

Intellectual Disability Reconceptualised and Redefined

In Chapter 1 I raised the question as to whether the current construct and definition of intellectual disability was still fit for purpose. In Chapter 7 I outlined in some detail why it is not. What I want to do in this chapter is: first, to consider what assumptions are reasonable to make with regard to intellectual disability and our ability to measure it; second, to consider what we require from a construct of intellectual disability; and, third, to suggest more appropriate concepts and definitions.

Assumptions

There are few facts in social science in general and in psychology in particular. What there is, is a body of empirical data, other observations, and suppositions leading to assumptions about what is factually the case. Some of these assumptions are based on more evidence than others though I would suspect that there is not a direct relationship between the amount of supporting evidence for an assumption and the degree of certainty that it is believed in. What I want to do is to explicitly state the assumptions that I think a new construct and definition of intellectual disability should be based on. Some of these assumptions will be shared by most others writing on intellectual disability at the moment. Some are assumptions that are not shared by most others; nonetheless I think there is considerable evidence for them. Others lack empirical evidence but are based on my experience of working in the intellectual disability field as a clinical psychologist for the past 30 years. I hope I have made it clear in the previous chapters where there is evidence for my assumptions and where I am basing them on my own experience.

1 Intellectual disability is a social construct

As we saw in Chapter 1 there are a number of human conditions that are naturally occurring; that is, they occur irrespective of whether society wants them to occur, will be recognised by most societies and will often continue to exist over millennia. Obvious examples are what sex one is or whether one is alive or dead. Other examples are some human diseases: such as smallpox, which is caused by an infection of the smallpox virus infecting an individual and Down's syndrome, which results from an extra chromosome on the twenty-first pair. These conditions will have existed before they were discovered and given a name. Once such conditions are identified they can be studied to get information about the exact nature of the condition and possibly ways found of reducing or eliminating them. As a result of this, Down's syndrome can be detected in early pregnancy and smallpox has now been eliminated by immunisation. Other conditions are social constructs, conditions that have been created by society to meet some need. I gave the example of a witch in Chapter 1, a construct that was required to explain things that were occurring that seemed not to have a natural explanation and so were blamed on witchcraft. A more up-to-date example would be 'criminal'. The term criminal has a meaning to most people, though what different people understand by the term may differ. When one considers what the actual meaning of the term is, one can see that it is not clear, and that it does need defining. A criminal could include all people who commit crime or have committed any crime, whether that is armed robbery, driving over the speed limit or making a personal phone call on a work phone. The problem with this definition is that it would include most people and the term would be virtually useless in differentiating people. One therefore has to arbitrarily define 'criminal' in terms of the seriousness of the crimes committed. If you then want to study the nature of criminals what you will find will be dependent on the definition you have used. If you have a loose definition then those that are included in the category criminal will be people of both sexes, all ages and all social classes. If the definition is changed so it just includes 'serious' crimes, then criminals will be predominantly male, between 15 and 30 years old from lower social classes.

Intellectual disability is clearly a social construct, the nature of which will depend upon how it is defined. Whether the majority of people in the category have low levels of adaptive skills will depend on whether low adaptive skills are included in the definition. The numbers who fit into the category of mild learning disability is a direct function of how many standard deviations below the mean, the IQ and adaptive behaviour cut-off points are drawn. The advantage of this is that the construct can be defined so that it achieves what is required of it. The disadvantage is that it often does not make a lot of sense to pose questions about the nature of the condition, as the condition is what we define it to be. For example, by definition, people who currently have the label of intellectual disability will usually have failed at school, have had more difficulty getting jobs and generally will have difficulty in coping.

2 Adaptive behaviour is an arbitrary social construct

As we saw in Chapter 4 adaptive behaviour was included as part of the definition of mental deficiency in 1959, in part to reduce the numbers of people from the lower social classes and minority ethnic groups who were being given a label of mental deficiency when the definition was based on IQ alone. It also put more emphasis on ability to cope in the real world. However, it has been consistently criticised for being an invented construct, with the scales developed to measure it having somewhat arbitrary content and lacing both theoretical and empirical support (for example Greenspan 1979; 1997; 1999). In Chapter 4 I noted that the different measures of adaptive behaviour do not agree very well with one another, which would mean that an individual who scores low on one measure of adaptive behaviour may score in the mid-range on another. I would also argue that, despite the similarity between the construct of adaptive behaviour and the concept of coping that I have used throughout this book, there is a lack of evidence that individuals who obtain a score more than two standard deviations below the mean, on an adaptive behaviour scale, are usually not going to be able cope in their real world environment. The concept is therefore an arbitrary social construct, which fails to do the job required of it.

3 Intelligence (g) is a naturally occurring construct

I think general intelligence or g, is a naturally occurring construct. This is because the abilities that are said to constitute intelligence are not only determined by theory but are also found and confirmed by factor analysis. These factor analytic studies have consistently shown g to be the main factor in hundreds of studies, going from Spearman's work in the 1900s to the standardisation of the WAIS-IV a hundred years later. IQ subtests and the items within these subtests are therefore not chosen at random but have been demonstrated to be measuring intelligence. It is therefore legitimate to ask questions about the relationship between intelligence and how people behave in the real world, though accepting that there may well be major problems in the measurement of true intellectual ability particularly at the extremes.

4 There may be confusion as to what is meant by intelligence and IQ

In Chapter 7 I made distinctions among measured IQ, true intellectual ability, absolute intellectual ability and genetic potential for intellectual ability. It seems apparent from the way that lay people and the media discuss intelligence that people are not aware of these distinctions and often confuse them. I would suspect that most of the controversies with regard to intelligence are due to a failure to distinguish between genetic potential and measured IQ. It seems to be assumed that because a particular group, for example, people in lower social classes or minority ethic groups, has on average a lower measured IQ, this is due to inferior genes for intelligence. This assumption ignores the fact that measured IQ is determined by many factors in addition to genetic potential for intellectual ability, notably how nurturing their environment has been over their lifetime as well as errors in the measurement of intellectual ability.

I would also suspect that many people involved in the development of definitions of intellectual disability and its diagnosis are not aware of these distinctions. This seems apparent from the assumptions that are made with regard to the accuracy with which true intellectual ability can be measured. These confusions matter: a deficit in intelligence has been part of the construct of intellectual disability for thousands of years and since the turn of the twentieth century it has been defined in terms of measured intelligence. It was the assumptions of the eugenics movement that intelligence was almost entirely genetically determined, which led to policies of forced sterilisation and, in the extreme case of Nazi Germany, the killing of those identified as having low intellectual ability. It needs to be recognised that a measured IQ is only a rough predictor of true intellectual ability and that true intellectual ability gives only a moderate indication of an individual's genetic potential for intelligence.

5 The accuracy to which low IQ and adaptive behaviour can be measured is very poor

It was the gradual realisation that we could not measure low IQ as accurately as is suggested in the test manuals that started me thinking about whether the current concept and definition of intellectual disability was appropriate. I have outlined in some detail in Chapters 3 and 4 why I do not believe we can measure low IQ and adaptive behaviour with sufficient accuracy to base a definition on specified cut-off points. In Chapter 7 I considered the consequences of trying to do this.

6 There is only a moderate to small relationship between adaptive behaviour and intellectual ability

I think this needs stating as an assumption as it differs from what seems to be believed by many writers. For example, Detterman and Gabriel (2006) and Schalock (2006) both explicitly state that there is a high correlation between IQ and adaptive behaviour, though without presenting evidence. However, in my review of the relationship between IQ and adaptive behaviour in Chapter 4, I show the relationship to be low.

People who score low on IQ are mostly not the same people who score low on adaptive behaviour and vice versa. The implications of this are: first, that measured IQ and adaptive behaviour cannot be used interchangeably. Second, measured IQ only predicts an individual's ability in a limited number of intellectually dependent tasks such as academic skills, literacy skills, planning and problem solving. It tells us very little about an individual's ability to perform basic domestic tasks or to interact socially with other people, skills that may be critical to being able to cope in the real world.

7 Intellectual disability is a judgment condition

I argued at the beginning of Chapter 1 that some human conditions are what I called judgment conditions. These are conditions where, although the defining attributes are commonly agreed, it is not possible to measure them so the only way to decide if somebody has this condition is by judgment. The example I gave in Chapter 1 was whether somebody was beautiful or not. It may be claimed by some that one could take physical measurements of an individual, feed the information into a computer and get a score for beauty, however, I think it is unlikely there would be more than a moderate degree of agreement between these scores and the ratings of individuals, so beauty is a judgment condition. It seems to me that intellectual disability is also a judgment condition, as its defining attributes of intellectual ability and adaptive behaviour cannot be measured with any accuracy. So the best one can do to decide if somebody belongs in the category is to make an educated and professional judgment.

8 Clinical judgment may be flawed

In recent AAIDD/AAMR manuals there has been a place for clinical judgment in the diagnosis of intellectual disability for those cases in which the IQ score falls in what is regarded to be the error range between 70 and 75. Clinical judgment (AAIDD 2010, Schalock and Luckasson 2005), involves getting information from a wide range of sources, evaluating that information and coming to an unbiased judgment. An experienced assessor should consider the evidence for and against the individual being assessed as having an intellectual disability and come to a conclusion. But there may well be problems with clinical judgment as it is inevitably subjective. Different assessors may well emphasise different factors, so there may well not be very good agreement between assessors. Also there is the possibility that factors other than how the individual presents may sway decisions, such as the financial implications of a decision or, in a forensic assessment, whether a diagnosis would suit the case of those instructing the assessor. However, clinical judgment has the advantage of being explicitly judgmental so that any judgments should be open to challenge.

9   There are some things that low IQ does predict

It is clear from the relatively high correlations between academic performance and intellectual ability and the apparent need for special education for those with low intellectual ability that people with low IQs are more likely to fail academically. In addition, individuals with low intellectual ability may well be more likely to be more naïve, gullible and fail to make sensible decisions, which may well be a major factor in their failing to cope (Greenspan et al. 2011).

10   Some people with low IQ cannot cope

It is abundantly clear that some people with low intellectual abilities cannot cope and need support to achieve an acceptable quality of life. It also seems likely that there is a relationship, though possibly not a particularly strong one, between a true intellectual ability and being able to cope, for those in the low IQ range.

11   Currently the relationship between a having a diagnosis of intellectual disability and being able to cope is not straightforward

As we saw in Chapter 5, the bulk of the people who would meet the current diagnostic criteria are not known to services and many of them may well be coping. There are, in addition, people with relatively low intellectual ability, though not sufficiently low to meet the current diagnostic criteria, who are not able to cope.

12   Society believes people who are not able to cope due to a low intellectual ability are deserving of care and support

In the absence of surveys that actually ask the general public what they feel about caring for people with low intellectual ability, it is not clear what society as a whole does want. However, it is clear that the dominant philosophy of care in the west, of Normalisation (Wolfensberger 1972), puts emphasis on treating people with intellectual disabilities as valued members of society. There is now legislation to that effect, for example, in the UK the White Paper, Valuing People (Department of Health 2001). It therefore seems reasonable to assume that society does have a minimum acceptable level of quality of life and is prepared to ensure that people do not fall below this level. I have used the terms coping and not coping throughout this book to denote where this level is.

13   The aetiologies of low intellectual ability are varied

As we saw in Chapter 6, the causes of low intellectual ability can be usefully divided into organic, where there is clear biological pathology, and familial, where the low intellectual ability is due to a combination of multiple genetic and environmental influences. It is clear that some specific organic conditions such as Fragile X and William's syndrome have behavioural and personality characteristics associated with them: people with Fragile X have autistic tendencies and those with William's syndrome are, on the whole, more friendly. People with familial intellectual disability will have a similar range of personality as those with higher levels of intellectual ability. A diagnosis of intellectual disability therefore tells us very little about what an individual is going to be like, apart from not being able to do well in intellectually demanding tasks. Similarly the reasons why an individual fails to cope will vary. Not only will this be influenced by an individual's level of true intellectual ability, personality factors such as motivation, autistic traits and mental illness but also by the nature of the environmental demands.

14   There is stigma associated with the label of intellectual disability

It seems quite clear that the diagnosis of intellectual disability carries with it a lot of stigma. One only has to consider how terms like 'moron', 'imbecile' and 'idiot', words that once had only a technical meaning, have now become terms of abuse. Having a low intellectual ability is something that virtually everybody would want to avoid and, if they did have it, may want to conceal. Stigma may well have a negative effect on an individual's self-esteem, confidence and mental health. However, it is likely that the issue of stigma is more acute for people with a milder degree of disability. They may well be far more aware of the stigma associated with the condition and wish to avoid the label even if this means not getting a service.

15 A useful distinction can be made between those with mild and more severe intellectual disability

There are a number of ways in which people with mild intellectual disability differ from those with moderate to profound degrees of disability:

- Aetiology is general different: those with a mild intellectual disability usually have a familial aetiology, those with greater degrees of disability having an organic aetiology.
- The inability to cope is much more obvious and permanent in people with more severe degrees of disability. Many people who currently get a diagnosis of mild intellectual disability may well appear normal to most of their peers and may well be able to cope most of the time.
- Whether people with mild intellectual disability cope or not is multiply determined by demands on them, other personality factors such as motivation and autistic spectrum disorders and mental health. For those with more severe degrees of intellectual disability a failure to cope may well be far more to do with their very low level of intellectual ability.
- People with more severe degrees of disability are much more likely to be known to services than are those with mild disabilities.
- As the aetiology of severe degrees of disability is most likely to be organic, the prevalence of moderate to profound disability is determined by the prevalence of these organic conditions, which may well change over time. For example, if we were able to reduce the incidence of brain injury at birth, we would also reduce the numbers of people with moderate to profound degrees of disability. However, the prevalence of mild disability is determined by definition of intellectual disability, which states that those who score below two standard deviations in IQ and in adaptive behaviour, irrespective of what the individual's absolute intellectual ability is or whether they are able to cope, are intellectually disabled.
- People with mild degrees of disability may be more affected by stigma and are more able to articulate what they want.

16 The definition will need to satisfy a number of stakeholders

There are a number of different stakeholders, such as service providers, educators, service planners, researchers, doctors, the criminal justice system and the individuals who are given the diagnosis themselves, who have an interest in the construct of intellectual disability. What each of these stakeholders wants from the construct may well be different.

17 Getting a diagnosis can have a major effect on an individual

Finally it is clear that getting or not getting a diagnosis can have a major effect on the individual. On the positive side it can result in an individual being provided with services to ensure that they cope and, in the extreme case of US death penalty, can result in them not being executed. On the negative side it is a stigmatising label that people may well want to avoid.

Intellectual disability reconceptualised

What I want to do in the following section is to look at the options we have for producing a new and better conceptualisation of intellectual disability based on the assumptions laid out above.

Stakeholders and what the construct will need to do

My first assumption is that intellectual disability is a social construct, designed to do a job or a number of jobs. I also assume that there are a number of different stakeholders who have different rudiments of the construct. It seems to me that the first task in producing a new construct of intellectual disability is to consider what each stakeholder will require of the construct and whether these diverse requirements can be incorporated within a single construct.

So who are the stakeholders and what do they want? What I present below is not an exhaustive list of stakeholders but the more obvious ones. I also give what I consider the requirements they would have from a construct and definition of intellectual disability.

Service providers will require a construct and definition that can be used to determine who is eligible for services and who is not. In discussing my ideas about construct and definition of intellectual disability with colleagues, the issue of gate keeping has frequently been raised. In these times of diminishing resources, we cannot have a service for people with intellectual disabilities that is given to everybody: there must be clear criteria to decide who should be given a service and, by implication, who should be refused one. There are times when I have suspected that what is being suggested is that it does not matter if some people do not get the service they need, provided that the greater good is serviced. I do not agree with this, and feel that the current construct and definition leads to a very arbitrary way of allocating services. However, I do think there is a legitimate requirement of service providers for a definition that can be used to ensure that those in need of a service, and who are entitled to one, get that service and those who are either not entitled to a service, or are not in need of it, do not get one.

Educators may need a definition that identifies children who are likely to fail in the mainstream education system because of a general intellectual disability, as opposed to failing in a specific aspect of education such as literacy or numeracy.

Planners will need a definition that allows them to predict what the future need for a service is likely to be. I think that essentially this would seem to be predicting how many people are likely to meet the criteria for having a service in the future. As such, the construct and definition required by planners may therefore need to be similar to that required by service providers.

Medical doctors may require a definition that tells them something about pathology, treatment and prognosis, so appropriate treatment can be prescribed (Reeve 2006). The current definition does not do this as it focuses in on function rather than pathology. If information with regard to pathology and prognosis is a requirement of the medical profession it may be inconsistent with what service providers and planners currently require.

Researchers. Clearly different research will have different requirements of the construct and definition but, in broad terms, it seems to me that most researchers will need a definition that describes the individuals who are the subjects of research in such a way that the study can be replicated accurately. Currently, the major way in which people with intellectual disability are described in the research literature is in terms of their level of intellectual ability (Laird and Whitaker 2011), suggesting that the primary concern of researchers is to study people who have low intellectual ability. Although, as I have emphasised throughout this book, there are problems with how accurately the level of intellectual ability can be assessed, it seems to me to be quite reasonable to base an academic definition on supposed intellectual ability, though any definition would have to take account of what we know about our ability to measure low IQ. I also feel it would be unhelpful for researchers to have the additional criteria of a deficit in adaptive behaviour or inability to cope in the definition, as this would exclude people with low intellectual abilities who are coping and so, at least in theory, one would not be able ask questions about why some people with low intellectual ability are able to cope. It therefore seems to me that the needs of researchers are very different from those of planners and service providers.

Legislators. In the UK there is some legislation specifically about people with intellectual disabilities. The White Paper, 'Valuing People' (Department of Health 2001), although not an Act, outlines various expectations as to what people with learning disabilities are entitled to for example:

> All people with a learning disability to be registered with a GP by June 2004. All people with a learning disability to have a Health Action Plan by June 2005. (p. 61)

However, as I showed in Chapter 5, only a small proportion of those who would fit the current international definitions are known to services. The same applies to the rather looser definition given in the Valuing People document (Whitaker 2004). The problem with these requirements of Valuing People for 'all' people with learning disability to be registered with a GP and to have a Health Action Plan, therefore, is that as we do not know who most of the people who would fit the current definition of intellectual disability are, it not possible either to provide all of them with a Health Action Plan or to ensure that they are registered with a GP. There is therefore a need for a definition that could be used so that 'all' people with an intellectual disability can be identified. This could be achieved by using an administrative definition such as 'People who are currently known to intellectual disability services'. However, this will be different from a definition that would have to be used by services to assess eligibility in the first place.

The criminal justice system. Whether an individual has an intellectual disability may be important in the criminal justice system for at least two reasons. First, there are cases where a diagnosis of intellectual disability will give an individual an entitlement to something. The most obvious example is preventing his/her execution in the US, if they have been convicted of a capital offence. Here I think the definition would need to reflect what the legislator intended. The reasons stated in the Supreme Court ruling for stopping the execution of individuals with mental retardation was because it was concerned that individuals with mental retardation were not as culpable as other criminals, and that they would not be as able to cope with the court proceedings as well as other criminals and so may well not be able to instruct their lawyers and, for example, take advantage of plea bargaining. The problem with the Supreme Court's decision is that they did not give a definition of mental retardation but rather left it up to individual sates to produce their own definition. On the whole these definitions are based on the AAIDD definition, which seems to lead to arguments in court with regard to IQ, and whether the individual had the disability before the age of 18, which may or may not reflect their capability for the crime or their ability to deal with the court proceedings. However, this does not apply to all states. Texas has a much less precise definition based on the level and degree of mental retardation, which a consensus of Texas citizens would agree with. This resulted in Marvin Wilson being executed in August 2012, in spite of having a measured IQ of 61 on the WAIS-III. What concerns me about this is not that Texas has its own rather looser definition as such, but rather that this definition resulted in a man who it is likely would have been found to have mental retardation in all other states being executed. In part this may have been due to too much emphasis being put on a lay interpretation of what intellectual disability is, which tends to see obvious signs of disability (Greenspan and Switzky 2006). In part it may be that the burden of proof may well have been too great for the defence, as a measured IQ of 61 on the WAIS-III, a test that, as we saw in Chapter 3, may measure too high by up to 12 IQ points, must suggest that the defendant is very likely to have a significantly low intellectual ability.

The second reason why a court may wish to know if somebody has an intellectual disability is when it is a pertinent factor in the case. For example, whether somebody has an intellectual disability may be important in a case where he/she was being taken advantage of by others or there was a question as to whether he/she would make a credible witness. It is quite apparent from reading accounts of court cases that establishing that somebody has a learning disability in UK courts and or mental retardation in US courts can be an important part of a case. However, it has been pointed out (Greenspan and Switzky 2006) that courts often fall back on lay ideas as to what intellectual disability is, which is somewhat different from what is intended by the formal definitions. What would seem to be needed here is a term that is understood by the court, indicating what an individual is likely to be able to do or not be able to do, particularly in relation to the case being considered by the court.

The individuals who are given the label. Particularly with the individuals themselves, I hesitate to say what they would require from a construct, definition and label that would be applied to them. However, the evidence does suggest that many people to whom the label is either applied or could be applied, find it stigmatising and would seek to avoid it. It therefore seems likely that they would rather not be labelled or if they have to be, they should be given a less stigmatising label.

Different consequences of an error in diagnosis

A further issue is the consequences of making an error in diagnosis, which could be very different for different stakeholders and in different circumstances. In a research study in which there are large groups of people, having a few people whose measured IQs differed in the order of 20 points from their true intellectual abilities would not make much difference to the study. At the other extreme, in a death penalty assessment, having a measured IQ only a few points higher than the individual's true intellectual ability could results in the execution of a person whom the Supreme Court had intended to be spared. It seems to me that the consequences of making an error should be taken into account when defining the construct, possibly having a definition that would have more false positives if the consequences of a false negative were severe.

Given these diverse requirements of a construct and definition, and the variation in the consequences of making an error in diagnosis, producing a construct and definition that satisfies all stakeholders with safeguards for the individuals to whom may be applied may be very difficult. But there are a number approaches to producing a construct and definition that could be considered.

Possible approaches for a new construct and definition

Keeping the current construct and accepting the increased error

The simplest solution would be to retain the current AAIDD (2010) construct and definition, just accepting that the error in the measurement of IQ and adaptive behaviour are greater than previously assumed. The AAIDD (2010) manual acknowledges that error exists and that clinical judgment should be used where an IQ score is not clearly either less than or greater than two standard deviations below the mean. It would, however, require adjustments to be made in the manual as to the amount of error that should be expected. A specific 'gold standard' test IQ would need to be specified, and the scores of all other tests should be altered for compatibility. However, there are a number of problems with this approach. First, the error is much greater than had previously been assumed and, as is argued in this book, I think is too great for it to be reasonable to actually give it a numerical score. Secondly, there is not sufficient data to quantify the degree of error in the low range. For example, as I write no work has been done to compare the WISC-IV and WAIS-IV at low levels so it is not known if the WISC-IV measures lower than the WAIS-IV and by how much in the low IQ range. Third, it would not fully satisfy any of the stakeholders. There would be too much error for service providers and planners, there is a lack of precision for researchers and the meaning of the term is probably too complex and technical for the legal system. For these reasons this does not seem to be a viable option.

Having a definition based on IQ only

Going back to a definition purely based on IQ has been suggested by a number of authors, notably Detterman and Gabriel (2006) and Zigler et al. (1984) who have been very critical of adaptive behaviour, which they considered an arbitrary construct. However, they believed that IQ could be measured reliably. Although I share their assumption with regard to adaptive behaviour, I do not feel IQ can be measured accurately and that this inaccuracy would lead to many people with true intellectual abilities below 70, who were not able to cope, being misdiagnosed as not having intellectual disability. So, from the point of view of a service provider, this would be an unsatisfactory construct. However, it may well suit researchers whose primary interest is in low intellectual ability, rather than whether people can cope or not.

Having cut-offs at one standard deviation

It is likely that IQ tests are more accurate at one standard deviation below the mean than at two standard deviations, as there are far more people in the standardisation sample with abilities at this level. Although we do not have specific data on the reliability of IQ and adaptive behaviour tests at one standard deviation below the mean, the reliabilities may well be the same as those given in the test manuals based on the performance of people with average abilities.

However, about 16 per cent of the population would have measured IQs below one standard deviation or IQ 85. This is considerably more than the 3 per cent who have measured IQs below 70 and much more than the proportion of the population who fail to cope because of intellectual problems. There is a danger that some would see a measured IQ of 85 not as just one of several criteria to be met for a diagnosis, but as the only necessary condition for having an intellectual disability. This may well lead to misdiagnosis and consequent social stigma for some people in the low average intellectual range. It would have to be emphasised in any definition of intellectual disability that IQ 85 was not considered to be a significant limitation in intellectual functioning but was stated only because one cannot be confident in the accuracy of lower IQ scores. Therefore, whether or not an individual with a measured IQ in the range one to three standard deviations below the mean should be considered to have an intellectual disability would have to be based on other information and clinical judgment. It seems to me that there would be very little to be gained by specifying a cut-off point at one standard as the vast majority of people who could be considered may have a significant limitation of intellectual ability would meet this criterion and therefore their diagnosis would depend on clinical judgment.

Have a definition that does not specify cut-off points

It may well be possible to formulate a definition without the use of specified cut-off points. This option would acknowledge that we currently cannot measure low IQ and adaptive behaviour sufficiently accurately to have a specified cut-off point. The assessment as to whether an individual had an intellectual disability would therefore have to be explicitly based on clinical judgment. So whether the individual fulfilled all the criteria of the definition, for example, low intellectual ability, low adaptive behaviour, or not being able to cope, would be a matter of judgment. If the assessor had to decide how likely it was that an individual's true intellectual ability was of the order of two or more standard deviations below the mean, they may take into account such factors as intellectual assessments done in the past, performance at school, functioning in his/her environment, and signs of gullibility or naivety. Part of this evidence may also be a newly administered IQ test. However, if new or old IQ data is used, the scores should be corrected for the Flynn effect and the floor effect, and then interpreted according to what is known about the test accuracy in the low range and any systematic deviation that test may have with other commonly used IQ tests. I do not think a judgment should be made that an individual has a significant degree of intellectual disability on the basis of an IQ score alone and certainly not a single IQ score (see Appendix II).

However, clinical judgment is not without its problems as I indicate below.

Basing the definition far more on clinical judgment

Clinical judgment (AAIDD 2010, Schalock and Luckasson 2005) involves an experienced assessor getting information from a wide range of sources, evaluating that information and coming to an unbiased judgment. However, as was noted in Assumption 8, above, there are potential problems with clinical judgment.

• There are likely to be disagreements between assessors, particularly if they are motivated to come to different diagnoses, if, for example, two assessors were from different sides in a criminal trial.

- It is likely that a clinical judgment, made under a particular set of circumstances, would not satisfy the needs of all stakeholders. For example, if a diagnosis were being made for reasons of service eligibility, then there would be emphasis on whether the individual could cope at that time. This may well exclude people with true intellectual abilities below two standard deviations, who were coping, who researchers may be interested in.

Any definition based on clinical judgment would have to take account of these potential problems. However, the advantages of the use of clinical judgment to make a diagnosis of intellectual disability are, first, as I argued above, intellectual disability is a judgment condition and so can only really be decided on judgment. Secondly, although clinical judgment is to some extent subjective, it is explicitly subjective, and so clearly open to question by others. This contrasts to the current definition, based on measurements that are supposedly objective and so appear to be beyond question, but are in reality inaccurate, resulting in incorrect diagnoses that will not be questioned.

Having a definition based on coping

I explain what I meant by this rather loose construct of coping in Chapter 5 and which I have used throughout this book. It reflects society's judgment as to what is an acceptable minimum of quality of life is and its preparedness to put in resources to stop people falling below that level. I would expect that what is regarded as coping to change over time and possibly from situation to situation. The fact that there are many people who have low intellectual ability who cannot cope is now the main reason for having the construct of intellectual disability. However, as I note in Assumption 11 above, there may well be many people who meet the current definition who can cope and some people who do not meet the current definition who cannot cope. Basing the definition explicitly round coping would help to ensure that only people who could not cope got a diagnosis. However, there are some problems with basing the construct round coping. First, a construct of not being able to cope would be over-inclusive and include not only people with low intellectual ability, but also people who could not cope for other reasons, such as mental illness, personality problems or addictive behaviour. A construct and definition of intellectual disability based on coping would therefore have to include additional criteria indicating that the inability to cope was primarily due to a low intellectual ability. Second, diagnosis would have to be based on clinical judgment, which as I note above has its problems. Third, although a definition of intellectual disability based on coping would meet the needs of service providers and possibly planners, it probably would not meet the needs of other stakeholders, such as researchers and the criminal justice system.

Not labelling the individual as such but specifying where they are failing to cope

The issue here is whether we need to label people at all. A piece of legislation in the UK that may be useful in considering this is the 2005 Mental Capacity Act (Department of Health 2005). Although this legislation is not specific to intellectual disability it does include it. The Act outlines how an individual should be assessed as to whether he/she has the capacity to make specific decisions. It is based on a number of principles:

- An individual should be assumed to be capable of making a specific decision at a specific time themselves unless it is demonstrated they cannot.
- An individual should not be regarded as not being able to make the decision unless all practical steps have been taken to help them.
- The individual should not be regarded as incapable of making the decision just because they may choose to do something that others regard as unwise.
- If an individual is felt to be incapable any decision made on their behalf should be in their best interests.
- Any action taken should be done in a way that has the least impact on the individual's rights and freedom to act.

There is therefore no requirement for an individual to have a specified diagnosis for him/her to be given help. There is also no assumption that because they may have a specific condition, such as intellectual disability, they will not be able to make a specific decision, or that because they are not able to make that specific decision at one time, they will not be able to make it at another time. The Act therefore requires a specific assessment to be made as to whether the individual can do something at a particular time and not whether they have a specific diagnosis. This model of not labelling an individual as such, but rather looking at his/her capacity to do specific things, could be adopted more when considering how we may treat people who today may be give a diagnosis of intellectual disability. It would have the advantage of reducing stigma as individuals would not be labelled as such so may well suit the individuals to whom it is applied better. However, it would not suit other stakeholders, such as researchers who may feel they need to have people clearly categorised as having an intellectual disability or not.

Abandoning the construct of mild intellectual disability

In Assumption 15 above, I made the point that people with mild intellectual disability are in many ways different from those with a moderate to profound disability. Because of this there may be an argument for abandoning the concept of mild intellectual disability. Individuals who would meet the current criteria for mild intellectual disability and have a need for a service could be classified as vulnerable adults or children in need. However there are a number of reasons why this may not be a good idea:

- Drawing a distinction between what is considered as mild intellectual disability and moderate intellectual disability, in individual cases, may be more problematic than is the distinction between mild intellectual disability and not having an intellectual disability, if it is to be based on IQ and adaptive behaviour cut-off points. The accuracy of IQ and adaptive behaviour tests may well be even worse at three standard deviations below the mean than they are at two standard deviations below the mean. Therefore the distinction would have to be based on clinical judgment.
- Although, in many respects, adults with mild intellectual disabilities may be similar to other vulnerable adults and children a critical difference is that people with mild intellectual disabilities will have a need for a service that focuses on low intellectual ability specifically. For example, psychological treatments for mental health and behavioural problems used with people of average intellectual ability have to be adapted so that they can be used with people of low intellectual ability.
- Abandoning the construct of mild intellectual disability may not suit all stakeholders, for example researchers.

Because of this I am not yet persuaded that doing away with the classification of mild intellectual disability is a way forward, although we should be aware that it may well be a very different sub-category of intellectual disability from moderate to severe.

Having multiple constructs and definitions

It is apparent that not all options suit all stakeholders: definitions based primarily on intelligence would suit researchers and ones based on coping may suit service providers. Also, error in diagnosis may well have very different consequences depending on the context in which it is made. However, as intellectual disability is a social construct, constructed to do a number of jobs, there is no reason why we should just have one definition. It would clearly be possible to develop different constructs and needs to suit different stakeholders.

Possible definitions

From what I have argued above I think it follows that any constructs and definition of intellectual disability should have the following properties:

- It should have an emphasis on low intellectual ability and, usually, an associated inability to cope.
- A cut-off score should not be specified for either IQ or adaptive behaviour.
- In the absence of cut-off scores any diagnosis will have to be based on clinical judgment.
- It should not suggest that the condition is permanent. It is perfectly possible that some individuals will cope for most of their lives, but have particular intellectual challenges, say bringing up children, that they are not able to cope with. They should therefore only be regarded as having the condition during that period.
- It is not likely, and indeed not necessary, that any one definition and construct will meet the needs of all stakeholders. There is no reason why, in most cases, stakeholders could not produce their own construct and definition. So any one construct and definition would not need to cover all circumstances in which low intellectual ability is an issue.
- Any construct, definition and name should be written in such a way as to minimise the stigma that could be associated with the term when it is applied to individuals.

In the past (Whitaker 2008a; Webb and Whitaker 2012) I have suggested a definition of intellectual disabilities without the specification of cut-off points. This, in a somewhat modified form, is as follows:

A person can be regarded as having an intellectual disability if he/she is judged to be in need of community care or educational services due to a failure to cope with the intellectual demands of his/her environment and are suffering significant distress, disadvantage and/ or are unable to take care or protect themselves or their dependants from significant harm or exploitation. Provided that there are indications that he/she did not meet or had difficulty in meeting the everyday intellectual challenges they were faced with in childhood and that this has continued since then.

I would like to suggest that this definition of intellectual disability could form the basis of other, related constructs and definition, which may have to be written to meet the needs of various stakeholders.

As it stands, this definition seems to fulfil many of the criteria outlined above. It put emphasis on not being able to cope in association with a low intellectual ability, does not specify any cut-off points for measured IQ or adaptive behaviour and makes it clear that it is a judgment condition. It does not and, I would emphasise, should not, imply that the condition is necessarily permanent. Unlike the current (2010) AAIDD definition it does not determine the prevalence of people who have a mild form of the condition; if the environment becomes less intellectually challenging then the prevalence will go down and if it becomes more intellectually challenging the prevalence will go up. It also puts the emphasis on the intellectual challenge of the environment rather than the lack of intellectual ability of the individual, which, hopefully, will help to reduce the stigma associated with the label intellectual disability.

The definition does, however, have a number of problems, which, although not critical, would have to be taken into account by any stakeholder wishing to use it as a basis for a definition. The main problem is that it is based on clinical judgment, which can be flawed, inconsistent and open to challenge. Any stakeholder who produces a definition will have to make it clear who will make the clinical judgment, how it should be made and what should be done in the case of a dispute over diagnosis. I would suggest that, as part of the specification as to how clinical judgment works, it is stated that, in the absence of full information about an individual's current and past level of functioning, an equivocal diagnosis could be made. So, for example, if there is insufficient information the diagnosis could be stated as follows: 'the individual probably/possibly can be considered to have an intellectual disability at the current time'.

The second issue is that this suggested definition will suit some stakeholders better than others. When I originally suggested the definition (Whitaker 2008a, Webb and Whitaker 2012), I was focusing on the needs of service providers: my main aim being to produce a definition that would ensure that those who needed a service were not refused one on the grounds of not scoring below an IQ cut-off point. The definition therefore may suit the needs of service providers more than legislators or researchers. Although it would be presumptive of me to produce definitions for specific stakeholders, it may be useful to consider the sort of approaches particular stakeholders could take.

Service providers. As I note above, my suggested definition may be best suited to making decisions on services eligibility for service providers. However, service providers may wish to alter the definition to suit their local needs. Also, in the context of deciding if somebody is eligible for a service it may not be necessary to give somebody a formal diagnosis or label at all, but simply state that they are eligible for the specified service. The services could be given a neutral name,say based on where the service was provided, for example, 'Lake Side'. Not labelling individuals should help to reduce stigma associated with the label. So the criteria for this service could stated be as follows:

> An individual is eligible for a service from Lake Side if he/she is judged to be in need of community care services owing to a failure to cope with the intellectual demands of his/her environment and is suffering significant distress, disadvantage and/or is unable to take care or protect themselves or their dependants from significant harm or exploitation. Provided that there are indications that he/her did not meet or had difficulty in meeting the everyday intellectual challenges they were faced with in childhood and that this has continued since then.

Clearly the term Lake Side can be replaced with any other natural term that indicates who the service providers are but not necessarily what they do.

Educators. Although in a sense educators are service providers, the service they provide is different from that provided by community teams for adults with intellectual disability: there may need to be more of an emphasis on failure to cope with the intellectual demands of education generally. The definition may therefore be required to identify children who are in need of special education in all academic subjects. So a definition that may suit educators might be as follows:

> A young person is eligible for general special education if he/she is judged to be failing to cope with the intellectual demands of the

mainstream school curriculum, and it is likely that this failure will persist and he/she will significantly benefit from special education.

Although a formal assessment of the child's IQ may be part of the assessment to see if the child fits this definition, since intelligence, as we saw in Chapter 2, is a relatively good predictor of educational achievement, critically the definition is not written in terms of an IQ score and does not require one. Also, if an IQ assessment is used, it should only be used as part of a much wider assessment of the child's academic abilities.

Legislators.   In writing legislation, whether it is in regard to the services people are entitled to, as in the case of the UK's White Paper, Valuing People, or what their legal entitlements are, such as in the US Supreme Court ruling against the death penalty, there is a need for a construct that is as clear as possible. However, there probably are differences in what would be required in these two examples.

In the case of Valuing People the definition would be required to identify which 1–2 per cent of the population, should be regarded as having an intellectual disability, at any one time. In the case of the death penalty a definition should determine if a specific individual has an intellectual disability or not. The consequences of getting the diagnosis wrong are also very different; in the case of the UK's Valuing People where the worst that can happen is that somebody is denied a service, in the case of somebody seeking exception for a death penalty they could be executed. Secondly, the death penalty legislation will be the basis of legal arguments in court and so needs to be framed in such a way that would make things clearer to courts. It is therefore unlikely that one definition would easily suit both these examples.

Valuing People.   With regard to legislation such as Valuing People, ideally there should be a definition that would identify all those who need a service. However, this may not be an achievable objective, as not all people who are eligible for and in need of a service are currently known to services. I would suggest that what may have to be done is to explicitly use an administrative definition, based on those who have already acquired a label, for example:

> People who are currently judged to be in need of community care or educational services owing to a failure to cope with the intellectual demands of their environment and are suffering significant distress, disadvantage and/or are unable to take care or protect themselves

or their dependants from significant harm or exploitation. Provided that there are indications that they did not meet or had difficulty in meeting the everyday intellectual challenges they were faced with in childhood and that this has continued since then.

As the people who are currently receiving a service will be known it is a straightforward process to determine to whom the legislation applies. There is, however, a potential problem if local services have radical different definitions of intellectual disability, or what constitutes coping. This could be reduced by more guidance in legislation as to what the legislators regard as a minimum standard of quality of life.

The US death penalty. Here there is a need to ensure that those whom the Supreme Court intended to spare the death penalty are not executed. Unfortunately the US Supreme Court did not specify in any detail who these people are, leaving it up to individual states to frame their own definitions. However, what is clear from the Supreme Court's ruling is the reason why it was made: that they were concerned that individuals with mental retardation were less culpable than other murderers and that they may be disadvantaged by failing to understand the legal system they were involved with, so may not be able to indicate where evidence was wrong, or plea bargain. I would therefore suggest that a definition of 'mental retardation' produced by a state, for use in death penalty cases, should put an emphasis on lack of culpability and ability to deal with the court proceedings. I would suggest that it could be based on the following definition:

> An individual should be considered to have mental retardation if, at the time of the offence and or when appearing in court his/her level of cognitive ability is impaired to such an extent as to significantly reduce his/her culpability for the crime and/or impair his/her ability to understand court proceeding and/or instruct his/her lawyers.

I am assuming in this definition that foolishness and naivety, which Greenspan et al. (2011) believe is the key characteristic of people with low intellectual abilities and may lead them to get involved in murder, will be taken into account when assessing culpability.

Researchers/academics. Here clearly it is up to each journal to define the condition they are interested in. However, as I suggest above, I think that editorial boards would want to have more emphasis on looking at people who have a low intellectual ability and not whether they can cope or not. I would therefore suggest a definition something like this:

An individual should be considered to have a low intellectual ability if, on the basis of intellectual assessments, that take into account the limitation of the assessments used with regard to both chance and systematic errors, and on the basis of commensurate difficulties with the intellectual demands in the real world since childhood, he/she probably has an intellectual ability at least one standard deviation below the mean.

There is more emphasis on measured IQ in this definition, though with safeguards to ensure that measurement error is taken into account and the cut-off point changed to 'about' one standard deviation below the mean, where the accuracy of the tests will be better. I think this is justified in the research context as there are fewer negative consequences for the individual getting a wrong diagnosis. However, as I suggested in Laird and Whitaker (2011), there is a need for journal editors to insist on more information being given with regard to how IQ was measured, for example what tests were used, and whether any corrections were made for the Flynn and floor effects.

Developing countries

I think the above definitions are relevant to developed western countries where the concept of intellectual disability has been about in some form or another for centuries, where there is an established system of social care provided by the state and where the environment has become increasingly intellectually demanding. One of the main points I am making is that definitions should be applicable to a local context and it would be presumptive of me to draw up a definition for developing countries, where the intellectual demands of the environment, the system of state care and the perception of need may be very different.

Helping people to cope and be seen as being valued

What I have tried to do in this book is to show a way forward to producing a construct and definition of intellectual disability that will do what is currently required of it, based on what I consider to be reasonable assumptions about the condition and our ability to assess it. Although there will be variation between stakeholders, in the main it can be summed up as an inability to cope with an intellectually demanding world. What I have not done is to look at what we need to do in order to help people who have the condition to cope more effectively or, from a normalisation viewpoint, be seen as more valued members of society. Helping people to cope and making them seem valued may be a considerable challenge. As I said in Chapter 2, when discussing the Flynn effect, I think the world is becoming more technological and intellectually demanding. There is a constant stream of new devices that seems essential for modern work and general living which we have to get to grips with. This more technological and intellectually demanding world has largely been designed by the people with high intellectual ability, for people with average intellectual ability, often for financial reasons. There is very little financial cost for those designing new technology if a few people with low intellectual ability are not able to cope. So, without legislation, I am doubtful that the world will become less intellectually demanding in the near future. I would also suspect that, although in principle we would like to regard people with intellectual disabilities as valued members of society, in reality this might be becoming more difficult for society as a whole. Modern society seems to put a lot of value on intellectual ability and a higher proportion of the current population seems to be actively trying to demonstrate it. In the UK, just less than 60 per cent of 16-year-olds achieve five good grades at GCSEs, the majority of the remaining 40 per cent get lower grades and only a few get no GCSEs at all. This contrasts with the 1960s, when only about 25 per cent of 11–12 year olds went to grammar schools and were expected to get academic qualifications. Also about 40 per cent of young people in the UK currently gain a qualification in higher education, which contrasts with about 15 per cent in the 1960s. The proportion of the population that is not academically able is therefore getting smaller, and so not having academic skills will stand out more as being different. The danger is that we end up with a stigmatised underclass of those without qualifications who may find the intellectual demands of many jobs difficult, are often unemployed and the subject of criticism by politicians and others in society for relying on benefits. At the bottom of this underclass will be people with a diagnosis of intellectual disability. So what can be done? Well, at a practical level, the simplistic answer is if somebody is not coping, then there should be an analysis as to why they are not coping and then they should be given the training and/ or support they need to help them cope. However, even the most well-resourced services may be limited in what they can achieve, as the gap between the intellectual demands of the environment and the intellectual capacity of the bottom few per cent of the population may well be increasing. As we saw in Chapter 2, the Flynn effect may well have stopped or gone into reverse in the low range, showing that people with low intellectual ability are no longer becoming more able to compensate for the increased intellectual demands of their environment. What may well be needed is legislation that ensures that the world does not become more intellectually demanding for those with the lowest ability. New consumer products should be checked for understandability, while employers should be encouraged to ensure that what should be basic manual jobs are not intellectually demanding, for example, requiring the ability to read or understand complex vocabulary or adjust to frequent change. There is also a need to present people with intellectual disabilities in as positive a light as possible, for example, in the media and other places, so they are seen as valued members of society. Over the last few years I have noticed a trend to have people with intellectual disabilities as characters on TV in plays, films and soap operas. I think this needs to increase: this will give a positive impression of intellectual disability in a way that will be seen by ordinary members of the public.

Making people aware of my ideas and changing attitudes

Currently intellectual disability seems to be regarded, both locally in the UK and internationally, as a naturally occurring condition, which can be diagnosed by the objective and scientific measurement of IQ and adaptive behaviour. What I am proposing is a paradigm shift, to one where intellectual disability is seen as a number of social constructs that have relevance under particular circumstances for particular reasons. That, as we are not able to measured IQ or adaptive behaviour with sufficient accuracy, is regarded as a judgment condition. There is likely to be resistance to this radical change in the current concept. Systems resist change naturally, and there will be people and organisations that may want to keep things the same. I think it is unlikely that the AAIDD will want to radically change their next definition of intellectual disability and, if they do not change, it is not likely that the other internationally recognised definitions of ICD-11 and DSM-V will change. It is also unlikely that, without a change in the AAIDD definition, individual states in the US will change their definitions. At a more local level there may well be a reluctance to give up an IQ cut-off point as a defining criterion, as it is often seen as a way of gatekeeping to ensure that services are not overwhelmed with referrals. Organisations such as the British Psychological Society may be reluctant to stick their necks out with a radically different approach defining intellectual disability, without there first being change in the internationally recognised definitions. At the level of professionals working in the intellectual disability field, although I am aware of many psychologists who are sympathetic to my views, I am also aware that there are psychologists who earn their living, or a significant part of it, by giving intellectual assessments in order to diagnose intellectual disability. I think it is unlikely that many of them would be willing to accept my suggestions unquestioningly. So why do I bother?

First, at least some of the resistance to this change will be in the form of logical argument against what I am suggesting. The logic for change seems compelling to me so I would hope that this resistance would be overcome by argument and make my position more widely known. From my point of view the most difficult approach to overcome would be from people who disagreed with me to simply ignore me. However, as I write in late 2012, things are going well in stimulating the debate: I have been interviewed on UK national radio about my ideas and the British Psychological Society is to call a conference to discuss the whole issue of the definition and diagnosis of intellectual disability next year, in part as a result of my findings and agitations.

Secondly, other, possibly more influential writers on intellectual disability, have also noted that there needs to be a change in how we use IQ tests and how we define intellectual disability. Flynn (2007), for example, has pointed out that IQ tests could go out of date which could lead to wrong diagnosis. Greenspan et al. (2011), though not acknowledging the greater error in the measurement of IQ and adaptive behaviour, have questioned the use of numerical cut-off points in a diagnostic definition of intellectual disability. So, although my ideas are somewhat different from those of Greenspan and of Flynn there seems to be a general realisation that there is a need for a radical change in the way intellectual disability is conceptualised.

Thirdly, in the UK at least, there is legislation that seems to be based on the same reasoning that has led me to believe a change in the construct of intellectual disability is needed. The recent Mental Capacity Act acknowledges that people may only be disabled or, as the Act puts it, not have capacity, with regard to specific decisions taken under specific conditions, at a particular time in their lives. So there is no need for them to have a specific diagnosis to lack capacity and if they have a particular diagnosis this does not imply that they lack capacity to do specific tasks.

Fair Access to Care Services (Department of Health 2003), sets out the basis that should be used by local authorities to allocate resources to people on the basis of the impact it would have if the services were not provided. This establishes the principle that services should be provided to people where his/her quality of life falls below a critical level, and that the assessment of this depends on both judgment and the ability to provide the necessary resources. This is essentially the same as the concept of coping that I have used throughout this book and is a key part of most of my suggested definitions.

Therefore, in order to produce the necessary paradigm shift, in the face of resistance to change, I would suggest the following:

- Further research should be done so that the weight of evidence is so great that it can neither be argued against nor ignored. In particular we need more studies that specifically address low intellectual ability such as the reliability and validity of IQ assessments, the Flynn effect in the low range and comparisons of IQ tests. These studies ideally should be multi area and done with large groups.
- There needs to be further opportunity for debate. Even without this research the evidence is actually quite convincing and it is important that people are aware of it and its implications. I and others therefore need to make sure the debate continues by taking every opportunity and debate the issue in public forums.

What I have tried to do in this book is to demonstrate that the current construct of intellectual disability is not currently fit for purpose and to suggest alternative constructs and definitions. I think I have succeeded in doing this, though I would suspect that this book will not be the final word on the subject.

Appendix I: The WISC-IV and WAIS-IV Subtests

Both the WISC-IV and the WAIS-IV give five main scores for index abilities and Full Scale IQ, which correspond to the factors derived from factor analytic studies:

Verbal Comprehension Index: A measure of an individual's ability to understand, learn and retain verbal information and to use language to solve novel problems.

Perceptual Reasoning Index: A measure of an individual's ability to understand visual information and to solve novel abstract visual problems.

Working Memory Index: A measure of an individual's ability to hold verbal information in short-term memory and to manipulate that information.

Processing Speed Index: A measure of mental speed, though the score may also be affected by other cognitive factors, such as attention, as well as ability to use a pen/pencil.

Full Scale IQ: A measure of an individual's overall cognitive ability based on the individual's performance on all the subtests that are used to measure the four index scales. This is what we are referring to when we speak about an individual's measured IQ.

Each of these scores is set to have a mean of 100 and a standard deviation of 15 for the population as a whole.

WISC-IV

Subtests

The WISC-IV has 15 subtests, 10 of which are core subtests that are usually used to measure the four index scores and Full Scale IQ. The other five are supplementary subtests that can be used if for some reason a core subtest cannot be used or is not appropriate for a particular child.

Verbal Comprehension Index has three core subtests, which are:

Similarities

The individual is presented with two words and asked how they are alike, for example, they may be asked how a peach and an apple are alike. The test is designed to assess verbal reasoning and the development of concepts.

Vocabulary

The individual is presented with words and is asked to define them. The test was developed to measure word knowledge and verbal concept formation.

Comprehension

The individual is asked questions about social and other situations, such as: Why should children not be allowed to work in factories? The test was developed to measure an individual's ability to understand complex questions and formulate answers.

There are two supplementary subtests that can be used to measure the Verbal Comprehension Index:

Information

The individual is given a series of general knowledge questions, such as: How far is it from London to Paris? The test was developed to measure an individual's ability to acquire, retain and retrieve information.

Word Reasoning

The individual is given a series of clues and has to say what the common concept is. The test was developed to measure verbal reasoning.

Perceptual Reasoning Index has three core subtests, which are:

Block Design

The individual is required to copy a pattern using coloured blocks. The item is designed to assess an individual's ability to understand complex visual information.

Picture Concepts

The individual is shown either two or three rows of pictures and has to choose one picture from each row that share a common characteristic. The test was developed to assess a child's ability to categorise items.

Matrix Reasoning

The individual is presented with a matrix of abstract pictures in which there is one picture missing. She/he has then to choose which of a number of possible options the missing picture is. The test was developed non-verbal problem solving.

There is one supplementary subtest that can be used to measure the Perceptual Reasoning Index:

Picture Completion

The individual is shown a picture in which there is a significant part missing, such as a man cutting down a tree using an axe without a head, and is required to say what is missing. The test was developed to measure visual understanding and organisation.

Working Memory Index has two core subtests, which are:

Digit Span

There are two parts to this subtest. In the first part (digits forward) the individual is read a series of numbers and is required to say them back to the examiner.

In the second part (digits reversed) he/she is again read a series of numbers but this time she/he is required to say them back to the examiner in reverse order. The test was developed to measure verbal short-term memory, and attention.

Letter-Number Sequencing

The child is read a series of letters and numbers and is required to repeat them back with the letters in alphabetical order and the numbers in numerical order. The test was designed to measure an individual's ability to hold verbal information in memory while he/she manipulates it.

There is one supplementary subtest that can be used to measure the Working Memory Index:

Arithmetic

This consists of a series of mental arithmetic questions such as: If Jo has 12 buns, he then eats 3 and gives 4 away how many does he have left? The test was designed to measure a number of mental tasks including the ability to hold information in memory while it is being manipulated.

Processing Speed Index has two core subtests, which are:

Coding

The individual is presented with a key in which the numbers 1 to 9 are each paired with a different symbol; his/her task is then to use this key to put in the appropriate symbols for a list of numbers between 1 and 9. The test was designed to measure speed of processing but also is affected by other cognitive abilities such as learning, short-term memory and concentration.

Symbol Search

The individual has to look at two target symbols and then examine a group of symbols to see if the target symbols are repeated. The test is designed to measure processing speed but is also affected by other cognitive abilities such as visual-motor coordination and concentration.

There is one supplementary subtest that can be used to measure the Processing Speed Index:

Cancellation

The child looks at a random sequence of pictures and is required to cross out target pictures. In addition to processing speed it is probably affected by other factors such as attention, and visual neglect.

All ten core subtests are used to measure Full Scale IQ.

The WAIS-IV

Subtests

As with the WISC-IV the test has 15 subtests, 10 of which are core subtests that are usually used to measure the four index scores and the Full Scale IQ. The other five are supplementary subtests that can be used if for some reason a core subtest cannot be used or is not appropriate for a particular individual.

Verbal Comprehension Index has three core subtests, which are: Similarities, Vocabulary, and Information. Comprehension is a supplementary subtest. They are essentially the same subtests as I describe above for the WISC-IV.

Perceptual Reasoning Index has three core subtests, which are: Block Design, and Matrix Reasoning, which are essentially the same as the subtest described for the WISC-IV, and a new core subtest Visual Puzzles.

Visual Puzzles

The individual is shown a pattern and has to choose three possible parts to make up that pattern. The subtest was developed to measure non-verbal reasoning and the ability to understand abstract visual information.

There are also two supplementary subtests that can be used to measure the Perceptual Reasoning Index; one is Picture Completion described above, the other is a new subtest Figure Weights:

Figure Weights

The individual is presented with a picture of a pair of scales in which there are missing weights, and they have to choose the correct weights to keep the scales in balance. The subset is designed to measure quantitative and analogical reasoning.

Working Memory Index has two core subtests, which are: Arithmetic (as described above for the WISC-IV) and a modified version of Digit Span.

Digit Span

This is a slightly modified version of the one described above for the WISC-IV. It has the two original parts of digits forward and digits reversed and there is a third part (digits sequential) in which the individual has to say the digits in order of magnitude. This requires the individual to hold the digits in immediate memory and then to sort them into ascending order, a task that requires working memory.

Letter-Number Sequencing is a supplementary subtest for the measurement of the Working Memory Index, which is similar to that used in the WISC-IV.

Two core subtests are used to measure the *Processing Speed Index*: Coding and Symbol Search; Cancellation is a supplementary subtest all three are very similar to those used in the WISC-IV, described above.

As with the WISC-IV all 10 core subtests are used to measure Full Scale IQ.

Appendix II: Getting the Best Estimate of True Intellectual Ability

It is a central theme of the book that true intellectual ability cannot be measured accurately in the low range. It follows from this that we should not be using cut-off points in diagnosis or making statements about what an individual's IQ is without a lot of qualification with regard to the test error. However, as things are at the moment, with intellectual disability still being defined in terms of an IQ cut-off point, it is likely that psychologists will be called upon to make an estimate of what somebody's true intellectual ability is. What I want to do in this appendix is to look at how we can get the best estimate of an individual's true intellectual ability.

Error in the measurement of low IQ

As I have explained in Chapter 3 there are a number of sources of both chance and systematic error in the measurement of low IQ:

Sources of chance error:

- Lack of internal consistency.
- Lack of stability.
- Scorer error.

Sources of systematic error:

- Flynn effect.
- Floor effect.
- Practice effect.
- Malingering.
- Additional error apparent from the difference between scores on different tests.

What I want to do is consider how each of these sources of error can be reduced and having done that whether we would be able to quantify how much error still remains.

Error due to lack of internal consistency

This error is due to test items being inconsistent, which in part is due to the varied experiences of the clients, possibly over many years. Neither the experiences of the client nor the individual test item can be changed in an individual assessment, so there is no scope of reducing this error for an individual assessment. However, according to the WAIS-IV manual the error is relatively small even in the low range, with a 95 per cent confidence interval of about four points. Therefore, if it is assumed that these errors will be the same in clinical settings as they were when the test was standardised, and there is no reason to suppose that there would be any difference, we can assume that a lack of internal consistency can affect scores by up to four points.

Error due to a lack of stability

If an individual is assessed twice on the same test his/her IQ score will usually not be the same. The difference in the scores is due to such factors as changes in the state of the individual, changes in the environment in which the test is given, or changes in the way the test is given between assessments. Here being very strict about only giving the test in optimum conditions should reduce this error. It is likely that many of the assessments that are done in clinical and criminal justice settings are not done under optimal conditions and this may be one reason why the test re-test reliability found by Whitaker (2008b) is lower than that found when the tests were standardised. For example, in criminal justice settings such as prisons, there may be distractions due to noise; the client may be depressed, anxious or not be motivated to do well; the examiner may not be used to giving assessments in such settings and/or to giving assessments in the low IQ range. However, even though these errors could be reduced, it will not be possible to tell by how much they have been reduced in numerical terms. Without further studies in which the test re-test is assessed under various conditions, one must rely on the studies that have been done up to now which I have suggested (Whitaker 2008), gives a 95 per cent confidence interval of 12.5 points for the stability of IQ.

Scorer error

Scorer error is due to inconsistency in the scoring of tests. According to the manuals the average scorer consistency, on the core subtests required to measure Full Scale IQ, is about .97 for the WAIS-IV and .98 for the WISC-IV. This would mean that the effective 95 per cent confidence interval for scorer error would be four points for the WAIS-IV and five points for the WISC-IV. However, I suggested in Chapter 3 that if the test re-test studies were done using different scorers for each assessment, then scorer error would be included in the error due to lack of stability. It may be possible to reduce scorer error by ensuring that all scorers are fully trained and by having tests scored by two separate scorers and any inconsistencies in scoring considered carefully so that a correct score was more likely. However, as with temporal error we are currently not in a position to say by how much this would reduce the error.

The Flynn effect

The Flynn effect is due to changes in the absolute intellectual ability of the population as a whole over time. This causes IQ tests to be inaccurate as the tests compare an individual's intellectual ability to the intellectual ability of the population when the test was standardised and not as it is when the test was given. The Flynn effect could be minimised by always using the latest standardisation of a test, since if a test has only just been standardised there will be no Flynn effect. If a test were less than four years old then the effect would be one point or less and so could be ignored. Flynn (2009) has argued that if a test is a few years old the effect can be corrected by subtracting .3 of an IQ point for each year since the test was standardised. On balance I feel that this is probably the best approach to take at the moment. However, it may not always be the case and does not seem to be the case in other areas of the world at the moment. There is evidence from Scandinavia that the effect may have gone into reverse in the low range (Teasdale and Owen 2005), resulting in tests underestimating IQ as they go out of date. It therefore cannot be assumed that this method of correction for the Flynn effect will continue to be valid, nor can we tell, without extensive studies, how valid it is at any one time.

The floor effect

This is due to tests having a minimum score that they can measure down to, so that if somebody's ability is less than that minimum score a test will over estimate his/her ability.

With the WISC-IV and WAIS-IV there are two sources of a floor effect: first, there is the conversion of raw scores to scaled scores where the minimum scaled score is one, which is given to all raw scores below a certain point. Secondly, there is the minimum IQ and index score on the tests, which for Full Scale IQ is 40 on both tests so that if an individual has a true intellectual ability below 40 their measured IQ of 40 will be an over estimate of this. In the main, these floor effects should only be a problem for measured IQs in the 40s and 50s on the WAIS-IV and in the 40s, 50s, 60s and 70s on the WISC-IV. I have suggested (Whitaker and Gordon 2012) that the floor effect could be corrected for by extrapolating the relationship between raw scores and scaled scores down below scaled score one, so that scaled scores of zero and less can be allocated to low raw scores. However, although this method seems logical and may be valid for a small correction, where a scaled score of zero or minus one is given instead of a scaled score of one, there is no empirical evidence to support the procedure. Therefore, although applying some correction for the floor effect may result in a more accurate assessment, it is not possible to say how much more accurate a corrected IQ score is than one that is not corrected. It is not recommended that any correction should be made below a scaled score of minus one.

The practice effect

The practice effect could be eliminated by not assessing an individual twice on the same assessment. If there is no way of avoiding doing this, then the error could be corrected by subtracting an appropriate number of IQ points from the second assessment. However, the problem then is deciding by how many points to reduce the second assessment. The practice effect will vary depending on which test is being given, the time interval between assessments, as well as factors within the individual such as his/her level of intellectual ability. Therefore one cannot be sure how accurate a corrected score is.

Malingering

Malingering is the technical term for an individual deliberately scoring less than they are capable of. Clearly one way to eliminate error due to malingering is not to assess individuals who may well be motivated to do poorly in the assessment. If an assessment has to be done, there does not seem to be any reliable way of detecting malingering (Salekin and Doane 2009), or of telling to what degree a score has been affected by it. The best an assessor could do therefore is consider what an individual's motivation may be with regard to the assessment and if necessary raise the possibility that the IQ score may have been reduced by malingering in the report.

Additional error apparent from the difference between scores on different tests

The error apparent from the differences between tests may be very difficult to correct for. It could only be done if there was firm evidence that one test was accurate and it was known by how much other tests' scores systematically differed from this gold standard test. Adding or subtracting the appropriate number of points from their obtained scores could then correct inaccurate tests. However, this is currently not possible for a number of reasons: First, although Gordon et al. (2010) have produced evidence that the WISC-IV systematically measured lower than the WAIS-III, the study was based on a small sample of 16-year-olds and so it cannot be assumed that the exact difference between the tests due to factors other than the Flynn effect is exactly 10 points. Secondly, the WAIS-III is now no longer used and there are no studies comparing the WAIS-IV and WISC-IV in the low intellectual range. Thirdly, although it could be argued that the WISC-IV is more likely to be accurate than the WAIS-IV as getting a representative sample of children with low IQs would seem to be less subject to error than getting one of adults (cf. Flynn and Weiss 2007), this is only speculation and in reality we do not know to what degree either of these gold standard tests is accurate or inaccurate or indeed if other less well known tests are more accurate in the low range.

Improving the accuracy of measured IQ

As we saw in Chapters 3 and 7, an individual's measured IQ and his/her true intellectual ability may differ by the order of 25 points. If this is acknowledged and the assessors are motivated to get the best estimate of true intellectual ability, there are a number of things that can be done:

- It should be made explicit in any reports that measured IQ and true intellectual ability are not the same thing and that measured IQ is only a rough estimate of true intellectual ability.
- The assessor should correct for the Flynn effect and the floor effect down to scaled scores of minus one. As these corrections may be contentious, the fact that they have been made should be indicated in any report, together with a justification for having made them, and a statement as to how much difference it made to the IQ scores. If it is clear that there is a floor effect but it cannot be corrected for either because there is a very low raw score or a raw score of zero then a definitive index score should either not be given or one should be calculated on the basis of an scaled score of zero or minus one and then made very clear in the report that both the index score and the Full Scale IQ are subject to floor effects and so are high estimates of true ability.
- If it is known that the test being used systematically measures lower or higher than another gold standard test, then this should be made very clear in the

report. So, for example, if reporting on the results of a WAIS-III or WAIS-IV, it should be noted that there is evidence that it measures higher than the equivalent the WISC-IV, and that it is not clear which test is producing the best estimate of true intellectual ability. Although this will not eliminate the systematic error it will make readers aware of it.

- If an assessor is doubtful about how motivated a client is to do well on a test then looking at previous assessment given at a time when the individual may have been motivated to do well on the test may give a better estimate of his/her true intellectual ability. However, in checking out previous assessments, if one does not get full information about how the individual was when assessed, when the assessment was given, what test was used and what the raw scores were, the values of these assessments as an estimate of true intellectual ability will be reduced. If one knows the test that was used and when it was given one can adjust for the Flynn effect and make it comparable with other tests. If the raw scores are available the score can be corrected for any floor effect. If there is information as to the conditions under which the assessment was given one can speculate as to whether the score was lower than would have occurred if the assessment was done in optimal conditions. However, simply giving an IQ score without any information about how the IQ was obtained is almost worthless.

- If there have been several intellectual assessments given the assessor should look for consistency in the different IQ scores. In order to do this all the scores should be corrected in the same way for the Flynn effect, floor effect and the difference between tests. A key question is then: do the scores give more or less the same result? If so, this consistency in measured IQ suggests that chance error has had only a relatively small effect on the scores. It will also provide evidence as to whether the individual's true intellectual ability is above or below any cut-off IQ point for a diagnosis of intellectual disability. However, it may still not possible to say whether an individual's true intellectual ability is above or below this point as the systematic error apparent from the difference between tests is not corrected for and, as we saw above, really cannot be corrected for.

It may well be the case that even when test scores have been adjusted there are still significant differences between the results of assessments done at different times and/or with different tests. In this situation it is not entirely clear what should be done, though there are a number of options, each with advantages and disadvantages. One possibility would be to take the average score. This would assume that the assessments were subject to errors, some of which increased the scores above true intellectual ability and some of which decreased scores below true intellectual ability, so that averaging the scores cancelled out the errors to give a good estimate of true intellectual ability. However, this would also assume that the individual's true intellectual ability were the same on each occasions he/she was assessed and that the errors was evenly distributed between those that increased scores and those that decreased scores. These are assumptions that the assessor is unlikely to have evidence for.

A second approach would be to argue that most error would decrease score, so that lower scores are therefore likely to be subject to more error and, therefore, the highest scores are more accurate. However, whereas it may seem reasonable to assume that high scores are more likely to be correct, this is not inevitable and the high scores could be due to systematic error or change in intellectual ability over time.

Thirdly, real world consistency could be looked for. How well an individual copes with the intellectually loaded everyday tasks could give support to a particular test score. In part this could be indicated by an assessment of the individual level of adaptive behaviour on a scale such as the Vineland-II (Sparrow et al. 2005). However, as we saw in Chapter 4, there are often only low correlations between adaptive behaviour and IQ. For example, the correlation between the Vineland-II Composite score and Full Scale IQ on the WISC-III is only .09. So ability to do some tasks, such as socialise with others or have daily living skills, is not indicative of high IQ. On the other hand IQ does correlate well with academic ability. So, indications that he/she was coping academically, for example, with SATs scores or academic qualifications, may very well be indicative of an average intellectual ability.

It is likely that, even if the above suggestions are followed, it will still not be possible to give an exact figure on an individual's true intellectual ability or produce an exact confidence interval indicating how accurate any estimate is. It should therefore be made clear in any report that the scores are not exact and the confidence intervals are considerably greater than that stated in the test manual.

If the IQ score is required for a diagnosis, the issues may not be so much what the exact IQ figure is, but rather whether it is below the cut-off point for a diagnosis of intellectual disability. To take an extreme example, if an individual had several measured IQs in the 90s, then, even though it would not be possible to put an exact figure on his/her true intellectual ability, one could say with a high degree of certainty that it was above 70. However, it is likely that the majority of individuals in which there is a question as to whether they should be considered to have an intellectual disability will have measured IQs in the 60s and 70s, in which case it will not be possible to say with any certainty that their true intellectual ability falls above or below 70. The best approach in such cases may be to give an estimate of the probability of the true intellectual ability falling above or below the critical figure in non-exact terms, using such words as 'possible', 'likely' or 'unlikely'.

Recommendations for an estimate of true intellectual ability

- Correct scores for Flynn and floor effects and if the information is available, adjust the scores so that different tests' scores are equivalent. Then make it clear which test the scores are equivalent to.
- Do not base an estimate of true intellectual ability on a single IQ test.
- Look for consistency between scores, both within tests and between test and with an individual's ability to cope with intellectually loaded tasks in the real world. The more consistent this is, the more confidence one can have in the scores.
- Do not give a definitive result unless this is clearly justified.

References

Abramowicz, H.K. and Richardson, S.A. (1975). Epidemiology of severe mental retardation in children: Community studies. *American Journal of Mental Deficiency*, 80, 18–39.

American Association on Intellectual and Developmental Disabilities (2010). *Intellectual Disability: Definition, Classification, and Systems of Support*, 11th edition. American Association on Intellectual and Developmental Disabilities.

American Psychiatric Association (2000) *Diagnostic and Statistical Manual of Mental Disorders*, 4th edition, text revision. Washington DC: American Psychiatric Association.

Anastasi, A. and Urbina, S. (1997). *Psychological Testing*, 7th edition. Upper Saddler River: Prentice-Hall Inc.

Atkinson, L. and Cyr, J.J. (1988). Low IQ Samples and WAIS-R factor structure. *American Journal on Mental Retardation*, 93, 278–82.

Baroff, G.S. (1999). General learning disorder: A new designation for mental retardation. *Mental Retardation*, 37, 68–70.

Baroff, G.S. (2006). On the 2002 AAMR definition of mental retardation.In H.N. Switzky and S. Greenspan (eds),*What is Mental Retardation? Ideas for an Evolving Disability in the 21st Century*, revised and updated edition. Washington DC: American Association on Mental Retardation.

Bergen, D.C. (2008). Effects of poverty on cognitive function: A hidden neurologic epidemic. *Neurology*, 71, 447–51.

Binet, A. and Simon T. (1905). Upon the necessity of establishing a scientific diagnosis of inferior states of intelligence. First published 1905, then in *The Development of Intelligence in Children*. Baltimore: Williams and Wilkins, 1916, pp. 9–36. Then in M. Rose, G.R. Clark and M. Skivitz 1976. *The History of Mental Retardation Collected Papers Vol 1*. Baltimore: University Park Press.

Birch, H.G., Richardson, S.A., Baird, D., Horobin, G. and Illsley, R. (1970). *A Clinical and Epidemiological Study: Mental Subnormality in the Community*. Baltimore: Williams and Wilkins.

Bolte, S. and Poustka, F. (2002). The relationship between general cognitive level and adaptive behavior domains in individuals with autisim with and without co-morbid mental retardation. *Child Psychiatry and Human Development*, 33, 165–72.

Borthwick-Duffy, S.A. and Eyman, R.K. (1990). Who are the dually diagnosed? *American Journal on Mental Retardation*, 94, 586–95.

Bouchard, T.J. (2009). Genetic influence on human intelligence (Spearman's g): How much? *Annals of Human Biology*, 36, 527–44.

Bresnahan J.A. (2008). A preliminary study of WISC-IV and WAIS-III IQ scores for students with extremely low cognitive functioning. Dissertation Abstracts International: Section B: The Science and Engineering. Fairleigh Dickinson University, Teaneck, NJ, USA.

Budimirovic, D.B. and Kaufmann, W.E. (2011). What can we learn about autism from studying Fragile X Syndrome? *Developmental Neuroscience*, 33, 379–94.

Burr, V. (2003). *Social Constructionism*, 2nd edition. Hove: Routledge.

Castles, K. (2004). 'Nice average Americans': Postwar parents' groups and the defences of the normal family. In S. Noll and J.W. Trent (eds), *Mental Retardation in America: A Historical Reader*. New York: New York University Press.

Chester, G. and Dale, P. (2007). Institutional care of mentally defectives, 1914–1948: Diversity as a response to individual needs and an indication of lack of policy coherence. *Medical History*, 51, 59–78.

Clausen, J. (1967). Mental deficiency – development of a concept. *American Journal of Mental Deficiency*, 71, 727–45.

Cocodia, E.A., Kim, J.S., Shin, H.S., Kim, J.W., Ee, J., Wee, M.S.W. and Howard, R.W. (2003). Evidence that rising population intelligence is impacting in formal education. *Personality and Individual Differences*, 35, 797–810.

Coffee, B., Keith, K., Albizua, I., Malone, T., Mowrey, J., Shermand, S.L. and Warren, S.T. (2009). Incidence of Fragile X Syndrome by newborn screening of methylated FMR1 DNA. *American Journal of Human Genetics*, 85, 503–14.

Dale, P. (2003). Implementing the 1913 mental deficiency Act: Competing priorities and resource constraint evidence in the south west of England before 1948. *Social History of Medicine*, 16, 403–18.

Davis, L.J. (1966). The internal consistency of the WISC with the mentally retarded. *American Journal of Mental Deficiency*, 70, 714–16.

DeMatteo, D., Marczyk, G. and Pich, M. (2007). A national survey of state legislation defining mental retardation: Implications for policy and practice after Atkins. *Behavioral Science and the Law*, 25, 781–802.

Department of Health (2001). Valuing People: a new strategy for learning disability for the 21st century – a White Paper. London: HMSO.

Department of Health (2003). Fair Access to Care. London: HMSO.

Department of Health (2005). Mental Capacity Act. London: HMSO.

Detterman, D.K. and Gabriel, L. (2006). Look before you leap: Implications of the 1992 and 2002 definitions of mental retardation. In H.N. Switzky and S. Greenspan (eds), *What is Mental Retardation? Ideas for an Evolving Disability in the 21st century*, revised and updated edition. Washington DC: American Association on Mental Retardation.

Devlin, B., Daniels, M. and Roeder, K. (1997). The heritability of IQ. *Nature*, 388, 468–71.

Dickens, W.T. and Flynn, J.R. (2001). Heritability estimates versus large environmental effect: The IQ paradox resolved. *Psychology Review*, 108, 346–69.

Doane, B.M. and Salekin, K.L. (2009). Susceptibility of current adaptive behavior to feigned deficits. *Law and Human Behavior*, 33, 329–43.

Doll, E.A. (1941). The essentials of an inclusive concept of mental deficiency. *American Journal of Mental Deficiency*, 46, 214–19.

Duvall, J.C. and Morris, R.J. (2006). Assessing mental retardation in death penalty cases: Critical issues for psychologists and psychological practice. *Professional Psychology: Research and Practice*, 37, 658–65.

Edawardraj, S., Murtaj, J.H., Kuruvilla, A. and Jacob, K.S. (2010). Perception about intellectual disability: a qualitative study from Vellore, South India. *Journal of Intellectual Disability Research*, 54, 736–48.

Emerson, E., Hatton, C., Felce, D. and Murphy, G. (2001). *Learning Disability the Fundamental Facts*. The Foundation for People with Learning Disabilities.

Farmer, R., Rohde, J. and Sacks, B. (1993). *Changing Services for People with Learning Disabilities*. London: Chapman and Hall.

Ferguson, P.M. (2004). The legacy of the almshouse. In S. Noll and J.W. Trent (eds), *Mental Retardation in America: A Historical Reader*. New York: New York University Press.

Floyd, R.G., Clark, M.H. and Shadish, W.R. (2008). The exchangeability of IQs: Implications for professional psychology. *Professional Psychology: Research and Practice*, 39, 414–23.

Flynn, J.R. (1984). The mean IQ of Americans: Massive gains 1932 to 1978. *Psychological Bulletin*, 95, 29–51.

Flynn, J.R. (1985). Wechsler intelligence tests: Do we really have a criterion of mental retardation? *American Journal of Mental Deficiency*, 90, 236–44.

Flynn, J.R. (1987). Massive gains in 14 nations: What IQ tests really measure. *Psychological Bulletin*, 101, 171–91.

Flynn, J.R. (1998). IQ gains over time: Towards finding the causes. In U. Neisser, (Ed) *The Rising Curve: Long-term Gains in IQ and Related Measures*. Washington DC: American Psychological Association.

Flynn, J.R. (2006). Efeito Flynn: Repensoado a inteligencia e seus efecitos [The Flynn Effect: Rethinking intelligence and what affects it]. In C. Florres-Mendoza and R. Colon (eds) *Introducao a Psicologia das Diferenncas Individuais* [*Introduction to the psychology of individual differences*] Porto Alegre: ArtMed, pp. 387–411.

Flynn, J.R. (2007). *What is Intelligence: Beyond the Flynn Effect*. Cambridge: Cambridge University Press.

Flynn, J.R. (2009). The WAIS-III and WAIS-IV: Daubert motions favor the certainly false over the approximately true. *Applied Neurology*, 16, 98–104.

Flynn, R.J. and Weiss, L.G. (2007). American IQ gains from 1932 to 2002: The WISC subtests and educational progress. *International Journal of Testing*, 7, 209–24.

Galton, F. (1908). *Memories of my life*. London: Methuen.

Gelb, S. A. (2004). 'Mental deficients' fighting fascism: The unplanned normalization of World War II. In S. Noll and J.W. Trent (eds), *Mental Retardation in America: A Historical Reader*. New York: New York University Press.

Goddard, H.H. (1910). Four hundred feeble-minded children classified by the Binet method. *Journal of Psycho-Asthemics*, 15, 17–30. Reprinted in M. Rose, G.R. Clark and M. Skivitz, (1976), *The History of Mental Retardation Collected Papers, Vol 1*. Baltimore: University Park Press.

Gordon, S., Duff, S. Davison, T. and Whitaker, S. (2010). Comparison of the WAIS-III and WISC-IV in 16 year old special education students. *Journal of Applied Research in Intellectual Disability*, 23, 197–200.

Gottfredson, L.S. (2008). Of what value is intelligence? In A. Prifitera, D.H. Saklofska and L.G. Weiss (eds), *WISC-IV Clinical Assessment and Intervention*, 2nd edition. San Diego: Academic Press.

Granat, K. and Granat, S. (1973). Below-average intelligence and mental retardation. *American Journal of Mental Deficiency*, 78, 27–32.

Greenfield, P.M. (1998). The cultural evolution of IQ. In U. Neisser, *The Rising Curve: Long-Term Gains in IQ and Related Measures*. Washington DC: American Psychological Association.

Greenspan, S. (1979). Social intelligence in the retarded. In N.R. Ellis (ed.) *Handbook of Mental Deficiency, Psychological Theory and Research*, Hillsdale: Lawrence Erlbaum Associates Publishers.

Greenspan, S. (1997). Dead manual walking? Why the 1992 AAMR definition needs redoing. *Education and Training in Mental Retardation and Developmental Disabilities*, 32, 179–90.

Greenspan, S. (1999). What is mental retardation? *International Review of Psychiatry*, 11, 6–18.

Greenspan, S. (2006). Mental retardation in the real world: Why the AAMD definition is not there yet. In H.N. Switzky, and S. Greenspan (eds), *What is Mental Retardation? Ideas for an Evolving Disability in the 21st century*, revised and updated edition. Washington DC: American Association on Mental Retardation.

Greenspan, S. and Shoultz, B. (1981). Why mentally retarded adults lose their jobs: Social competence as a factor in work adjustment. *Applied Research in Mental Retardation*, 2, 23–38.

Greenspan, S. and Switzky, H.N. (2006). Lessons from the Atkins decision for the next AAMR manual. In H.N. Switzky, and S. Greenspan (eds), *What is Mental Retardation? Ideas for an Evolving Disability in the 21st century*, revised and updated edition. Washington DC: American Association on Mental Retardation.

Greenspan, S., Switzky, H.N. and Woods, G.W. (2011). Intelligence involves risk-awareness and intellectual disability involves risk-unawareness: Implications of a theory of common sense. *Journal on Intellectual & Developmental Disability*, 36 (4), 246–57.

Gresham, F.M. (2009). Interpretation of intelligence test scores in Atkins cases: Conceptual and psychometric issues. *Applied Neuropsychology*, 16, 91–7.

Grossman, H.J. (ed.) (1973). *A Manual on Terminology and Classification in Mental Retardation*, revised edition. Washington, DC: American Association on Mental Deficiency.

Grossman, H.J. (ed.) (1983). *Classification in Mental Retardation*, revised edition. Washington, DC: American Association on Mental Deficiency.

Hamelin, J.P., Frijters, J., Griffiths, D., Conillac, R. and Owen, F. (2011). Meta-analysis of deinstitutionalisation adaptive behaviour outcomes: Research and clinical implications. *Journal of Intellectual & Developmental Disability*, 36, 61–72.

Hansen, H. (1978). Brief report decline of Down's syndrome after abortion reform in New York State. *American Journal of Mental Deficiency*, 83, 185–88.

Harrison, P.L. (1987). Research with adaptive behavior scales. *Journal of Special Education*, 21, 37–68.

Harrison, P.L. (1990). Mental retardation, adaptive behavior, assessment and giftedness. In A.S. Kaufman (ed.) *Assessing Adolescent and Adult Intelligence*. Needham: Allyn and Bacon.

Harrison, P.L. and Oakland, T. (2003). *Adaptive Behavior Assessment System*, 2nd edition. San Antonio, TX. The Psychology Corporation.

Haworth, C.M., Wright, M.J., Luciano, M., Martin, N.G., de Geus, E.J., van Beijsterveldt, C.E., Bartels, M., Posthuma, D., Boomsma, D.I., Davis, O.S., Kovas, Y., Corley, R.P., Defries, J.C., Hewitt, J.K., Olson, R.K., Rhea, S.A., Wadsworth, S.J., Iacono, W.G., McGue, M., Thompson, L.A., Hart, S.A., Petrill, S.A., Lubinski, D., Plomin, R. (2010). The heritability of general cognitive ability increases linearly from childhood to young adulthood. *Molecular Psychiatry*, 15, 1112–20.

Haworth, C.M.A., Wright, M.J., Martin, N.W., Martin, N.G., Boomsma, D.I., Bartels, M., Posthuma, D., Davis, O.S.P., Brant, A.M. Corley, R.P., Hewitt, J.K.,

Iacono, W.G., McGue, M., Thompson, L.A., Hart, S.A., Petrill, S.A., Lubinski, D., and Plomin, R. (2009). A twin study of the genetics of high cognitive ability selected from 11,000 twin pairs in six studies for four countries. *Behavioral Genetics*, 39, 359–70.

Heber, R. (1959). A manual on terminology and classification in mental retardation (Monograph Supplement). *American Journal of Mental Deficiency*, 64 (2).

Heber, R. (1961). A manual on terminology and classification in mental retardation (2nd edition) (Monograph Supplement). *American Journal of Mental Deficiency*.

Her Majesty's Stationery Office (1989). Children Act. London: HMSO.

Her Majesty's Stationery Office (2004). Children Act. London: HMSO.

Herrnstein, R.J. and Murray, C. (1994). *The Bell Curve: Intelligence and Class Structure in American Life*. New York: Free Press.

Howe, S.G. (1848). Report of commission to inquire into the conditions of idiots of the Commonwealth of Massachusetts. Boston: Senate Document No. 51, 1–37. Reprinted without the tables in M. Rosen, G.R. Clark and M. Skivitz (1976) *The History of Mental Retardation Collected Papers Vol 1*. Baltimore: University Park Press.

Huberty, T.J. (1987). Factor analysis of the WISC-R and the Adaptive Behavior Scale-School Edition for a referral sample. *Journal of School Psychology* 25, 405–10.

Hull, C.L. (1928). *Aptitude testing*. New York: Word Book Co.

Ireland, W.W. (1882). On the diagnosis and prognosis of idiocy and imbecility. *Edinburgh Medical Journal*. Reprinted in M. Rose, G.R. Clark and M. Skivitz (1976), *The History of Mental Retardation Collected Papers, Vol 1*. Baltimore: University Park Press.

Jacobson, J.W. (1990). Do some mental disorders occur less frequently among persons with mental retardation? *American Journal on Mental Retardation*, 94, 596–602.

Johnson, W., Bouchard, T.J., McGue, M., Segal, N.L., Tellegen, A., Keyes, M. and Gottesmand II (2007). Genetic and environmental influences on the Verbal-Perceptual-Image Rotation (VPR) model of structure on mental abilities in the Minnesota Study of Twins Reared Apart. *Intelligence*, 35, 542–62.

Kamin, L.J. (1974). *The Science and Politics of IQ*. Potomac MD: Erlbaum.

Laird, C. and Whitaker, S. (2011). The use of IQ and descriptions of people with intellectual disabilities in the scientific literature. *British Journal of Developmental Disabilities*, 57, 175–83.

Lynn, R. (1990). The role of nutrition in secular increases in intelligence. *Personality and Individual Differences*, 11, 273–85.

Lynn, R. (1998). In support of the nutritional theory. In U. Neisser, *The Rising Curve: Long-Term Gains in IQ and Related Measures*. Washington DC: American Psychological Association.

Lynn, R. (2009). What has caused the Flynn effect? Secular increase in the developmental Quotient of infants. *Intelligence*, 37, 16–24

Lynn, R. and Harvey, J. (2008). The decline of the world's IQ. *Intelligence*, 36, 112–20.

Mackintosh, N.J. (1998). *IQ and Human Intelligence*. Oxford: Oxford University Press.

MacMillan, Siperstein, G.N. and Leffert, J.S. (2006). Children with mental retardation: A challenge for classification practices – revised. In H.N. Switzky and

S. Greenspan (eds) *What is Mental Retardation? Ideas for an Evolving Disability in the 21st century*,revised and updated edition. Washington DC: American Association on Mental Retardation.

McCulloch, T.L. (1947), Reformulation of the problem of mental deficiency. *American Journal of Mental Deficiency*, 52, 130–6.

McLennan, Y., Polussa, J., Tassone, F. and Hagerman, R. (2011). Fragile X Syndrome. *Current Genomics*, 12, 216–24.

Martorell, R. (1998). Nutrition and worldwide rise in IQ scores. In U. Neisser, *The Rising Curve: Long-Term Gains in IQ and Related Measures*. Washington DC: American Psychological Association.

Mattinson, J. (1970). *Marriage and Mental Handicap*. London: Duckworth.

May, D. and Hogg, J. (1999). Is there a 'hidden' population of adults with intellectual disabilities? Evidence from a follow-up study. *Journal of Applied Research in Intellectual Disabilities*, 12, 177–89.

Mayfield, K.L., Forman, S.G. and Nagle, R.J. (1984). Reliability of the AAMD Adaptive Behavior Scale. Public School Version. *Journal of School Psychology*, 22, 53–61.

Mercer, J.R. (1973). The myth of 3% prevalence. In G. Tarjon, R.K. Eyman and C.E. Meyes (eds), *Sociobehavioral Studies in Mental Retardation*. Washington DC: American Association on Mental Deficiency.

Minogroni, M. (2004). The secular rise in IQ: Giving heterosis a close look. *Intelligence*, 32, 65–83.

Neisser, U. (ed.) (1998) *The Rising Curve: Long-Term Gains in IQ and Related Measures*. Washington DC: American Psychological Association.

Nichols, P.L. (1984). Familial mental retardation. *Behavior Genetics*, 14, 161–70.

Nisbett, R.E. (2009). *Intelligence and How to Get It: Why Schools and Culture Count*. London: W.W. Norton & Company.

Noll, S. and Trent, J.W. Jr (2004). Introduction. In S. Noll and J.W. Trent (eds), *Mental Retardation in America: A Historical Reader*. New York: New York University Press.

Nuttall, M. (1998). States and categories: indigenous models of personhood in northwest Greenland. In R. Jenkins (ed.), *Questions of Competence: Culture, Classification and Intellectual Disability*. Cambridge: Cambridge University Press.

Platt, L.O., Kamphaus, R.W., Cole, R.W. and Smith, C.L. (1991). Relationship between adaptive behavior and intelligence: Additional evidence. *Psychological Reports*, 68, 139–45.

Reeve, A. (2006). Adaptation, remission, and growth: Conceptual challenges to the definition of mental retardation – medical implications and applications. In H.N. Switzky and S. Greenspan (eds), *What is Mental Retardation? Ideas for an Evolving Disability in the 21st century*, revised and updated edition. Washington DC: American Association on Mental Retardation.

Reschly, D.J. (2009). Documenting the developmental origins of mild mental retardation. *Applied Neuropsychology*, 16, 124–34.

Richards, P.L. (2004). 'Beside her sat her idiot child': Families and developmental disability in the mid-nineteenth-century America. In S. Noll and J.W. Trent (eds), *Mental Retardation in America: A Historical Reader*. New York: New York University Press.

Roeleveld, N., Zielhuis, G.A. and Gabreels, F. (1997). The prevalence of mental retardation: A critical review of recent literature. *Developmental Medicine and Child Neurology*, 39, 125–32.

Russell, A.J., Munro, J.C., Jones, P.B., Hemsley, D.R. and Murray, R.M. (1997). Schizophrenia and the myth of intellectual decline. *American Journal of Psychiatry*, 154, 635–9.

Rutter, M., Tizard, J. and Whitmore, K. (1970). *Education, Health and Behaviour*. London: Longman.

Salekin, K.L. and Doane, B.M. (2009). Malingering intellectual disability: The value of available measurements and methods. *Applied Neuropsychology*, 16, 105–13.

Saudino, K.J., Plomin, R., Pedersen, N.L. and McClearn, G.E. (1994). The etiology of high and low cognitive ability during the second half of the life span. *Intelligence*, 19, 359–71.

Schalock, R.L. (2006). Scientific and judgment issues involved in defining mental retardation. In H.N. Switzky and S. Greenspan (eds), *What is Mental Retardation? Ideas for an Evolving Disability in the 21st century*, revised and updated edition. Washington DC: American Association on Mental Retardation.

Schalock, R.L. and Luckassson, R. (2005). *Clinical Judgment*. Washington DC: American Association on Mental Retardation.

Scheerenberger, R.C. (1983). *A History of Mental Retardation*. Baltimore: Paul H Brookes Publishing Co., Inc.

Schooler, C. (1998). Environmental complexity and the Flynn effect. In U. Neisser (ed.) *The Rising Curve: Long-Term Gains in IQ and Related Measures*. Washington DC: American Psychological Association.

Shin, M., Besser, L.M., Kucik, J.E., Lu, C., Siffel, C. and Correa, A. (2009). Prevalence of Down Syndrome among children and adolescents in 10 regions of the United States. *Pediatrics*, 124, 1554–71.

Sigman, M. and Whaley, S.E. (1998). The role of nutrition in the development of intelligence. In U. Neisser (ed.) *The Rising Curve: Long-Term Gains in IQ and Related Measures*. Washington DC: American Psychological Association.

Simeonsson, R.J., Granlund, M. and Bjorck-Akesson, E. (2006). The concept and classification of mental retardation. In H.N. Switzky and S. Greenspan (eds), *What is Mental Retardation? Ideas for an Evolving Disability*, revised and updated edition. Washington DC: American Association on Mental Retardation.

Smith, J.D. (2002) The myth of mental retardation: Paradigm shift, disaggregation, and developmental disabilities. *Mental Retardation*, 40, 62–4.

Smith, J.D. and Wehmeyer, M.L. (2012). Who was Deborah Kallikak?, *Intellectual and Developmental Disability* 50, 169–78.

Snell, M.E. and Voorhees, M.D. (2006). On being labeled with mental retardation. In Switzky, H.N. and Greenspan, S. (eds) *What is Mental Retardation? Ideas for an Evolving Disability in the 21st Century*, revised and updated edition. Washington DC: American Association on Mental Retardation.

Sparrow, S.S., Balla, D.A. and Cicchetti, D.V. (1984). *Vineland Adaptive Behavior Scale*, 2nd edition Survey Forms Manual. Circle Pines, NM: American Guidance Service, Inc.

Sparrow, S.S., Cicchetti, D.V. and Balla, D.A. (2005). *Vineland-II: Vineland Adaptive Behavior Scale*, 2nd edition Survey Forms Manual. Circle Pines, NM: AGS Publishing.

Spitz, H.H. (1986). Disparity in mental retarded persons' IQs derived from different intelligence tests. *American Journal of Mental Deficiency*, 90, 588–91.

Spitz, H.H. (1988). Wechsler subtests pattern of mentally retarded groups: Relationship to g and to estimates of heritability. *Intelligence*, 12, 279–97.

Spitz, H.H. (1989). Variations in the Wechsler interscale IQ disparities at different levels of IQ. *Intelligence*, 13, 157–67.

Spitz, H.H. (2006). How we eradicated familial (hereditary) mental retardation-updated. In H.N. Switzky and S. Greenspan (eds), *What is Mental Retardation? Ideas for an Evolving Disability in the 21st century*, revised and updated edition. Washington DC: American Association on Mental Retardation.

Strømme, P., Bjømstad, P.G. and Ramstad, K. (2002). Prevalence Estimation of Williams Syndrome, *Journal of Child Neurology*, 17, 269–71.

Sundet, J.M., Barlaug, D.G. and Torjussen, T.M. (2004). The end of the Flynn Effect? A study of secular trends in the mean intelligence test scores of Norwegian conscripts during the half a century. *Intelligence*, 32, 249–62.

Sundet, J.M., Borren, I. and Tambs, K. (2008). The Flynn effect partly caused by changing fertility patterns. *Intelligence*, 36, 183–91.

Switzky, H.N. (2006). The importance of cognitive-motivational variables in understanding mental retardation in the 21st century. In H.N. Switzky and S. Greenspan (eds) *What is Mental Retardation? Ideas for an Evolving Disability in the 21st century*, revised and updated edition. Washington DC: American Association on Mental Retardation.

Teasdale, T.W. and Owen, D.R. (1989). Continuing secular increases in intelligence and stable prevalence of high intelligence levels. *Intelligence*, 13, 255–62.

Teasdale, T.W. and Owen, D.R. (2005). A long-term rise and recent decline in intellectual test performance: the Flynn Effect in reverse. *Personality and Individual Differences*, 39, 837–43.

Teasdale, T.W. and Owen, D.R. (2008). Secular decline in cognitive test scores: A reversal of the Flynn effect. *Intelligence*, 36, 121–6.

Thompson, G.H. (1916). A hierarchy without a general factor. *British Journal of Psychology*, 8, 271–81.

Thompson, G.H. (1939). *The Factual Analysis of Human Ability*. London: University of London Press.

Thompson, L.A., Detterman, D.K. and Plomin, R. (1993). Difference in heritability across groups differing in ability, revisited. *Behavior Genetics*, 23, 331–6.

Thorndike, E.L. (1925). *The Measurement of Intelligence*. New York: Teachers College, Columbia University.

Thurstone, L.L. (1938). *Primary Mental Abilities*. Chicago: University of Chicago Press.

Thurstone, L.L. (1947). *Multiple Factor Analysis*. Chicago: University of Chicago Press.

Thurstone, L.L. and Thurstone, T.G. (1941). *Factorial Studies of Intelligence*. Chicago: University of Chicago Press.

Weaver, T.R. (1946). The incident of maladjustment among mental defectives in the military environment. *American Journal of Mental Deficiency*, 51, 238–46.

Webb, J. and Whitaker, S. (2012). Defining learning disability. *The Psychologist*, 25, 440–3.

Wechsler, D. (1939). *Wechsler-Bellevue Intelligence Scale*. New York: The Psychology Corporation.

Wechsler, D. (2003). *WISC-IV Technical and Interpretive Manual*. San Antonio, Texas: Harcourt Associates Inc.

Wechsler, D. (2004). *Wechsler Intelligence Scale for Children – Fourth UK Edition: Administrative and Scoring Manual*. London: The Psychological Corporation.

Wechsler, D., Coalson, D.L. and Raiford, S.E. (2008). *WAIS-IV Technical and Interpretive Manual*. San Antonio, Texas: Pearson.

Whitaker S. (2004). Hidden learning disability. *British Journal of Learning Disability* 32, 139–43.

Whitaker, S. (2008a). Intellectual disability: A concept in need of revision. *British Journal of Developmental Disabilities*, 54, 3–9.

Whitaker, S. (2008b). The stability of IQ in people with low intellectual ability: An analysis of the literature. *Intellectual and Developmental Disabilities*, 46, 120–8.

Whitaker, S. (2010a). Are people with intellectual disabilities getting more or less intelligent? *British Journal of Developmental Disabilities*, 56, 49–55.

Whitaker, S. (2010b). Error in the estimation of intellectual ability in the low range using the WISC-IV and WAIS-III. *Personality and Individual Differences*, 48, 517–21.

Whitaker, S. (2011). Are people with intellectual disabilities getting more or less intelligent II? US data. *British Journal of Developmental Disabilities*, 57, 157–64.

Whitaker, S. (2012). The measurement of low IQ with the WAIS-IV: critical review. *Clinical Psychology Forum*, 231, 45–8.

Whitaker, S. and Gordon, S. (2012). Floor effects on the WISC-IV. *International Journal of Developmental Disabilities*, 58, 111–19.

Whitaker, S. and Porter, J. (2002). Letter to the editor on Valuing People: a new strategy for learning disability for the 21st century. *BILD*, 30, 133.

Whitaker, S. and Wood, C. (2008). The distribution of scale score and possible floor effects on the WISC-III and WAIS-III. *Journal of Applied Research in Intellectual Disabilities*. 21, 136–41.

Williams, W.M. (1998). Are we raising smarter children today? School- and home-related influences on IQ. In U. Neisser (ed.) *The Rising Curve: Long-Term Gains in IQ and Related Measures*. Washington DC: American Psychological Association

Wolfensberger, W. (1972). *Principals of Normalization in Human Services*. Toronto: National Institute on Mental Retardation.

World Health Organization (1985). *Mental Retardation: Meeting the Challenge. Joint Commission on International Aspects of Mental Retardation*. WHO Offset Publication no. 86. Geneva: World Health Organization.

World Health Organization (1992). The ICD-10 Classification of Mental and Behavioural Disorders. Geneva: World Health Organization.

Zendaerland, L. (2004). The parable of the Kallikak family. In S. Noll and J.W. Trent (eds), *Mental Retardation in America: A Historical Reader*. New York: New York University Press.

Zigler, E. (1967). Familial mental retardation: A continuing dilemma. *Science*, 155, 292–8.

Zigler, E., Balla, D. and Hodapp, R. (1984). On the definition and classifications of mental retardation. *American Journal of Mental Deficiency*, 89, 215–30.

Zimmerman, I.L. and Woo-Sam, J.M. (1997). Review of the criterion-related validity of the WISC-III: the first five years. *Perceptual and Motor Skills*, 85, 531–46.

Index

Printed and bound in the United States of America